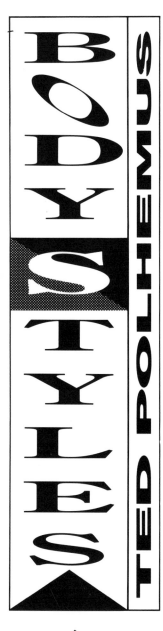

BODY STYLES

TED POLHEMUS

A CHANNEL FOUR BOOK

Lennard Publishing
1988

Lennard Publishing 1988
In association with Channel Four Television Company Limited

Lennard Publishing
A division of Lennard Books Ltd, Lennard House,
92 Hastings Street, Luton, Beds, LU1 5BH

British Library Cataloguing in Publication Data
Polhemus, Ted
Body Styles
1. Costume – Sociological perspectives
1. Title
391
ISBN 1 85291 008 9

First published 1988

Based on the television series 'Body Styles'
produced for Channel Four Television by Arbor Productions Limited.

Designed by Pocknell and Company

Dedication

For the world's remaining tribal peoples and those who work on their behalf.
Throughout the world tribal societies are in danger and if you would like to find out more about this urgent situation and/or to make a donation please contact Survival International (310 Edgeware Road, London W2 1DY; 2121 Decatur Place, NW Washington DC, 20008 USA)

'The body is the totality of meaningful relations to the world.' – Jean-Paul Sartre, *Being and Nothingness*

Personal Acknowledgements

I would like to thank the following people for their support and assistance: Nicole Ogrodnik; Sarah Menon; Lynn Procter; Marcus Podilchuk; Ken Kensinger; Jane Richardson-Hanks; my family; Susanna Yager and Sandy Holton at Channel Four; Mary Jane Walsh; Arbor Films; Michael Lee and Adrian Evans of the Hutchinson Picture Library; The boys at P.I.P.; Chris Going; the friendly and helpful staff of the library of the Royal Commonwealth Society; Roderick Brown, Eileen Williams, Claire Sawford and Christine Monk at Lennard Publishing; Brig Davies; Ruth Grunthall; Adel Rootstein; Siegel and Stockman; Nick Tracken; Debbie and Robyn; Robyn Beeche; the staff of the Holton Picture Library; Grace Lau; Eddie Babbage; Dover Books; Neelam Sharma; John Taylor; Lal Hardy; Henry Fergeson and Body Art Magazine; Timsway Holidays; Fiesta Magazine; Trevor Watson; Kay Devanthey; Gemini Entertainment Agency; Tanta Fash; Tim Woodward and Skin Two Magazine; Krystine Kitsis of Ectomorph; Kim West; Kevin Davies; the press office of Buckingham Palace; WEEF; Shelly Shoes; Jean Muir; Allie at Mikel Rosen Promotions; Zandra Rhodes; Vivienne Westwood; Benny Ong; Casey Tolar; Gina Fratini; Roland Klein; British *Vogue*; The Costume Department of the Museum of London; The National Chopper Club of Great Britain; Babs Fotherby; Lynn Franks PR; Amstrad; Anna Goodman; Anita Bingeman; Angela Coles; Cathy Meade; Caroline Evans; Fran Cottell; Gerry Denn, Graham Nash Labs; Jo Ann Kaplan; Lisa Cooper; Lotte Hughes; Louise Haines; Prue Harrison; Buster and Pris, and *all* of the people who allowed me to photograph them. I also thank Methuen and Co for Jean-Paul Sartre, *Being and Nothingness*, quoted at the start of this book

Contents

1 Beauty

1 Mirrors 4
2 Social Bodies 9
3 Artificial Bodies 13
4 Living Dolls 21
5 The Pursuit of the Perfect Body 24

2 Adornment

6 Customized Chameleons 29
7 The functions of Adornment 32
8 Messages in Make-up 43
9 Tattoo 48
10 Peacock Power 54
11 First Impressions 68

3 Modesty

12 Naked Savages 72
13 The Pursuit of an Innocent Eden 75
14 The Naked and the Nude 79
15 The Politics of Modesty 91

4 Eroticism

16 Unnatural Desires 95
17 Fetishism 99
18 Underwear 114
19 Dressing for Sex 117

5 Clothing

20 Stitches in Time 120
21 Costume and Fashion 123
22 The Bourgeoisie's New Clothes 126
23 Costume Today 129
24 Fashion Today 135

Acknowledgements 140
Bibliography 141
Index 143

1 Beauty

1 Mirrors

Imagine that you and I are sitting opposite each other riding on a train. We do not know one another, but our physical appearances provide us with some clues. Outside the train darkness falls and the window beside us becomes a mirror.

There are three types of relationship present in this scenario: Firstly there is the relationship between you and me (probably a superficial and fleeting relationship consisting only of a few facial expressions acknowledging the existence of the other, but one which could theoretically become significant and long lasting). Secondly, there is the relationship which each of us has with our own image in the mirror. And thirdly, there is the relationship which our reflected images have with each other – a purely comparative and non-interactive relationship, but one which is important nevertheless.

All three of these relationships are physical, in that each involves our bodies in some way. All three are also social. This is obvious in the case of the relationship between you and me. The social nature of the other relationships, although less immediately obvious, is no less real and significant: for it is our social histories which give meaning to the images reflected in the glass.

The theme of this book is the interface between social and physical experience. In subsequent chapters we will explore in greater detail how the body, and its second skins of adornment and clothing, play a vital part in our social relationships. Here we will begin to consider the social nature of the human body and, specifically, the body's reflected image. We will begin by sketching out a phenomenology of that seemingly simple, but actually very complex, activity of looking at oneself in a mirror.

In the course of our lives the most important relationship any of us ever has is between 'ourself' and our reflection. This is not simply a question of vanity or narcissism:

it is through this relationship that we affirm, re-affirm, define and re-define who we are. When I *confront* myself in the glass, I confront *myself*; the experience brings me to the conclusion that I not only have a body, but that I *am* a body.

Or at least it should do. Many people who suffer from certain psychological disorders may – despite the evidence of the mirror – feel that their bodies are alien entities. This is known as depersonalization and it has been defined by Alexander Lowen as 'a loss of feeling of the body, with accompanying sensations of strangeness and unreality' (Lowen:1975:p.2). In his book *The Betrayal of the Body*, Lowen cites many case histories of such depersonalization:

'The other day I looked in the mirror, and I became frightened when I realized it was me. I thought, this is what people see when they look at me. The image was a stranger. My face and my body didn't seem to belong to me . . . I felt very unreal.' (Lowen:1975:p.2)

In a sense, it is not just Lowen's patients who suffer from this problem. Our entire dualistic tradition in philosophy is founded on the principle of depersonalization (or, as I would prefer to call it, disembodiment). From St Augustine (who wrote: 'When the question is, of what elements is man made up, I am able to answer – of a soul and a body') to Descartes (who reasoned: 'The essential Self must be the Self-that-thinks, i.e., the mind as opposed to the body'), we find the foundations of an estrangement from our physicality.

Where philosophy has led, science and science fiction have followed with enthusiasm. In Arthur C. Clarke's novel *Childhood's End* the descendants of *Homo*

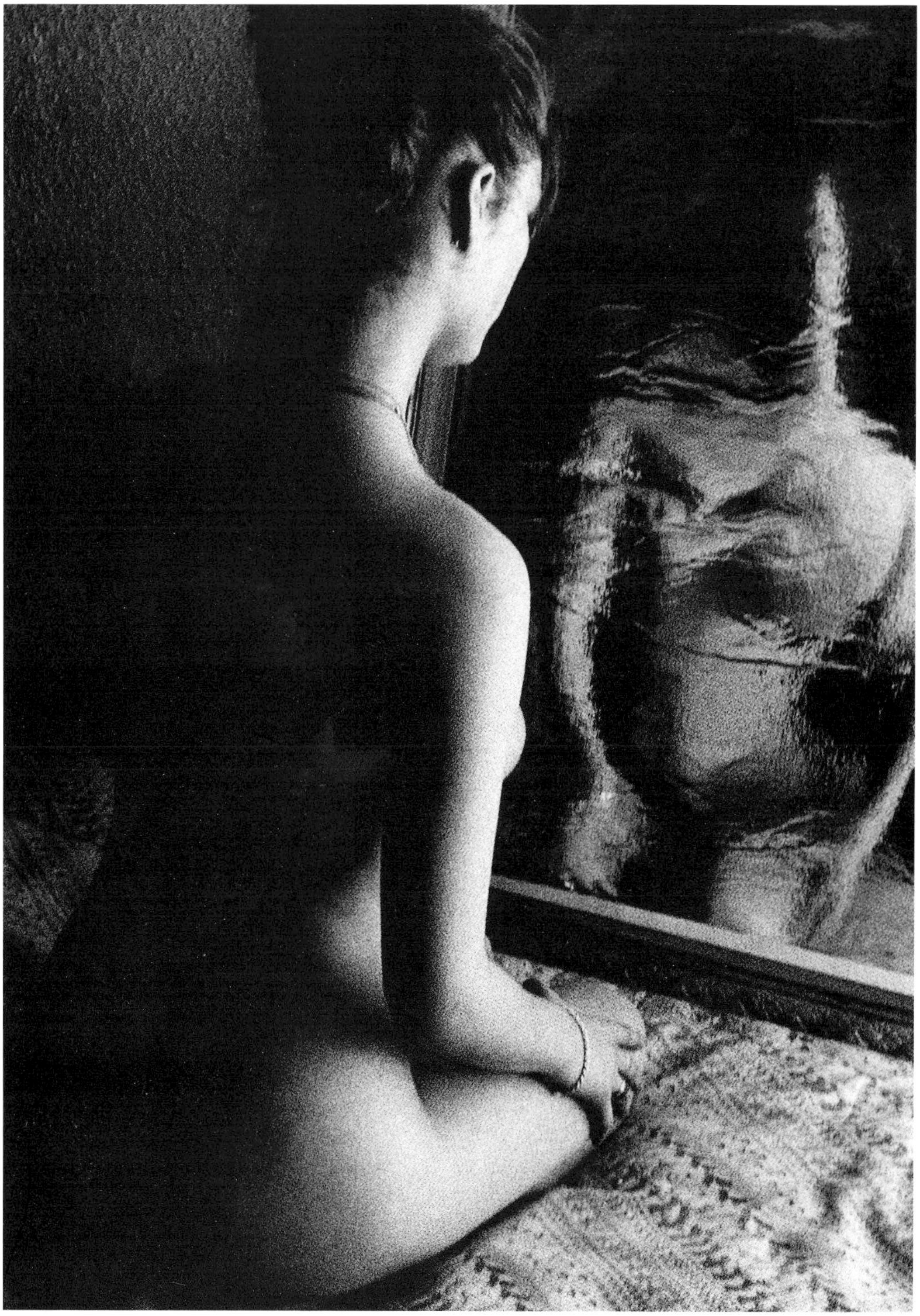

sapiens de-materialize their bodies and their world into the eternal and universal OVERMIND and thereby leave behind the 'childhood' of physical existence as a butterfly leaves behind its chrysalis.

Writing in 1969, Dr José M.R. Delgado of Yale University looked forward to a day when research into electrical stimulation of the brain would create the possibility of a 'psycho-civilization' in which direct mind-to-mind contact would bypass the need for physical contact and experience. Professor Tom Stonier predicted that mankind would move (as one newspaper headline put it) 'Into the Cerebral Future . . . Without the Body'. Only in this way, he argued, could humankind hope to cope with future problems of war, economic depression and overpopulation and achieve a truly global community.

For Stonier, Delgado, Clarke, Descartes, St Augustine and Lowen's patients, the body which peers back from the mirror is not a part of their essential selves. For them, the physical entity of the body (and its reflection) is at best a sort of 'house' and at worst simply an encumbrance to their being. It is not sufficient simply to describe this view as dualistic. It is a very *unequal* dualism, with the body riding far at the back of the ontological bus.

Now, allow me to put my own cards on the table. I believe that, far from simply providing a housing for the self and far from being an existential encumbrance, the body is an essential part of our most fundamental ground of being. Devoid of physicality, human beings would not be human beings, and this book is an attempt to explore the myriad ways in which this is the case. The reader who would like to escape his or her physicality and merge with the OVERMIND is advised to read something else.

For those of us left, let us return to our respective reflections in the train's darkened glass. If we conclude from this experience that we 'are' one of those bodies looking back from the glass, we will also note that those bodies are different. Even in the case of identical twins, there is always some unique physical feature which separates one from the other. Most of us exhibit more marked differences. In my own case, I am 5′11″, blue-eyed, blond, caucasian, male, thinnish (at least when I keep up with the Canadian Airforce exercises), with a mole on my abdomen, a scar on my right palm, a large bump of unknown origin on the right side of my head, a prominent freckle on my right hand, etc. You and your body are different.

This fact of life also has a science fiction antithesis: a future age when bodies are cloned to identical, assembly-line perfection. This is not as far-fetched as it sounds. Biological engineering can already produce virtually identical plants and livestock. But – aside from the political and ethical questions raised by the production of a master race of human clones – would it not be an existential catastrophe if we were to lose our physiological differences? Surely, just as I *am* my body, I am also – in a sense – the freckle on my right hand. A cloned world would negate this element of my/your reality.

Nor is the dream of physical uniformity entirely modern. As we will see in subsequent chapters, all societies have a tendency towards the neutralization (through adornment, body modification, etc.) of physical differences. Whether in a traditional tribal community in the Amazon, a peasant community in Roumania, a Western 'tribe' of punks or Hell's Angels, or some clique of 'fashionable society', there is always an impulse toward glossing over our physical differences to achieve a uniform ideal. Modern plastic surgery and genetic engineering only offer a technical advantage in fulfilling this ideal.

The merits and demerits of this socially based drive towards physical uniformity will be considered in due course. For now, let us simply note that, until scientists are let loose to sculpt and clone us all into identical replicas, our reflections in a mirror will continue to be different and unique, and this will remain an important factor in both our definition of self and our reactions to the Other. If I or you were to look in the mirror and see *anybody*, our entire being-in-the-world, our existential reality, would be profoundly altered. (Certainly the relationship between 'me' and my reflection or 'you' and your reflection would be strained, to say the least.)

But let us put aside science fiction horror stories and return to present realities. I look in the mirror and I see 'me'. This 'me' is unique and *I* am the product of this relationship.

What of the mirror, the medium of this relationship? Measured against the span of human history, the mirror as we know it is a relatively recent development. Polished metal surfaces have been around for thousands of years but it is only in modern times that the majority of the population has had access to mirrors. Indeed, the modern world is a world of mirrors – even on the street (or on a train) we are constantly confronted by our image in some reflective surface.

And, as our entire planet is Westernized, so our mirrors are bartered and sold to all of humankind from the New Guinea Highlands to the Arctic wastes. It could well be argued that mirrors are that product of Western civilization of which tribal peoples are most covetous. Certainly it is now a common sight to see tribal peoples putting on their traditional body decorations hunched over a hand mirror which they have acquired from anthropologists, missionaries or traders.

Which is not to say, of course, that the experience of seeing one's own reflection is a modern phenomenon. Still water has always provided this opportunity (as Narcissus discovered too late). Although some animals (my cats, for example) do not seem to recognize their reflections, it seems likely that it was very early in human evolution that some distant ancestor of ours first recognized him or herself as a reflection in still water.[2] Some tribal peoples make use of bowls of water to make this activity more convenient. The development of the modern mirror has simply extended this convenience and made the experience of seeing 'oneself' omnipresent in daily life. (It has also made rituals of adornment and grooming more personal and less social, as we – and now those tribal peoples who possess mirrors – can deal with these matters individually, whereas previously the decoration of the body was generally a communal activity. Considering the fact that mutual grooming in animals has the effect of strengthening social relations, I doubt that this technological advance is also a social advantage.)

Although the technology of image reflection (e.g., hand mirrors *vs* still water) may have had some effect on social usage, the activity of confronting one's image is the same phenomenologically regardless of the devices used. Throughout human history and throughout the world, the subject sees a version of his or her 'self' looking back with right and left side reversal.

There may, however, be differences from one culture to the next in the degree of objective reality which is accredited to the reflected image. It might be, for example, that in some tribal societies the reflected image is seen as a ghost or a spirit and that this is perceived to be less or more 'real' than living human beings (but I know of no ethnographic data to confirm or deny this suspicion). Nevertheless, it would be foolish to presume that our own assumptions concerning the ontology of the reflected image are laws of nature.

In at least one Marx Brothers film there is a scene in which one of the brothers plays the part of someone else's reflection in a 'mirror'. Although this is only intended as a joke (albeit a very effective one) it points to our assumptions about the objective reality of reflected images. Like the character in the film, we are fooled into believing that the 'mirror doesn't lie' and that 'the real world' is reflected in glass. We may readily accept that a fairground mirror will distort our reflections beyond recognition, but we also assume that 'real' mirrors reflect a 'real' world.

The truth, of course, is that the creature in the mirror exists only in our seeing, and seeing should never be believing. The problem goes well beyond the optical accuracy of the mirror itself. It is our own perception which constitutes the ultimate cause of the distortion, for our eyes are directly connected to our brains and it is there that the image is interpreted and, in a very real sense, *created*. If we could switch off our brains while looking in a mirror, we would see nothing but an incomprehensible pattern of reflected light. This is true of all images but it is particularly telling when it comes to dealing with our own reflections in the looking glass.

Just as the reflected image of our body is created in our mind's eye, so are two other 'bodies'. Firstly there is what psychologists call our *body image* – an on-going, cumulative assessment by each of us of what we look like. This vision of our physical selves is generated and modified over the course of our lives. Although personal, body image is actually a product of social interaction. It arises from the comments about and reactions to our appearance which we receive throughout our lives from other people. Early experiences of relatives saying things like 'What lovely big brown eyes you have – just like your mother's' or of children at school teasing us about being too fat, thin, short, tall, etc., obviously have a particularly important part to play. The process, however, continues throughout our lives. Only at the moment of our death is our body image fixed forever.

Although no one's body image is a 100% accurate appraisal of their objective physical reality, some people's are a lot more inaccurate than others. For example, people suffering from anorexia nervosa generally have such distorted body images that it is impossible for them to accept the fact that they are wasting away from not eating enough. Researchers at the Royal Free Hospital in London devised a test of this in which anorexics were asked to adjust two horizontal lights until they represented their perceived width of face, chest, waist and hips. The results show graphically how the anorexic patients (but not a control group of healthy individuals) wildly overestimated how fat their bodies were, often by more than 50%. From this research we can see that anorexia nervosa involves not just extreme dieting, but an actual perceptual breakdown. When an emaciated sufferer looks at him or herself in a mirror, he or she sees a fat, overweight person looking back. In other words, the mirror *does* lie.

Anorexia nervosa is an extreme example but it should serve to remind all of us that our body image – how we generally see ourselves – is a subjective rather than an objective phenomenon. As a photographer, I never cease to be amazed at how often an attractive person, when shown a photograph which I and others see as flattering, reacts with comments like 'Take it away, please rip it up, I look *terrible*!' We all know people who won't even allow their picture to be taken, arguing that they will 'break your camera'.[3] When we consider that anyone's body image is ultimately built upon a foundation of subjective assessments by other people (who may or may not have serious problems about their own body image) it is hardly surprising

1. I am here using the visual phenomenon of observing one's reflection as a short-hand for all forms of sensory feedback between 'self' and 'body'. We all encounter our bodies through touch and various proprioceptive systems as well as the visual. For a blind person, the relationship between 'self' and 'body' is obviously conducted using non-visual means and is no less significant because it is non-visual.

2. My reason for suspecting the antiquity of this phenomenon stems from its widespread present-day occurrence. Anthropologists generally assume that any activity found in widely distant places must have a long history.

that many are so unrealistic.

Let us now return to the scenario on the train where you or I catch a glimpse of our reflections in the darkened windows: obviously what we see is not a straightforward, objective account of what is there. The configuration of light bouncing off the glass is always modified and distorted by existing preconceptions. (For example, if you and I look at my image in the glass on the train, we will each see different things.) When we look at our reflections, what we 'see' in the final analysis is a dialogue between the image focussed on the retina at that point in time (as interpreted in the mind's eye) and the conceptual image of ourselves which we carry around throughout our lives. And as if this process were not complicated enough, there is a third body-in-the-mind which (like a caller on a crossed line) is continually butting in on the conversation. This we will call the *ideal body*.

While body image is a personal vision of my body or your body, the ideal body is an alien other. Not a real person, the ideal body is an amalgamation of all the information which we have acquired throughout our lives concerning how a person *ought* to look. The dolls which we are given to play with as infants are often the first instalments in this process. Childhood and adolescent experiences in which other children are praised for their looks further contribute to the creation of this vision of perfection and in adult life advertisements, magazines, television, film and figurative fine art forms reinforce our ideal of beauty. And as in the case of body image, the ideal body is constantly being revised – especially in a society like our own in which ideals of beauty are in a perpetual state of flux because of changing fashions.

But no matter how transitory and illusory the ideal body may be in historical terms, it is, at any point in time, always very real and very powerful at a personal level. Although we may know in the back of our minds that this ideal is a product of history and culture, we tend to ignore this fact, and the result is that the simple act of looking in the mirror is a three-party conference between the immediate reflection in the looking glass, one's cumulative body image, and the ideal body which is the creation of society and history.

It is the latter which gives meaning to the former by providing a basis for critical evaluation. The ideal body tells us whether we are looking good, not bad or terrible. (Rarely, if ever, does it tell us that we are looking 'perfect', since the ideal body is, by definition, unattainable.) If, for example, I look in the mirror and disdainfully conclude that I am too fat or too thin it is because of the discrepancies between what I see in the mirror and my (i.e., my society's) vision of the ideal body.

It goes without saying that the ideal body is the source of untold human misery. It is the gremlin which makes us turn from the mirror in disgust. Lately it has become fashionable to presume that this devil is the creation of the modern media. It is certainly true that giant billboards, TV commercials, pictures in magazines, pin-ups, etc., bombard us with images of perfect beauty which serve as unavoidable reminders of our own physical imperfections. But it is a mistake to conclude that this beautiful gremlin is a child of modern technology, capitalism, urban life, industrialization, etc., for – in its various guises – it has been around throughout human history and long before.

Sexual mating is perhaps the parent of this gremlin. A male baboon has a fixed ideal of what a desirable female baboon should look like. A certain shape and colour of backside is essential, and male baboons battle with each other to get access to those females which fit this ideal most perfectly. The same general principle is true of any animal which reproduces by sexual selection. But there is an important difference between baboons and ourselves. For other animals the physical ideal is 100% instinctively determined. Thus all baboons of a particular species pursue the same ideal (which is biologically produced at a particular point in the female menstrual cycle). For humans, on the other hand, ideals of beauty are *learned*.

We know this because of the simple fact that people in different societies and different historical periods strive for radically different – often completely opposite – physical ideals. In some traditional areas of West Africa, girls whose fathers can afford it are sent to live in the fattening house so that they will emerge plump enough to interest potential suitors. Meanwhile, women (and men) in our own society may diet to achieve precisely the opposite body ideal. Clearly, in a worldwide and historical framework, there is no such thing as natural human beauty. (Yet *within* any particular social environment an individual who closely resembles the going definition of beauty is always thought of as just that.)

The ideal body is always outside an individual's control. No one person can change it. Indeed, it is a *political* phenomenon. Marx argued that the ruling class or dominant social group inevitably controls not just how we act but how we think. Let us add a footnote to Marx to suggest that this includes how we perceive physical beauty. In any revolution the established body ideal is one of the first things to be overturned or redefined, but some other ideologically appropriate body ideal always takes its place. Only a complete state of anoma and social collapse would allow us to contemplate our reflections in the mirror without that beautiful gremlin to laugh at our imperfections. However, in such a world our own image would be bereft of meaning and our reflection would be nothing but patterns of light trapped in glass. We would, like Dracula's victims, cast no reflection in the looking glass.

3. A fascinating expression which, rightly, credits the extraordinary power of appearance – a magical power capable, in this case, even of breaking a machine.

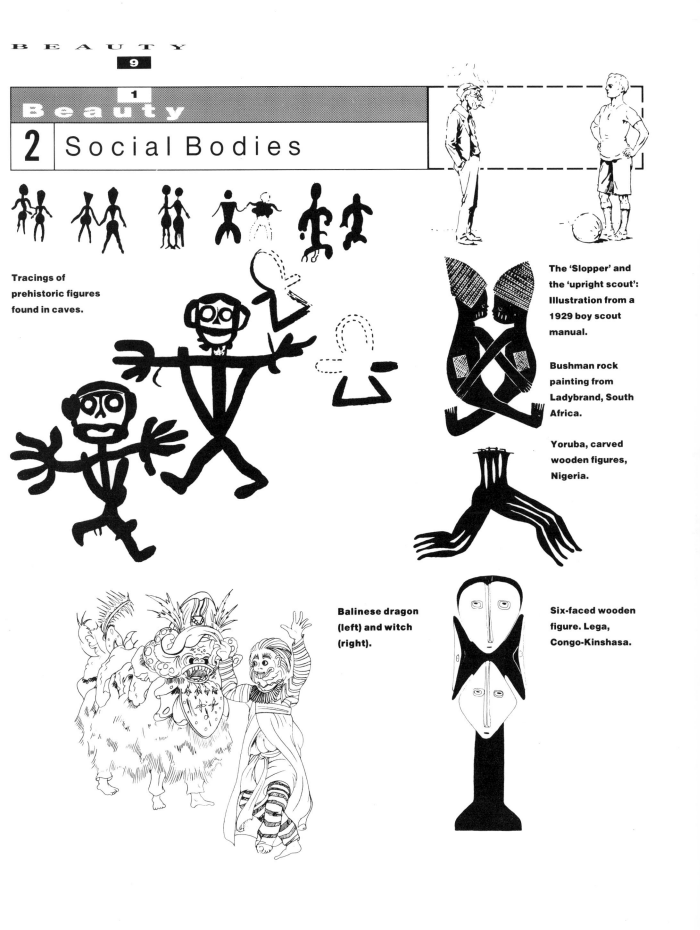

1 Beauty

2 Social Bodies

Tracings of prehistoric figures found in caves.

The 'Slopper' and the 'upright scout': Illustration from a 1929 boy scout manual.

Bushman rock painting from Ladybrand, South Africa.

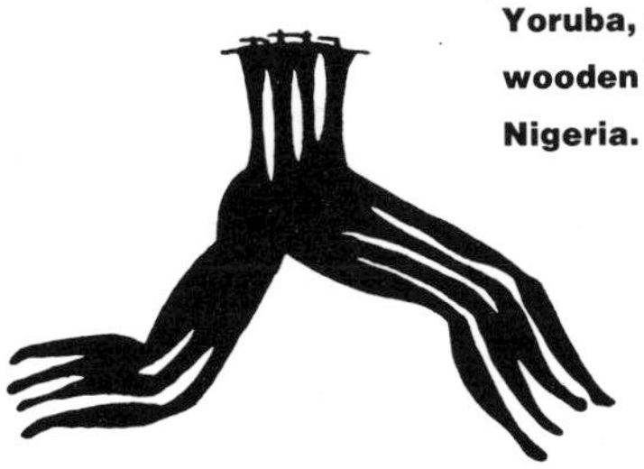

Yoruba, carved wooden figures, Nigeria.

Balinese dragon (left) and witch (right).

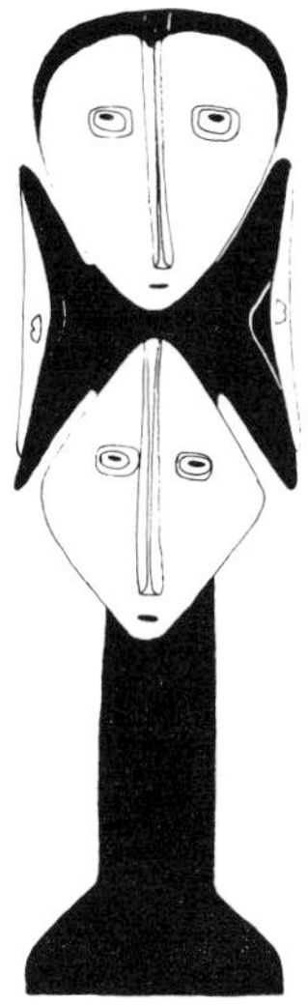

Six-faced wooden figure. Lega, Congo-Kinshasa.

Although the ideal body is neither my body nor your body, it is, in a sense, *our* body. While a body image is personal and unique, the ideal body is shared between all the members of a society.

Because modern Western 'society' is actually a conglomerate of lots of different societies which overlap and conflict with each other, and because each of these social groups has its own definition of the ideal body, it is difficult for those of us who live in 'the modern world' to properly appreciate the social basis of beauty ideals. In our world there are so many ideal bodies (the curvacious pin-up, the svelte fashion model, the extraterrestrial punk, the earth-mother hippy – to name only a few of the current female ideals) that the phenomenon seems random and purely a matter of personal inclination.

The social nature of the ideal body can, however, be seen much more clearly in small-scale, tribal or peasant communities. From the highlands of New Guinea to the Sahara desert, and from the Andes to the forests of Eastern Europe – wherever traditional and homogeneous communities have withstood the onslaught of Westernization – one finds within each community a remarkable homogeneity of opinion about exactly what constitutes the ideal body. For example, the Masai (of Kenya and Tanzania) ideal body for women . . .

'Calls for a well-built and slim body with lightly rounded forms. In contrast to the greater number of other negroes . . . a Masai beauty should not be fat. Limbs should be just sufficiently rounded not to seem angular. The other signs of beauty are: An oval face, white teeth, black gums, as light a facial complexion as possible, protruding buttocks (one cannot however speak of steatopygia), strong thighs, a deep navel. Lips should not obtrude either in shape or colour so that small dark lips are considered beautiful . . . With girls emphasis is placed on thin bones, small and delicate hands and feet, and upright semi-spherical breasts.' (Merker:1904:p.123)

This summary overly generalizes perhaps, but the point is clearly made that the Masai share (or shared) a definition of the body ideal which everyone in a given community (one would not be surprised to find regional differences within a tribe as large as the Masai) accepts as correct.

In the same way, the members of the Siriono tribe (Bolivia) share a very different definition of the ideal body:

'Besides being young, a desirable sex partner – especially a woman – should also be fat. She should have big hips, good sized but firm breasts, and a deposit of fat on her sexual organs. Fat women are referred to by the men with obvious pride as *ereN ekida* (fat vulva) and are thought to be much more satisfying sexually than thin women, who are summarily dismissed as being *ikaNgi* (bony). In fact, so desirable is corpulence as a sexual trait that I have frequently heard men make up songs about the merits of a fat vulva . . .

In addition to the criteria already mentioned, certain other physical signs of erotic beauty are also recognized. A tall person is preferred to a short one; facial features should be regular; eyes should be large. Little attention is paid to the ears, the nose, or the lips, unless they are obviously deformed. Body hair is an undesirable trait and is therefore depilated, although a certain amount of pubic hair is believed to add zest to intercourse. A woman's vulva should be small and fat, while a man's penis should be as large as possible.' (Holmberg:p.181)

Although infuriatingly few ethnographic reports bother to mention the body ideals of the people they deem to study (something which I suspect the natives themselves would find a strange deficiency), Clellan Ford and Frank Beach in *Patterns of Sexual Behaviour* managed to obtain enough information to assemble a chart of the female body ideals of various small-scale societies from around the world.

Societies Showing Preference for Selected Female Traits

Plump body build Abelam, Chiricahua, Chuckchee, Ganda, Hidatsa, Maricopa, Nama, Pukapukans, Ramkokamekra, Siriono, Tarahumara, Thonga, Wogeo.
Medium body build Apache, Hopi, Pima, Sanpoil, Thompson.
Slim body build Chenchu, Dobuans, Ila, Masai, Palaung, Tongans.
Broad pelvis and wide hips Chuckchee, Hopi, Kwakiut, Maricopa, Siriono, Wogeo.
Narrow pelvis and slim hips Yakut
Small ankles Kwakiutl, Lenge, Tongans.
Shapely and fleshy calves Ila, Kwakiutl, Maori, Tongans, Wogeo.
Elongated labia majora Dahomeans, Kusaians, Marquesans, Nama, Ponapeans, Thonga, Trukese, Venda.
Large clitoris Easter Islanders.
Long and pendulous breasts Azande, Ganda.
Large breasts Alorese, Apache, Hopi, Kurtatchi, Lesu, Siriono, Thonga, Trukese, Wogeo.
Upright, semi-spherical breasts Manus, Masai.

Even limited data such as this leads us to some important conclusions about the ideal body:

Firstly, there is no such thing as a universal ideal body. (The ideal body, therefore, is not the product of genetically determined instinct as it is in other animals.)

Secondly, variation in the ideal body corresponds to the boundaries of social groups. (Where tribe A ends and tribe B begins is also the point where one physical ideal is supplanted by another.)

Thirdly, within each small-scale, traditional group there is a high degree of consensus about what constitutes the ideal body. (A Masai male who preferred plump women, or a Siriono male who preferred slim women would be classified as deviant.)

All of these characteristics of the body

ideal point to its social and inter-personal nature, but there is yet another sense in which body ideals are social: they constitute a symbolic expression of the social group itself. In order to explore this theme we will need to draw upon certain ideas from semiotics and theoretical anthropology with which the reader may not be familiar.

Semiotics is a 'science of signs' – a theoretical framework for the analysis of any form of communication – which was first suggested by the Swiss linguist Ferdinand de Saussure and subsequently developed by Roland Barthes and other French intellectuals. For our purposes, the most important distinction which semiotics makes is between 'natural' symbols and arbitrary signs.

Both signs and symbols are composed of two elements: a signified (SD) which is described as the 'plane of content' and a signifier (SR) which is described as the 'plane of expression'. The signified is conceptual while the signifier is materialistic.

SIGNIFIER	=	**PLANE OF EXPRESSION**	=	**SOUNDS/ OBJECTS/ IMAGES**
SIGNIFIED	=	**PLANE OF CONTENT**	=	**CONCEPT/ IDEA/VISION**

In symbols there exists some 'motivated', 'natural' relationship between the signifier and the signified. For example, a drawing of a whale looks like what it represents and is therefore a symbol.

In signs, the relationship between signifier and signified is 'arbitrary' so that, for example, the word 'whale' represents the concept of a particular category of animal simply because of lexicographic convention. There is nothing 'whale-like' about the word 'whale' and in other languages a different term is used to describe the same category of animal.

Symbols are not literally 'natural' since perceptions, visual/auditory conventions and the concepts which they represent differ from one society to the next. (I will therefore use the term 'natural' within quotation marks.)

However, given the fact that within any society symbols enjoy a direct linkage with all relevant cultural systems, they are always perceived within that society as 'natural' and incapable of being other than what they are. Signs, on the other hand, except with regard to that which they signify, relate only to their own linguistic system.

From theoretical anthropology we will need to make use of certain ideas about the nature of social systems:

1. A society is more than simply a population of individuals. (As Durkheim put it, a society is more than the sum of its parts.)
2. Every society (or culture, to use the American terminology) constitutes a system of rules governing relationships, a system of values and beliefs (world view) and so forth, which is inter-generational.
3. In the final analysis, a society is only a set of ideas – a conceptualization or vision of how life ought to be lived.
4. Although only concepts, societies are arguably the devices which allowed *Homo sapiens* to develop into the dominant creature on our planet. Without them, that which is learned in the course of day-to-day trial and error experimentation is lost when an individual dies. By creating inter-generational frameworks which could last for centuries, social systems made it possible for knowledge and wisdom to be accumulated over long historical periods.

The essential problem for humankind, therefore, has been to find some means of expressing the particular vision of life and how to live it which is a society – for only in this way can a culture become objectively and inter-generationally 'real'. In semiotic terms, the concept signified of 'society' (and its attendant values, beliefs, rules of behaviour, etc.) requires some material of expression which will allow it to be communicated from person to person and from generation to generation.

Throughout human history the most appropriate and obvious material of expression of the plane of content of the social system has been the ideal body. There are many reasons for this 'choice' of signifier:

1. Both the human body and any society are assemblies of separate parts.
2. Both the human body and any society are integrated systems in which the whole is more than the sum of its parts.
3. Because all the members of any society obviously have bodies, the ideal body is a material of expression to which everyone can readily relate.
4. Because the human body is complex and multi-faceted it can be made to express any signified.

The idea that the body can serve as a symbol of a social system is nicely illustrated in Margaret Mead and Gregory Bateson's studies of Balinese culture. Balinese villages periodically stage a play about the exploits of a witch and a dragon. The part of the ideal body is played by the dragon, which is actually two men who move smoothly and gracefully together inside one ornate costume.

The witch, on the other hand, is for the Balinese the epitome of ugliness: she moves in a jerky and uncoordinated fashion and her costume – which has large stripes of black and white covering most of it – suggests that she is literally falling apart. In the play the witch is incensed when the king refuses to marry her hideous daughter and brings pestilence, famine and plague to the land. To overcome her, the king transforms himself into the mighty dragon and in this guise eventually wins the day.

The Balinese characters of the dragon and the witch are much more than models of good and bad deportment. The dragon represents a highly integrated social system in which everyone works smoothly together for the common good. The witch, on the other hand, shows what can happen when the parts of the social system (i.e., individual persons) act independently as separate entities. Thus the body of the dragon is a symbol of a

Utopia and the body of the witch is a symbol of distopia – a society which is falling apart.

Likewise in our own society we can find plenty of examples of the human body as a symbol of society and its values. We divide 'The Body Politic' into left and right. We compartmentalize 'The Social Body' into upper, middle and lower segments which are governed by a 'head'. Most, if not all, of our ways of describing behaviour are at once corporal and social. A person is 'upright', 'straight', 'bent', 'loose', 'uptight', 'hard-headed', 'up front', 'together', 'soft', 'hard', 'forward', 'backward', 'balanced', 'tough', 'big', etc. Likewise, 'inside' and 'outside' describe both physical and social boundaries.

The symbolic interface of the body and the social body has been analysed perceptively by the anthropologist Mary Douglas who, in her book *Natural Symbols*, concludes:

'The social body constrains the way the physical body is perceived. The physical experience of the body, always modified by the social categories through which it is known, sustains a particular view of society. There is a continual exchange of meanings between the two kinds of bodily experience so that each reinforces the categories of the other.' (Douglas:p.65)

'The human body is always treated as an image of society and . . . there can be no natural way of considering the body that does not involve at the same time a social dimension.' (Douglas:p.70)

Anthropologists, in seeking to explain the mechanics of social systems, have long made use of 'the organic analogy' whereby a society is likened to a physical organism such as the human body and on one level it could be said that what Douglas and I are suggesting is simply that *all* human beings do the same thing; that the body is an invaluable metaphor for visualizing the structure and patterns of organization of social 'organisms'. However, we are going one stage further. While the organic analogy is based on the simple (one way) premise that a 'social body' is like a physical body, we are also suggesting the reverse: that, as Douglas writes in the quote above, 'The human body is always treated as an image of society'.

Obviously, for this to make sense, it is necessary that one appreciates that 'the body' which participates in this two way, inter-active exchange of meaning is (at least in the first instance) not the 'real', biological body of flesh and blood, it is the ideal body which is itself a concept. In a sense, therefore, the ideal body and the social body should be viewed as a single, inter-active conceptual complex. This socio-physical ideal is different from society to society and from historical period to historical period and is itself always involved in an internal dialogue: the 'body' is forever in the process of becoming the 'social body' (the *corp*oration) and vice versa.

In other words, the ideal body *is* the (ideal) social body and it is for this reason – the extraordinary extent to which the ideal body is caught up in the task of serving as a symbol or metaphor of how life ought to be lived – that it is inevitably pulled away from the biological reality of the body. The implications of this are far reaching and of the greatest importance:

1) Because every society is different so too is every social group's vision of socio-physical perfection. It is for this reason that the ideal body is defined so very differently throughout our species.

2) Because 'the body' is a reflection not of the 'real' body, but rather, of the social body, it is always conceived in terms which – biologically speaking – are rather bizarre and unnatural. (Of course, *within any social system or culture*, the accepted definition of beauty is always perceived to be entirely 'natural'; it is only *other societies'* beauty ideals which seem physiologically bizarre – but this is simply a tribute to the extent to which a society is capable of imposing its own perception of 'the natural' upon everything within its social construction of reality.)

3) Because an ideal of beauty is a symbolic and social (as opposed to biological) creation, it is only artificial bodies created by artists from inorganic and therefore infinitely plastic materials, which can succeed in perfectly fulfilling its vision. (This is the subject of the next chapter.)

The gap between biological reality and social symbol is, in any society or historical era, enormous and in the attempt to bridge this gap is born the need for all the extraordinary forms of body decoration and modification which are characteristic of human beings. From this gap is also, of course, born the disappointment which we all feel when we look in a mirror – for our bodies are the product of biological rather than symbolic processes. But so important is 'the body' as a social symbol that even this universal dissatisfaction with one's own body is but a small price to pay.

If the ideal body was somehow stripped of its symbolic responsibilities, if beauty was returned to a purely biological dimension, then humanity would be robbed of its most important 'natural' symbol in the form of 'the body'. At first glance this might not seem like much of a loss, but closer examination reveals that such a thing would be catastrophic. We human beings are what we are because we live in social groups, each with its own culture; its own rules of behaviour, its own beliefs and values, its own vision of itself and of how life ought to be lived. Without all this we really would be 'just a bunch of animals'. And without the ideal 'body' to serve as a symbolic focus – a map, icon or corporate logo – of the 'social body', the latter would be without form or substance. If that should happen then 'society' would vanish into thin air. There would then be no social order, no cultural framework within which to live our lives and every man and woman would indeed be an island. As the Balinese might put it, the witch would triumph over the dragon.

1 Beauty

3 Artificial Bodies

Jean Paul Goude, the French artist, photographer and film director, makes beautiful women. He is most famous for his re-creation of the pop singer Grace Jones, but the way he works as an artist is perhaps best illustrated by the case of 'Toukie'. In his book *Jungle Fever* Goude describes her as 'a masterpiece of nature' and then immediately comments, 'Naturally I set about to see what I could do to improve her'. Firstly Goude took photographs of Toukie, chopped them up, put them back together and airbrushed them to exaggerate her proportions. He then had a life-size cast made of her which, using a pentagraph, he reduced to a 12″ high doll-like replica. But even this wasn't enough:

'I couldn't help myself; I had to improve the masterpiece. The real Toukie was a step in the right direction but she was not quite like my drawings. I had to see my dream girl for myself and also show others my concept of beauty. So I started chopping the replica as I had done with the photographs, elongating limbs and widening shoulders. On the original statue, Toukie's tits looked unnatural, like silicon jobs – because they had been cast while floating. So I chopped them off and made them more natural with big prune-like nipples.

I had always admired black women's backsides, the ones who look like race horses. Toukie's backside was voluptuous enough, but nowhere near a race-horse's arse, so I gave her one. There she was, my dream come true, in living colour.' (Goude:1981:p.41)

Toukie, we are not surprised to learn, was not thrilled with Goude's re-creation of her physique. Nor does it come as a surprise to learn that Jean Paul Goude and his creations have been harshly criticized by feminists. For myself, I cannot see that what Goude does is any different from what artists have done since art was invented: he idealizes the human form.

Illustration from *Science Wonder Stories* (June 1929) showing machine for transforming the ideal beauty of statues into living flesh.

Some 27,000 years ago a forever nameless artist took clay and fashioned the figure which we know today as the Venus of Willendorf. In terms of technique and in terms of the physical ideal portrayed, there is a world of difference between the Venus of Willendorf and Goude's re-creation of Toukie, but in terms of the artistic process whereby real flesh becomes an idealized vision there is surely no difference. If what Goude does is seen as sinister, the same must be said of the creator of the Venus of Willendorf and every other artist who has produced non-realistic, figurative art.

However, there *is* a moral problem associated with all such artistic creations which we ought to consider. Many of the world's religions (Judaism, Islam and some fundamentalist Protestant sects, such as the Menonites) explicitly prohibit the creation of 'graven images'. (For example, Deuteronomy 4:16 – 'Beware lest you act corruptly by making a graven image for yourselves in the form of any figure, the likeness of male or female.') The reason for this prohibition is clear: like Frankenstein, the artist who creates a 'body' mimics God. (On the other hand, of course, religions such as Catholicism, Hinduism, Buddhism and Greek Orthodoxy, actively encourage the production of figurative art as a didactic and spiritual medium.)

I am not eager to become involved in this theological debate, but it is important to point out that the artist who creates artificial bodies is indeed tampering with powerful forces. Because 'the body' is always heavily loaded with symbolic meaning, its creation and re-creation should never be approached capriciously. Like Dr Frankenstein and the well-meaning but naive creator of the Golem (a statue which, according to Eastern European mythology, was brought to life to protect the Jewish people but turned on those it was supposed to protect) the artist who creates graven images may find that his/her endeavours unleash forces which cannot easily be controlled.

Why then do artists persist in creating 'bodies' and why do most of us encourage their efforts? To answer this question we must return to the themes which we began to explore in the previous two chapters and carry them a little further.

A society or culture is a system of values, beliefs, prescriptions and proscriptions of behaviour, assumptions about social categories, a typology of role models and a model or map of itself. In order that these ideas should be communicated between persons and between generations it is

necessary that they be translated into some material of expression. Verbal language plays an important part in this process (e.g., in folk tales, songs, etc.) but the arbitrary nature of verbal language systems places limitations on its contribution. (Imagine trying to 'translate' the London Underground map into a non-pictorial language.)

The limitations of verbal language are particularly evident when it comes to the expression of fundamental concepts. Theologians, for example, find great difficulties in using verbal language to discuss the basic tenets of faith or to describe God. 'Love' is another example of a concept which often defies precise linguistic expression. And the same is true of all the components of a socio-cultural system itemized above.

However, what is difficult or impossible to express in arbitrary signs can often be 'said' using 'natural', iconographic symbols. Although practically anything can serve as a symbolic material of expression (an environmental feature such as the moon, a graphic shape such as the cross, a plant such as the olive branch, a colour such as black for mourning, etc.), one symbolic form – 'the human body' – is of special importance. (In

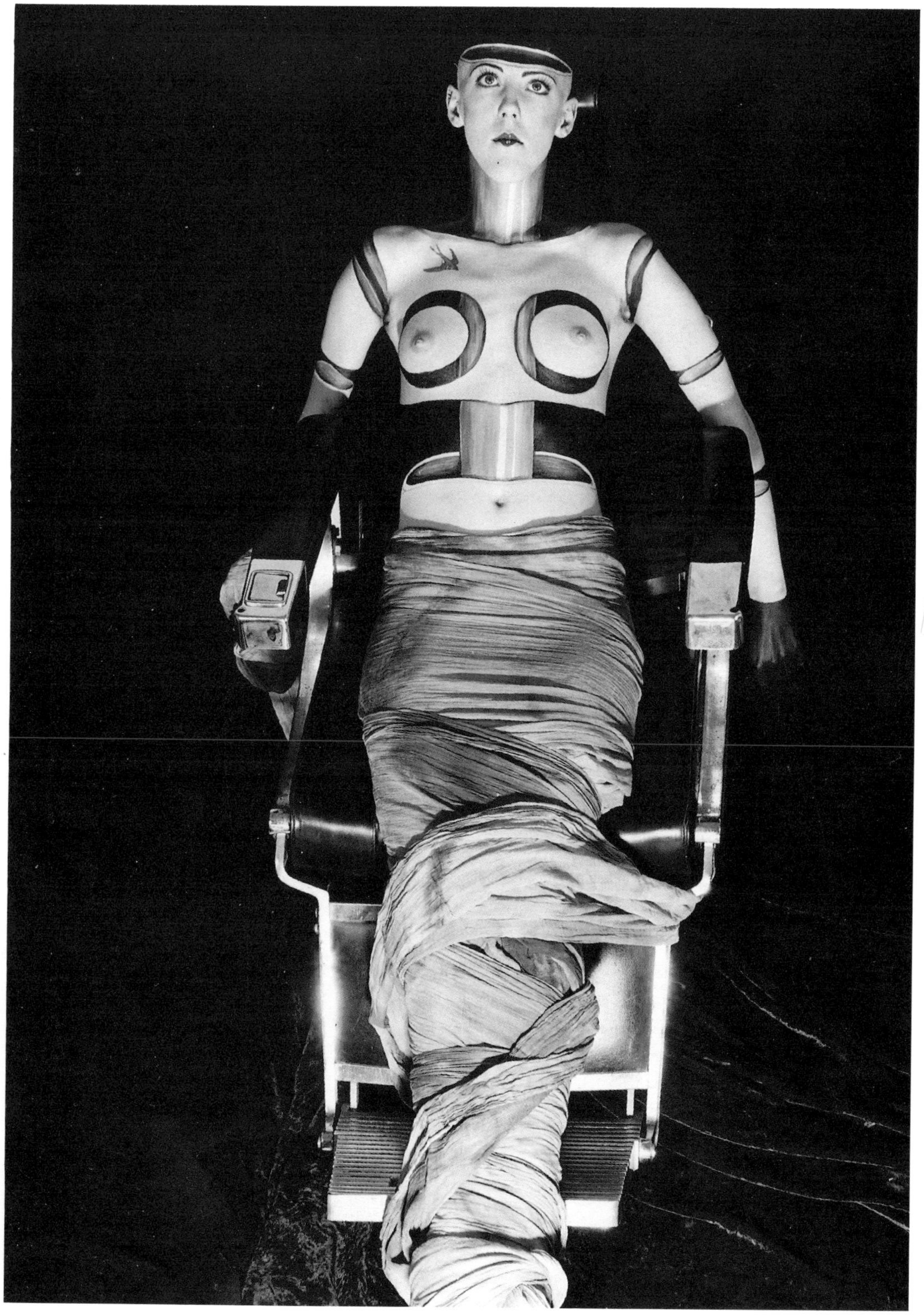

Photograph by Robyn Beeche (model: Scarlot; body painting: Richard Sharples).

Marquesas islanders with statue as depicted in Robert Brown, *The Races of Mankind* (1873).

the previous chapter we outlined many of the reasons for the popularity of the body as a symbol.)

The human form can serve as a symbol of any signified – including, of course, itself (as is the case of an illustration in an anatomy textbook). More frequently, however, representations of 'the body' are intended to convey a non-corporal meaning. For example, a caricature or portrait is a symbol of a particular person and the stylized symbols found on the doors of toilets signify difference of gender.

The most important category of signifieds of 'the body' is ideas about society and behaviour. As we saw in the last chapter, corporal metaphors and icons are – throughout the world – invaluable devices for expressing all of the beliefs, values and rules which, taken together, constitute a socio-cultural system. Thus the meaning of the Balinese ideal of the body as displayed in the form of the dragon is social integration. On the other hand, the emphasis on vertical segmentation (36″–24″–36″) in our traditional Western ideal body image suggests that one of its meanings is social hierarchy (lower class/middle class/upper class). Likewise, the 'upright' body of the scout (illustrated in the previous chapter) seems intended to serve not only as a model of proper deportment, but simultaneously as a model of proper behaviour.

The problem is, of course, that there are physical limitations to just how upright, segmented, together, etc., a living human body can be. And because the plane of content of the ideal, symbolic body is usually preoccupied with socio-cultural rather than physiological facts, there is often a huge gap between 'the body' as a social symbol and the physiological possibilities of the 'real' bodies which you and I are.

Throughout this book we will consider the various and extraordinary ways in which human beings (ourselves included) attempt to drag their own bodies into line with some socio-symbolic ideal. But there are limits to just how far such modification can go, and it is for this reason that artists have throughout history turned to some inanimate medium as a material expression of 'the body'. By successfully bridging the gap between social ideas and corporeal realities, the artist may be able to 'say' that which our 'real' bodies cannot. (Or, at least, that which our physical bodies cannot express so precisely and succinctly.)

Thus an artistic representation of the body 'tells a story'. There are difficulties in decoding this message into verbal language (if information of this type could be as effectively and efficiently expressed in verbal form, there would never have arisen the need for such a cumbersome material of expression as 'the body'). And there are difficulties in interpreting body symbol 'languages' from one culture to the next. (Which is just as problematic in the West, where, as I suggested earlier, there is not a single unified social system but a jumble of separate systems living cheek by jowl next to each other.) But let's give it a try. What, for example, is the socio-cultural meaning of the prehistoric Venus of Willendorf or Jean Paul Goude's re-creation of Toukie?

Obviously both of these figurative forms are, on the most immediate level, expressing different ideals of and attitudes towards femaleness. The Venus of Willendorf is usually described as a fertility symbol. No one really knows, of course, if that is what she was sculpted to be but she certainly possesses what are commonly called 'child-bearing hips' and breasts which look designed for suckling. We do know that at the time she was created, infant mortality was very high and so great value would have been placed on the woman-as-mother.

Goude's Toukie, on the other hand, appears to represent woman-as-erotic-animal. In one of his drawings of Toukie which is reproduced in *Jungle Fever* Goude has made our job easier by actually scribbling verbal comments on the figure. He describes his customized, idealized version of Toukie as

Approximate outline of the hypothetical body shape of (left) prehistoric figure known as the 'Venus of Willendorf' and (right) artist Jean-Paul Goude's reconstruction of 'Toukie'.

Bushman rock painting design, South Africa.

having a 'pinhead' and a 'horse's arse'. Certainly, as Fig.3.1 shows, her rear end is about four times the size of her head.

What is the meaning of the enormous backside? Firstly, as Goude's own comments suggest, the idea being expressed is that women (or at least some women) are animals. Secondly, given that a protruding buttock is, in evolutionary terms, the original primate sexual trigger, the other half of the message is of woman-as-sexual being. Thus instead of woman-as-mother, Goude's creation could be seen to signify woman-as-erotic-beast (and clearly indicates that he sees this as a desirable female characteristic).

But there is another message in these two figures, one which they have in common and one which has nothing *per se* to do with ideals of femininity. The Venus of Willendorf is fat. Indeed, she is the embodiment of corpulence. In Neolithic times (as in many parts of the Third World today) food was no doubt in short supply and in such an environment obesity would inevitably have been a symbol of pros-perity. Thus, like a Nigerian girl fresh from the fattening house (only more so), the Venus of Willendorf's flesh is a status symbol.

Goude's Toukie, on the other hand, aside from her enormous backside, is as thin as a rail. But in the social environment in which she was created this thinness implies not poverty but the exact opposite. In the modern West, where having enough to eat is the norm, status is signified by having enough money to buy non-fattening foods and enough spare time to exercise. (Which is not, of course, to suggest that people on low incomes cannot manage to stay slim – we are dealing here with symbols, not facts.) Therefore, despite the fact that these two figures portray completely opposite ideals of beauty, changing environmental and social

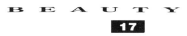

Bushman rock painting, South-West Africa.

circumstances enable them to convey the same message: prosperity.

Finally there is the matter of age. Whereas the age of the Venus of Willendorf is irrelevant (she could be 15 or 50) Goude's Toukie, with her pert breasts and firm skin, is most definitely youthful. She shares this characteristic with almost all modern, Western representations of beauty – thereby expressing the social message that young = good, old = bad. So omnipresent is our bias against age that we are puzzled by cultures such as that of the Venus of Willendorf which do not seem to automatically equate beauty with youthfulness.

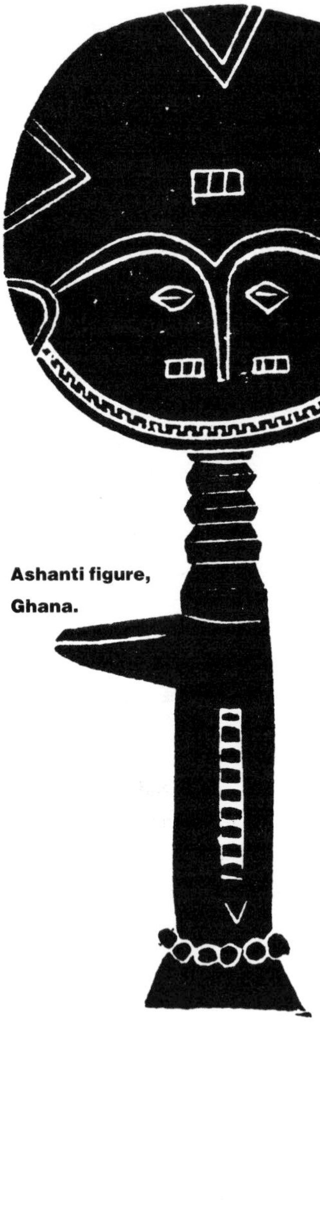

Ashanti figure, Ghana.

We could go on trying to coax meanings out of these works of art forever, but all that is really important here is to establish the fact that figurative art signifies – that it conveys meaning.

These significations are especially evident in the unrealistic nature of such artificial bodies and remind us that the task of conveying meaning inevitably wrenches such representations of the ideal body away from biological possibility. No human being could have legs as long as Goude's Toukie or as short as the Venus of Willendorf's. These idealized figures have such implausible appendages because their function is to represent ideas (e.g., about the role of women,

Bafo wooden mask, Cameroon.

social status, etc.) rather than to portray the human body as it really is. Both artists would have been perfectly capable of biological realism but that was not their objective.

Several important points follow from this:

Firstly, if we do not find attractive the ideas represented by figurative forms we will tend to find the idealized bodies which express them ugly rather than beautiful. (I'm sure that many readers will have found Goude's Toukie and the ideas she expresses especially unattractive.) In our complex modern society where we have cultural pluralism and conflicting ideologies existing side by side, this is our prerogative. In a traditional society such as that which produced the Venus of Willendorf, however, ideological homogeneity and a resulting consensus on the definition of beauty and the ideal body is the norm.[1]

Secondly, figurative art can be more or less conceptual and symbolic, or more or less realistic. In the former case it is possible to see a work of art as purely abstract when it is actually figurative. Marcel Duchamp's 'The

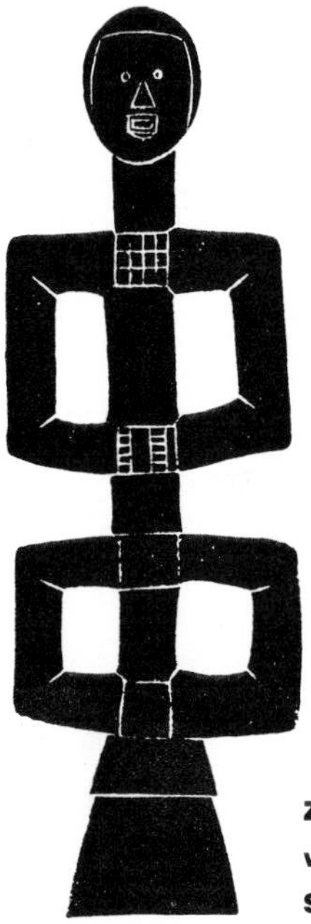

Zulu carved wooden figure, South Africa.

Bride Stripped Bare By Her Bachelors, Even' is a case in point. We know from Duchamp's own comments on his work that the upper part of 'The Large Glass' (as it is known) is an idealized female body while the bottom half is an idealized male body (or group of male bodies). But so laden are these figures with symbolic meaning and so revolutionary are the ideas about men and women which they express that the casual viewer may see nothing physical about them at all.

Not all idealized representations of 'the body' in art are so unrealistic, but all figurative art which carries a social message is pulled away from biological reality by the job of conveying that message. The end result of living with these corporal symbols, which in any society define ultimate beauty, is the disappointment we all have known when we look in the mirror. Human flesh is not nearly as malleable as clay, plaster, wood, metal, fibreglass, stone and the other materials from which idealized, symbolic bodies are made. A sculpture, a doll, a drawing, an air-brushed photograph or a shop window mannequin can achieve any ideal of beauty more perfectly than we can. This fact of life triggers a love/hate relationship between us imperfect human beings and the perfect beauties which artists create.

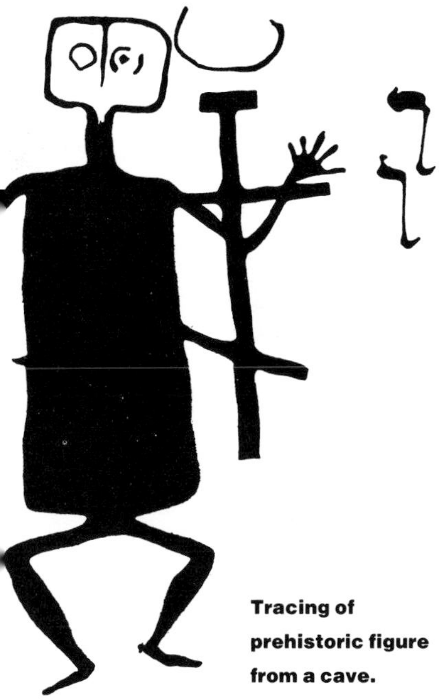

Tracing of prehistoric figure from a cave.

Like Jean Paul Goude and Pygmalion, we love particular artificial bodies for what they represent and for the fact that they can represent it so much more perfectly than real people ever can. On the other hand, we hate them because they mock our own physical imperfections. No doubt there were women in 2500 BC who hated the Venus of Willendorf just as Toukie hated the doll which Jean Paul Goude extrapolated from her own body. The biological body has its own imperatives: it cannot be too thin, too fat, too angular, too spherical, too symmetrical, too amorphous, and so on. Beyond a certain point of modification it will die. We are not, in other words, really cut out to be abstract symbols.

And we mere mortals age. The Venus de Milo may have lost her arms but she hasn't grown fat or wrinkled. Toukie's body, on the other hand, is today no doubt not quite the image of youthful beauty which Goude took as the starting point of his re-creation of her. And men and women who have been re-moulded as mannequins may wish that it was their representations (like Dorian Gray's) which aged, rather than their own bodies. One way or another, we are all mocked by artificial bodies which can achieve a standard of perfection (as defined by our socio-physical ideals) which we never can.

This is the other moral problem which confronts the artist who would play God: in the process he or she brings human misery. Because of Goude's experiments, poor Toukie may have ended up thinking that her own legs were too short, her own waist too fat and her own backside too small.

Likewise the creator of the Venus of Willendorf must have brought unhappiness to every woman who saw it and felt that in comparison she was too skinny; and Michaelangelo's 'David' mocks every male who, like me, desperately exercises to keep 'in shape'. In other words, like Don Juan we are defeated by statues – even if, in our own case, this defeat is only symbolic.

But what if we were to rise up and slay the artists and trample their creations into dust? In doing so we might free ourselves from odious comparisons but we would then have to depend completely on our own flesh to do the job that they do so well – the job of expressing and giving form to our most cherished and fundamental ideals, values and dreams.

In 'The Horror of the Waxworks', Vincent Price, the creator of the waxworks, has had his hands destroyed in a fire and can no longer sculpt the absolute beauty which is his obsession. His solution is rather grizzly: he searches for a living model who epitomizes his ideal so that he can kill her and plunge her still warm body into molten wax. What makes the film unbelievable is that he actually succeeds in finding a 'living doll' who completely fulfils his vision of beauty. As we will see in the next chapter, some living human beings may indeed approximate their societies' ideals, but as a medium for the expression of socio-cultural abstractions, they can never entirely compete with the unlimited possibilities offered by inanimate materials. In the 'real' world, Vincent Price's part would be played by Jean Paul Goude and, unable to find a woman who completely embodied his vision of social and physical perfection, he would end up doing a Dr Frankenstein and attempting to graft a horse's arse onto her posterior.

1. Ideals of beauty in the West are not always meaningful, however, because in our society they are frequently subject to changing fashions. As we will explore in more detail in Chapter 21, fashion 'looks' are often meaningless in so far as they exist only to demonstrate a change from last year's look. Fashionable ideals of beauty may therefore signify nothing other than change for the sake of change – in which case we would be frustrated in any attempt to decode their intrinsic meanings. Fashions in beauty are only arbitrary signs in the language of fashion: taken *together* they signify 'change' and 'progress'; but on their own they are as empty of meaning as are individual letters of the alphabet. Within the context of fashion, hips or breasts may get bigger or smaller, legs and necks may get longer or shorter, waists may get higher or lower, etc., without any significance other than the demonstration of the relentless march of fashion change.

Catherine Dyer and the Adel Rootstein mannequin which was modelled after her. (Photo: David Bailey)

Three display mannequins by Adel Rootstein;

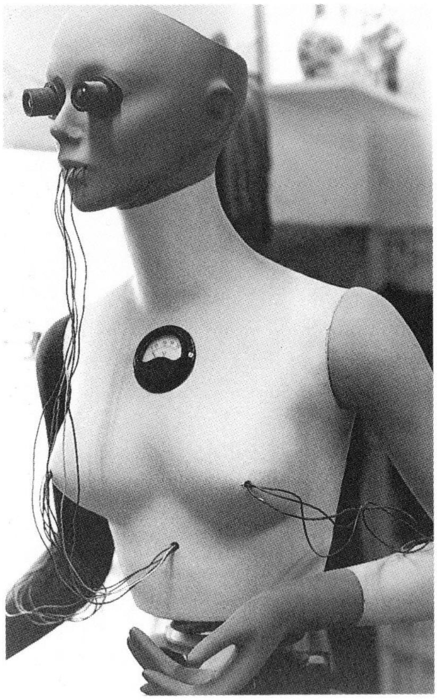

Modified display mannequin, Ibiza.

Adel Rootstein display mannequin modelled on Twiggy.

1 Beauty

4 Living Dolls

Every year at the height of the rainy season some 3000 members of the nomadic Fulani tribes of the West African savanna come together to hold a beauty contest. They call this event the *gerewol* and it lasts for seven days. The contestants are all the young men of the tribe and the prize to be won is not a car or a trip around the world it is a wife (for amongst the Fulani it is young women who choose their husbands). Otherwise there is a lot of similarity between the *gerewol* and our own Miss World or other beauty contests.

The Fulani festivities begin with a welcoming dance and a song as the contestants are first shown to the assembled crowd and the judges (the would-be wives), who carry colourful umbrellas to denote their status. Already the contestants have spent hours making themselves beautiful. The Fulani ideal of beauty which the judges are looking for is a long slender nose, long face, large white eyes, white even teeth and a tall lean body. To accentuate these features the contestants shave their foreheads, paint a white line from their hair-line to the tip of the nose and blacken their eyelids and lips.

By the afternoon, with luck, the contestants will be ready to take part in the *yaake*, a line-up in which they sing and dance, stand on tip-toe and make faces, rolling or crossing their eyes and grimacing to show off their teeth to the judges. They keep this up for hours, aided by the consumption of stimulating drugs beforehand. Throughout all this, old ladies in the crowd hurl criticisms at those who do not live up to the Fulani ideal of beauty.

As in Western beauty contests, although physical attractiveness is the primary factor which will affect the judges' decision, the Fulani also rank the contestants on 'personality'. In this case, instead of an eagerness to 'make the world a happy place', personality is defined by an ability to endure pain unflinchingly. This is put to the test in the next part of the *gerewol* ceremony, when each of the contestants is given a good whipping. If he cries out or shows even mild discomfort he will lose points. The winners of this round of judging are those who languidly contemplate their beauty in a mirror as if nothing was happening while great weals are cut into their backs (which, by the way, they will take pride in throughout their lives, rather as duelling scars used to be prized in Europe).

Then it is back to the dancing on tip-toe (rather like wearing high heels but without the heels), rolling their eyes and grimacing frantically. At the end of seven days of this the judges, one by one, step forward and with a slight gesture indicate their choice of winner.

If the Fulani *gerewol* ceremony shows us that the beauty contest isn't an exclusively Western phenomenon, Lucretius's description of the Roman pageant of Cybele in the first century AD demonstrates that it isn't a purely modern phenomenon either. Unfortunately, Lucretius doesn't tell us how the winner of this contest was chosen but he does describe a triumphal victory procession which leaves Miss World's in the shade:

> 'Adorned with emblem and crown . . . she is carried in awe-inspiring state. Tight-stretched tambourines and hollow cymbals thunder all around to the stroke of open hand, hollow pipes stir with Phrygian strain . . . She rides in procession through great cities and mutely enriches mortals with blessing not expressed in words. They strew her path with brass and silver, presenting her with bounteous alms and scatter over her a snow-shower of roses.'

In all societies and throughout human history, individuals who, by the luck of the genetic draw, happen to have bodies which approximate to their society's and their historical period's ideal of beauty (the socio-physical body ideal), have been put on a pedestal of adoration. As Lucretius's comment about mere 'mortals' suggests, these individuals become (if only for a day) gods and goddesses. For, like deities, they bestow a great blessing upon us: they offer conclusive proof that abstract, ethereal concepts of beauty (and what they symbolically represent) can be more or less realized in human flesh. For it is never enough to represent such ideals in the form of artificial bodies – to leave it at that is to exclude humanity itself from the pantheon of symbolic meaning.

In Chapter 2, I suggested that one of the reasons why 'the body' is a suitable metaphor for fundamental, but verbally inexpressible concepts is the fact that it is a metaphor to which we can all relate. Clearly, however, this is only the case if bridges are built between our real bodies and those non-corporal abstractions which define ideal beauty. The first such bridge is formed by the artificial bodies which our artists create. These give substance to abstract social ideals but they are themselves difficult to relate to because they are not and can never be 'one of us'. Therefore a second bridge is needed in the form of those living dolls who, by virtue of a fortuitous genetic inheritance, can try to compete with artistic perfection.

Whereas the artistic processes which produce artificial beauty are intentional and directed, the genetic processes which produce living dolls are haphazard and random. In any group of human beings some will be fatter, some thinner, some taller, some shorter. This is true of any physical characteristic including, of course, the long thin noses of which the Fulani are so fond. Perhaps, given enough time, evolution in the form of sexual selection can bring biological facts more into line with socio-physical ideals. But the time-scale of those changes is such that even relatively stable, traditional societies with ideals of beauty which are centuries old can rarely benefit from them. (And is there any evidence that 'the beautiful people' of any society actually produce more offspring? I suspect not.)

Let us pause for a moment to consider in this light the long noses of the Fulani. If we look at photographs of the youths participating in the *gerewol*, and if we mentally subtract the optical illusion created by the lines which they paint from their foreheads to the tips of their noses, we see that although some of these noses are long and thin, others are short and fat. Natural selection does not appear to have resolved this problem for the Fulani. Nor does the Fulani practice of mothers patiently pulling on the noses of their offspring seem to have helped.[1]

Genetic processes in all life forms produce variations of physical characteristics – a biological fact which has many social advantages for human beings. Biologists have long appreciated the role which genetic variation plays in improving the biological organism in the course of evolution, but social organisms (i.e., societies) also benefit from this phenomenon in that physical diversity ensures that *some* individuals will inevitably be born whose bodies approximate to any given ideal of beauty. Just as biological evolution makes use of 'freaks', so does any social system.

In both situations (be it a particular biological or a particular social environment) some of these freaks of nature will fail to find a suitable niche, while others will be born into the right environment and will prosper.

Contestant in British beauty contest, 1964.

Ultimately it is just a matter of chance – being in the right place at the right time. (And if that age-old science fiction dream of cloning identical individuals was ever put into practice both biological and social processes would be put in jeopardy.)

In evolutionary terms the right place at the right time refers to the physical environment. In terms of living dolls, on the other hand, being in the right place at the right time refers to a fortuitous social and cultural environment where the ideal of beauty (that is, the image of 'the body' which is attractive because it conveys the right social and cultural meanings) is similar to one's own physique.

Beautiful bodies may in some cases be naturally created by biology, but their classification as beautiful is always in the eye of the beholder. And, as we have seen, what is in the eye of the beholder is put there by the society of which he or she is a member. It is all culturally relative. Miss World wouldn't stand a chance in a traditional (un-Westernized) African tribe which equates beauty with obesity. Mr Universe wouldn't stand a chance in the Fulani's *gerewol* pageant.

Luck lies not so much in your genes as in what society and in which era you are born. Living dolls are generally freakish extremes of nature. In one society such extremes of appearance would make any who possessed them a miserable outcast. In another society, however, the very same extremes of appearance would cause that individual to be seen not as a freak but as a 'natural beauty'.

In its title and format the Miss World beauty contest attempts to deny this fact of life. Yet clearly Miss World is only Miss Westernized World. The fact that the Miss World contest can have the name it does simply reflects the success of Western imperialism, for the definition of beauty is ultimately a matter of politics. If the advance of the Arab world had not been stopped in Spain in the 15th century or if the industrial revolution had begun in, say, India instead of England, Miss World would look very different; for one of the most significant ways in which one culture dominates another is by the replacement of the indigenous ideal of beauty with that of the conquering society.

Nor does Miss World even represent the beauty ideals of everyone in the West – perhaps not even a majority. As we have seen, ours is an increasingly pluralistic world where many different cultures, each with its own vision of beauty, reside side by side. Miss World represents but one of these social bodies. Others are represented by fashion models, pin-ups and pop, cinema, television and athletic stars.

Finally, we should remember that Miss World reigns for just one year. Because Western society is subject to both rapid socio-cultural change and the clockwork oscillations of fashion, our ideals of beauty are short-lived. A modern Mr Fulani might have been a contender 20 or even a hundred years ago, but the first Miss World who was crowned in 1951 wouldn't stand a chance today.

But it is not my objective to denigrate Miss World or any other living doll. I may question her title and I may personally find the ideal of socio-physical beauty which she represents unattractive, but I cannot disagree with the fact that she has an important job to do. Without her and those like her humanity would be unrepresented in the Olympics of ideal beauty. In such a world it would be just us ordinary mortals versus them – the artificial bodies. We may loathe living dolls for pointing out our own imperfections but they are at least 'one of us'. They bring beauty and all that it signifies a little nearer our grasp and thereby bring our social ideals and values – even our society itself – one step closer to being a reality. They are to absolute beauty what Christians believe Christ is to God – the spirit made flesh.

1. The Fulani obsession with long noses would seem to stem from the time when, some scholars believe, this tribe migrated from the Upper Nile. Their noses would have been much longer and thinner than those of the indigenous population of the Niger, and to celebrate their presumed superiority over their fat-nosed neighbours the Fulani developed the idea that thin noses are beautiful whereas fat noses are ugly. We would be wasting our time, therefore, to look for a symbolic significance in this aspect of the Fulani ideal of beauty, for its meaning (as in the Black is Beautiful movement in America in the 1960s) is a product of historical circumstance rather than socio–cultural symbolism.

1 Beauty

5 The Pursuit of the Perfect Body

We began with a look at ourselves in the mirror and discovered that this strange creature is meaningful and real only in relation to an ideal body which is a reflection not of a person but of the social body of which we are a part. We went on to consider the conceptual and symbolic nature of this ideal and to see how far removed it can be from our physical being. Then we considered how this symbolic vision of 'the body' can be realized, both in the artificial bodies which artists create and in the bodies of those freaks of nature who happen to approximate to their society's socio-physical ideal. It remains only to bring the circle full round to where we started – the individual, human body.

Whereas 'living dolls' are born with the 'right' bodies (that is, physical forms which correspond to the social body and are therefore found to be attractive), most of us have to go to extraordinary lengths to bring our bodies into line with our socio-physical ideals:

* For centuries, women of the Padung tribe of Burma stretched their necks to three or four times their natural length by progressively inserting gold or copper rings between their heads and their shoulders.
* Amongst the Chinook tribe of the North-West coast of North America, the still malleable heads of babies were strapped between wooden boards for a year or more so that their heads would be attractively pointed.
* Upon achieving adulthood, males of the Tchikrin tribe of South America have a small piercing in their lower lip stretched until it will accommodate a wooden plug, which is often about four inches in width. They wear these plugs daily, despite difficulties eating and drinking.
* When Balinese boys and girls reach adolescence their teeth are filed flat without the benefit of an anaesthetic.
* In pre-communist China the feet of some 'lucky' young girls were tightly bound so that, as they grew, their arches would be forced inwards, creating tiny feet on which they were often unable to walk or stand unassisted.

Three Padaung women from Burma with stretched necks on a visit to London in 1966.

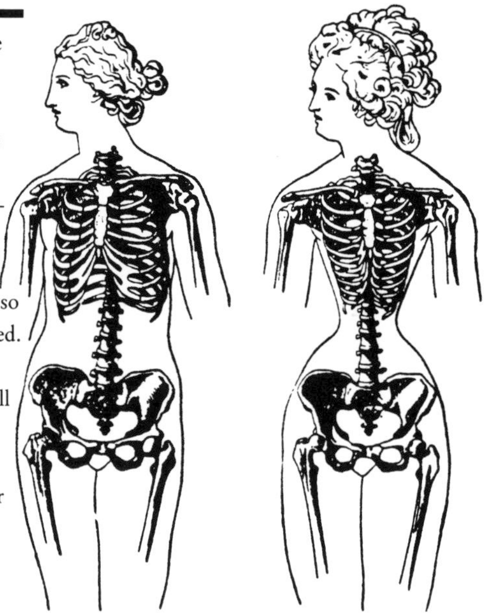

The effects of wearing tight corsets as shown in a study by Dr Samuel Soemmerring, 1793.

Nor is it only outside the boundaries of the West[1] where such drastic bodily modifications have been practised. Until quite recently cranial deformation was the norm in many European peasant communities (for example in France, Germany and Holland). Fashionable women in Victorian Europe and America practised extreme tight lacing from an early age which had the effect of compressing the rib cage and internal organs so as to produce a waist measurement of seemingly impossible dimensions.

Today we diet, exercise and tan our bodies to bring them into line with an ideal which we describe as 'healthy' but which – at least in extreme cases – may in fact be deleterious to health. Body builders (increasingly of both sexes) use specially designed equipment and, in some cases, steroids to 'pump up' their muscles in order to achieve an effect which could never be produced naturally.

And modern, Western plastic surgery has devised a technology of body modification which puts in the shade the attempts of tribal or peasant people to alter the shape of their bodies. Thanks to this technology we can today change practically every aspect of our bodies' appearance and, throughout the West (but especially in America), an ever-growing number of people of both sexes are submitting to the plastic surgeon's scalpel in order to alter the shape of their facial and bodily features. Most people are satisfied with 'correcting' only one feature of their physical appearance, but there are a growing number of 'plastic surgery junkies' who go on to transform their bodies in as many ways as possible.

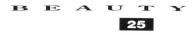

In *Beyond the Looking Glass* Katherine Perutz outlines the history of a woman in her mid-thirties who seems to have spent her entire adult life having her face and body 'perfected'. Susie began with dermabrasion of her skin to remove wrinkles (which involves using a sort of sanding machine on the skin), went on to have a full face-lift ('They take the skin from the frame and cut the skin from the tissue, you know, of the face, and then they pull it and they trim it out and sew it back on.'), went back for more dermabrasion (to get rid of freckles), decided to get breast implants ('They're plastic bags, I guess'), then changed her mind and had her breasts reduced to their original size. At the time that Perutz interviewed her, Susie was looking forward to having a thigh lift (to remove excess fat from the upper thighs) and getting her hands 'done'. This was in the 1960s, when plastic surgery was in its infancy.

From New York to Burma, Bali to the Amazon, the end product of these alterations to the human form are seen as not only 'attractive' but also 'natural'. This is because such modifications help to bring the physical body into line with the ideal body, which is itself a 'natural' symbol of the social system and which defines reality for all its members.

Before and after photographs showing effect of a stay in a fattening house in Old Calabar, West Africa.

Body building competition. (Photo: Grace Lau)

The congruence of meanings between all the cultural systems within a particular society obliterates any perception of artificiality. In any given society, that which is perceived as 'natural' is that which fits snugly within a culture's social construction of reality. Thus, from within traditional Padung society it would have seemed unnatural for women *not* to have stretched necks.

Exactly what such natural symbols might signify is often difficult to extrapolate. To discover the meaning of Padung stretched necks, Tchikrin lip plugs or Chinook pointed heads we would need to know the significance of the neck (or perhaps height), the lips (or perhaps the mouth) and the head in each of these societies which, unfortunately, we do not. Indeed, to a certain extent one would need to know all that the native informant might know about his or her society in order to unravel these symbols which are, after all, an expression of the social order itself.

It may also be the case that some body modifications are accidents of history which simply 'caught on' (perhaps as a way of accentuating a contrast with a neighbouring tribe, for example) but it is difficult to imagine that any such fundamental alterations of the body could be carried out in complete ignorance of the socio-physical construction of reality. The human body is too existentially omnipresent to avoid being 'clothed' in meaning and any alterations to the body would affect that meaning.

But while it may be impossible for us to get sufficiently inside Padung, Tchikrin or Chinook realities, we can perhaps make some guesses about our own pursuit of the perfect body. Despite the pluralism of modern Western society and its resulting pluralism of

Female body builder (Photo: Grace Lau)

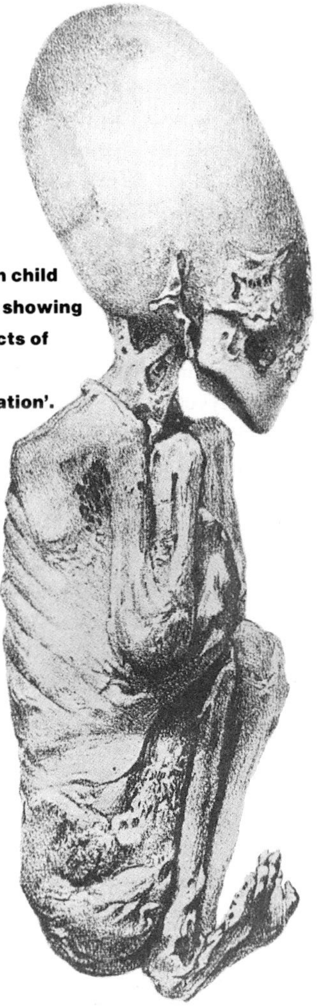

Peruvian child mummy showing the effects of cranial 'deformation'.

ideal body types, there do appear to be some common denominators of social meaning expressed by many of them. The rippling muscles of the body builder, the eternally firm and youthful flesh of the plastic surgeon's customers and the rake's progress of the compulsive dieter all point to a generic Western body ideal which is youthful rather than old, firm rather than flabby, lean rather than fat.

These characteristics of our ideal body are clearly sociologically as well as physiologically descriptive and suggest a social body which is itself 'youthful', 'firm' (if not 'hard'), 'lean' and 'healthy'. That we should, at this point in Western history, emphasize these particular socio-physical characteristics is probably because they precisely characterize all that our 'flabby', 'degenerate', 'bloated', 'decrepit' and 'ailing' (if not downright 'sick') society would like to be. In other words, the perfect body which we pursue with such diligence is perhaps a reaction to, rather than an expression of, our social facts – a desperately hoped-for Utopia born of a non-utopic reality.

However, the interpretation of socio-physical symbolism is prone to subjective bias. What is indisputable is the extent to which people in all societies and throughout history have striven against the odds to bring their own imperfect physical bodies into line with some ideal of beauty which is both specific to their own society and (because its plane of content is the social rather than the physical body) inherently unlike their own bodies. So why then, given the plasticity of artistic media and the good luck of those individuals who happen to have been born with particularly 'beautiful' bodies (both of which are so much closer to the ideal than our own), do the rest of us pursue so doggedly the actualization of these ideals *in our own flesh?*

Part of the answer to this question has already been hinted at: all human beings need to participate personally in their own (that is, their societies') socio-physical reality. It simply will not do for 'them' (the living dolls and the artificial bodies) to embody this universe of meaning while the rest of us are outside looking in, participating in our own social systems only by proxy. In such a situation our own bodies would be *insignificant*.

There is another reason why human beings transform the shape of their bodies (and why they transform the external appearance of their bodies with decorations and clothing). *Bodily modification constitutes an ultimate confirmation of social commitment*. The Tchikrin male or the Padung female publicly and permanently demonstrate their allegiance to their respective societies by putting their own bodies 'on the line'. Talk, as they say, is cheap, but a stretched lip or a stretched neck, although 'expensive' in terms of its cost in inconvenience and pain, offers indisputable proof of social commitment.

The permanence and severity of these acts of bodily modification may seem barbaric to us, but we would be negligent if we failed to appreciate their importance and functional efficacy, for it is by such means that the integrity and historic continuity of the social unit is safeguarded.

Social incorporation by means of physical modification is the most effective device ever invented for ensuring that a society will have a future and can, therefore, go on providing a framework for group effort and a data-bank for the accumulation of the knowledge and wisdom that is born of experience. Without such seemingly barbaric activities as body 'deformation' (and, as we will see, the transformation of physical appearance through adornment), humankind would not have become the dominant life form on what has increasingly become *our* planet.

If in the West we do not generally demonstrate commitment to our society by such drastic means of physical transformation, this is perhaps both a requisite and an entailment of the formlessness of our rapidly degenerating social system. Margaret Thatcher recently remarked that 'There is no such thing as society, there are only individuals and their families' and I for once have to agree with her but not her enthusiasm for this situation).[2] If there is – in the West and the Westernized world – no such thing as 'society', if our socio-cultural reality is falling apart, then this is perhaps related to our society's refusal to encourage the expression of social commitment through 'barbaric' acts of

1. Throughout this book I will use the term 'the West' to refer to that umbrella of social systems whose culture historically derives from Western Europe but which today has spread across the entire planet.

physical modification.

As it happens many people throughout Western society drastically modify their bodies through plastic surgery, dieting, weight training, etc., but there are essential differences between these practices and those encouraged in traditional tribal societies. Besides differences in the sought-after ideals of beauty and differences of technical expertise, there is also the fact that in the West the pursuit of the perfect body is motivated by *personal* rather than social objectives.

To be sure, the Tchikrin man who stretches his lip does so, in part, because it is only in this way that he personally can become attractive to the opposite sex and only in this way that he can achieve adult status. It is also clear that the man in Los Angeles who gets his face lifted, or his body fat removed, does so because his social and cultural environment defines beauty in the way in which it does. Nevertheless, we cannot equate these two actions sociologically and functionally. The Tchikrin man's action confirms an ultimate and irrefutable commitment to his tribe while the Los Angeles man's commitment is ultimately only to himself.

Part of the reason for this difference in the 'why' of body modification is the disintegration of our Western social system. Another reason is our Western disdain for social conformity and our celebration of individuality. We (and I would certainly include myself in this) cherish a belief in personal freedom – not only as regards our ideas but equally as regards our bodies. This view is forcefully expressed in an episode of the *Twilight Zone* TV series which was called 'Number 12 Looks Just Like You'.

Rod Serling begins this episode with the question:

'Given the chance, what young girl wouldn't happily exchange a plain face for a lovely one? What girl could refuse the opportunity to be beautiful? For want of a better estimate, let's call it the year 2000. At any rate, imagine a time in the future when science has developed a means of giving everyone the face and body he dreams of. It may not happen tomorrow – but it happens *now* in the Twilight Zone.'

The story focuses on a plain, but not ugly, 18 year old girl who – despite the arguments of her mother (a number 12), her uncle (a number 17) and her best friend Valerie (a number 8) – refuses to undergo the transformation that will make her beautiful according to a catalogue of body types from which she can choose. It seems that the girl's father had committed suicide several years previously, immediately after himself being transformed into a number 17. Before his death he had filled his daughter's head with all sorts of heresy: that if everyone is beautiful, then no one truly is. That the authorities aren't really interested in making people beautiful, their object is simply to make everyone conform.

Eventually our heroine is forced into having the operation. She becomes a perfect number 8 just like her friend Valerie. Clearly her mind has also been transformed for she is delighted with her new and beautiful body and delighted with the fact that now she is just like everyone else. As the ever-suave Rod Serling concludes:

'Portrait of a young lady in love – with herself. Improbable? Perhaps. But in an age of plastic surgery, body building and an infinity of cosmetics, let us hesitate to say impossible. These and other strange blessings may be waiting in the future – which after all, *is* the Twilight Zone.'

'No 12 Looks Just Like You' is an essay in the relationship between the pursuit of the perfect body and social conformity. The authors (Charles Ceaumont and John Tomerlin) are clearly against conformity and in favour of personal freedom, including the freedom to be 'ugly' as defined by one's society and historical era. Few of us would disagree with that message.

Yet if we take away the technological wizardry, what happens to our heroine is fundamentally no different from that which happens in any traditional society. The Balinese teenager who has his or her teeth filed, the Tchikrin male who has his lower lip stretched to accommodate an enormous plate or an Ibibio girl who spends a year of her life in a 'fattening house' all give up their personal freedom and individuality for the sake of the society in which they live.

As an anthropologist, I feel great respect for other ways of life and I see in bodily modifications, the purpose of which is to symbolically and irrevocably incorporate the individual into the social body, a highly effective and practical means of ensuring the stability and cohesiveness of social systems. But, on the other hand, as a liberal, freedom-loving Westerner, I also respect and embrace the anti-conformity message of 'No 12 Looks Just Like You'. Is there no way in which personal freedom and social conformity can co-exist?

Interestingly, the modern world seems to be in the process of generating just such a compromise solution in the form of the new 'tribes' which are springing up like mushrooms in our midst. Imagine, if you will, a future world where Western society has become simply an umbrella encompassing lots and lots of radically different and distinctive mini-societies, each with its own vision of beauty and each with its own values, beliefs and ideologies symbolically encoded in its ideal of physical perfection. In such a world there would be personal freedom to choose which socio-physical body appealed to you. And once that choice was made there would be social and physical conformity within its satisfying embrace.

Sheer fantasy? Hardly. Just such a world already exists all around us here in the twilight zone of Western civilization.

2. At least as regards mainstream, middle class Western Society. Sub-groups such as Hell's Angels, hippies and punks will be considered in due course.

Miss World contestants from Spain, Ireland and Israel having their hair permed, 1974.

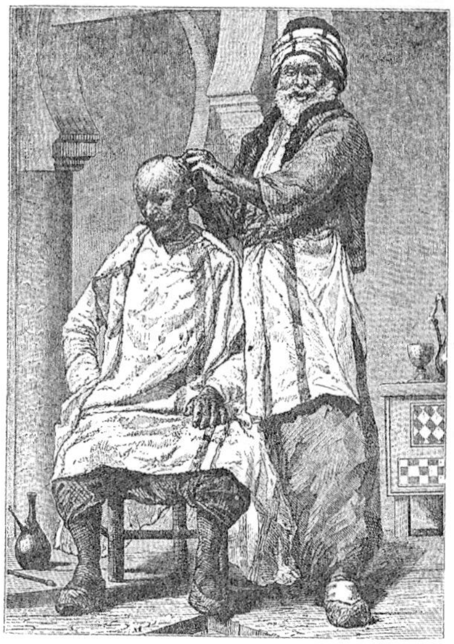

Turkish barber at work.

A Venetian woman bleaching her hair in the sun from Cesare Vecellio's *De gli Habti antichi et Moderni di Diverse Parti de Mondo* (1590).

Victorian man shaving.

2
Adornment

6 Customized Chameleons

From 1760 to 1770 a Jesuit missionary named Sanchez Labrodor lived amongst the Caduveo tribe of the Amazon. Many things about this people's way of life shocked and annoyed Labrodor and perhaps none more so than the amount of time they spent each day painting intricate arabesque patterns on their faces.

The Jesuit argued that, as they had little to eat, they should be spending this time hunting, gathering or growing crops and, further-more, that in painting their bodies they were tampering with God's handiwork. For their part, the Indians were shocked and amazed that anyone could object to their body painting. 'Don't be so stupid,' they chided Labrodor, 'If we didn't decorate ourselves then we would be just like the beasts of the jungle'.

For the Caduveo and many other tribal peoples it is the action of decorating, adorning or modifying the body which is seen as that which separates humankind from the animal kingdom. For some such peoples, as with the Caduveo, the distinction hinges on whether the body is painted. For other tribes it is a matter of wearing enormous lip plugs in piercings made in their flesh. Many tribal peoples from the Arctic to the South Seas define humanity by the action of tattooing or scarring the body. For the Balinese, it is filing the teeth flat which separates people from animals. And for still other tribal peoples the dividing line between humans and beasts is the action of shaving body, head or facial hair (a belief which has been a source of considerable difficulty for many bearded anthropologists). As Victoria Ebin puts it in *The Body Decorated:*

'The first and essential fact of body decoration is that it distinguishes man as a social being, distinct from animals of the forest and other humans outside his own particular group – for he regards both as equally alien. Through decorating his body in some permanent form the individual expressly conveys his allegiance to his own group, making a precise distinction between those in society and those beyond its confines: it is the crucial factor in his relations with the rest of the world, the distinction between beauty and the beast.

The Bafia people of Cameroon, for instance, say that without their sacrifications they would be indistinguishable from pigs or chimpanzees. The Maori woman of New Zealand claims that if she neglected to tattoo her lips and gums she would resemble a dog with her white teeth and red mouth. The Nuba of the Sudan perceive that the crucial difference between men and animals lies in men's ability to shave their heads and bodies and to make their skins smooth. This capacity distinguishes them from every other species: even language was once shared between men and monkeys.

In New Guinea the Roro people, who tattoo themselves extensively, describe the un-tattooed person as 'raw', comparing him to uncooked meat. Claude Lévi-Strauss draws a fascinating distinction between raw and cooked meat on the one hand, and fresh and rotten fruit on the other. The former is transformed by a cultural process, the latter by a natural one. The Roro see the tattooed man as 'cooked meat', transformed by a human process and thus given a social identity. Therein lies the distinction between a social being and a biological entity.' (pp.23–24)

Photograph by Robyn Beeche (Make-up: Phylis Cohen, collar by: Richard Sharples, Courtesy of Vidal Sassoon).

But whereas tribal peoples may define humankind as the species which modifies its natural appearance, we in the West have very different ideas about what distinguishes us from the animal kingdom. Traditionally the

Judeo-Christian view was (and for many still is) that we are unique in that we are children of God and possess a soul. But as our world has grown more secular another, apparently more objective, marker of human nature was called for and students of human and animal behaviour have pursued the problem with diligence.

It has, for example, been argued that what is special and unique about our species is our ability to make and use tools. The concept of *Homo faber* lost favour when it was discovered that chimpanzees and other primates living in the wild regularly fashion tools such as the twigs which they trim and lick to extract termites from their mounds.

So attention turned to the view that humankind alone possesses, and is defined by, a capacity for sophisticated language. *Homo loquans* has, however, also been pushed from his or her pedestal by recent discoveries. A few years ago primatologists working in the US decided to see if they could teach gorillas, chimps and orangutans to use the sign language system of the deaf. (They chose a non-verbal language because non-human primates have very different vocalizing apparatus from humans.) The primates, to everyone's surprise, learned sign language quickly, developed reasonable vocabularies, demonstrated creativity in linguistic usage (signing 'watermelon' as 'water-fruit' and calling one researcher 'crocodile' because of the logo on his shirts) and in the latest experiments many of the primates have gone on to teach sign language to their offspring. Simultaneously, researchers working in the field have discovered that the vocal and non-vocal communication of non-human primates in the wild is actually much more sophisticated than had previously been realized.

So is it language which makes us unique? The technical answer is that it depends upon one's definition of language and it looks, therefore, as if the issue will never be resolved to anyone's satisfaction. But one thing is clear from such recent studies of our non-human primate relatives: neither language nor tool use can provide a simple and clear-cut boundary with which to delineate the special qualities of human nature. Why then do we not simply embrace the logic of the Caduveo and other tribal peoples and celebrate *Homo sapiens* as *Homo depictus* – the only self-adorned species?

To answer this we need look no further than our own prejudices. No matter how objective we might strive to be in our analysis of human and animal behaviour, our theories and assumptions are inevitably embedded in our own culture. For the last few hundred years Western society has, in the main, dismissed body decoration, adornment, fashion and style as unimportant leisure activities which only the frivolous relish and which only the foolish take seriously. (Put another way, this has usually meant that we in the West categorize such activities as 'feminine'.)

It is hardly surprising, therefore, that 'serious-minded' primatologists, physical anthropologists, linguists, animal behaviourists and such like (usually men) should balk at the idea of allocating body decoration a central role in the definition of human nature. To do so would involve students of animal and human behaviour in an uncomfortable reappraisal of *their own* physicality (and their own body decoration – or lack of it). And because of the tendency in the West (during the last couple of hundred years only) to dismiss body decoration as a feminine pursuit, such an approach would have resulted in an emasculation of mankind itself. It is hardly surprising, therefore, that (unlike the Caduveo and other tribal peoples) we reject the idea that our unique capacity for self adornment is, and always has been, a central feature of our humanity.

With this in mind, let us go back some 24,000 years to the late palaeolithic era when our earliest *Homo sapiens* ancestors first began forging a unique way of life:

---

1. Instead of living in packs, these creatures resided in tribal groups each of which possessed a culture with its own rules of behaviour which were learned rather than genetically programmed.
2. Each group possessed its own language of vocalized sounds and non-verbal gestures.
3. Fire had been brought under control for warmth, cooking and protection.
4. Tools made of stone and other materials were regularly manufactured.
5. Within each tribal group there was probably a specialization of the labour force whereby men hunted in groups while women gathered and prepared foodstuffs and reared the young (who, unlike the young of other species, required many years to learn that which they needed to know for adult life).
6. The dead of at least some of these groups were ritualistically buried.
7. There was art in the form of painted pictures on the walls of caves and small clay figurines.
8. And there was art in the form of body decoration – with pigments such as red and yellow ochre and charcoal used to paint (or perhaps tattoo) the skin, and jewellery in the form of bracelets, necklaces and 'crowns' made of shells and animal teeth.

How one yearns to know what designs they painted on their bodies, and why! Did they decorate themselves daily or just on special occasions? Besides bracelets, necklaces and headpieces made of shells and animal teeth, did they adorn themselves with things such as feathers and leaves? (Decorations which, if they were used, would have inevitably perished with the passage of time.) Did everyone decorate their bodies or just individuals with some special status? Unfortunately, short of inventing a device for time-travel, we have no way of answering any of these questions.

Our only viable alternative is to look at the way body decoration is used in those tribal societies which still exist today. There are, of course, serious problems in making such a comparison. Like us, such people have some 24,000 years separating them from the late palaeolithic, during which time they too have evolved and changed. But, unlike us, these surviving tribal people are traditionalists whose way of life is highly resistant to change. And, like the early *Homo sapiens* of the palaeolithic, they live in small, tribal groups. This means that, whatever other modifications they may have made to their lifestyle, the members of these contemporary groups face many of the same problems and difficulties which our mutual ancestors must have faced.

When we look around the world at surviving groups of tribal peoples we see a fantastic degree of variation of lifestyle. Some are monogamous, some promiscuous. Some are peace-loving, some ferocious fighters. Some are highly religious, some are not. Some are highly competitive proto-capitalists, some are proto-communists. Some have highly hierarchical social structures, some are egalitarian. Some wear clothes, while some (at least to our eyes) go naked.

But, there is one thing which all tribal peoples have in common: they all practise some form of body adornment, decoration or modification.

No explorer, missionary, trader or anthropologist has ever discovered a group of peoples who, when it comes to the appearance of their bodies, are prepared simply to let nature run its course. From Africa to Asia, the Arctic to the South Pacific, tribal peoples cut, shave, dye or decorate their hair; paint, tattoo, scar or pierce their flesh. Many practise circumcision or clitoridectomy. Some bind the heads of their infants, stretch their necks or compress their waists. Most groups attach feathers, shells, bones, flowers, leaves or ornaments made of metals or some other material to their bodies. No group of which I am aware does all these things but – what is more important – *no group does none of them.*

Combining this information with the findings of those physical anthropologists who have excavated the caves and burial sites of the earliest *Homo sapiens*, we come to the inevitable conclusion that *throughout the history of our species and everywhere in the world, human beings are self-adorned animals* – creatures who steadfastly refuse to let nature alone dictate their appearance.

We are the only known life form which does such a thing. Chameleons, squids, some frogs and a few other animals may change their colouration, but (unlike us) all of these animals change their appearance *purely according to genetic programming*. Only human beings are a designer species.

Perhaps it could be argued – given the universality of this activity – that our tendency to adorn and modify our bodies is instinctive. However, *the particular way* in which each group of *Homo sapiens* decorate themselves is clearly a result of learned and cultural factors. That a Nuba male covers his body with paint while a Dinka male covers his with a corset made of glass beads is not a result of biological instinct. Even though these two men live relatively near each other in the Sudan, and must share a very similar genetic inheritance, what each does to his body in the way of decoration is clearly a result of their different socio-cultural (as opposed to genetic) backgrounds. In other words, although body decoration is universal to the human species, the end product – what the customized body actually looks like – is specific to each culture.

There *is* therefore a fundamental and clear difference between human beings and other animals in terms of body decoration. The Caduveo are right. By painting, tattooing, scarring, piercing or decorating our flesh and by cutting, colouring or shaving off our hair we set ourselves apart from the other beasts. This doesn't explain *why* human beings do these things (that is the subject of the next chapter) but it does help us better to understand and, to a certain extent, define human nature. We human beings are many things, but at what is perhaps the most fundamental and basic level of our humanity we are an animal which is born rather drab and monochromatic but which (be it through the adornment of the skin and hair or, in clothed societies, through the adornment of clothing) goes through life in technicolour display. We are customized chameleons – visibly and existentially (and the point of this book is that the two are always related) self-made organisms.

If the evidence from surviving tribal societies is anything to go by (and it is a rule of thumb in anthropology that any phenomenon which is geographically widespread is inevitably very ancient) our earliest *Homo sapiens* ancestors must have also looked pretty extraordinary. Imagine the contrast they must have made – patterns of black charcoal or red and yellow ochre on their skin, leaves, feathers or flowers in their hair – with the other monochromatic primates.

Is this – our obsession with altering our appearance – the reason why we lost our fur and became, except for small patches of hair, 'The Naked Ape'? A coat of fur is both protective and beautiful but you just can't *do anything with it*. Flesh and hair, on the other hand, are materials of expression which offer almost unlimited possibilities for customizing.

It seems too much of a coincidence that the one and only self-adorned animal should have ended up with the perfect medium for artistic expression purely by chance. Biological evolution is probably far too slow a process to respond to individual societies' definitions of ideal beauty but, given the hundreds of thousands of years of human history, it might well have responded to the practical advantages of body decoration and modification and provided us with the perfect canvas for the expression of ourselves personally and communally.

What I am proposing is nothing less than a radical (for us, but not for the Caduveo) redefinition of humanity itself – that *Homo sapiens* left the rest of the inhabitants of this planet far behind because we discovered the benefits of changing our spots.

2
Adornment

7 The Functions of Adornment

Why should just one species of animal – *Homo sapiens* – spend time and precious resources decorating and changing its appearance? One would have thought that, particularly in palaeolithic times, or in the more inhospitable parts of the world today, practical necessities such as finding enough to eat would have precluded such an apparently frivolous activity.

Yet the jewellery and piles of red and yellow ochre found in palaeolithic excavation sites prove otherwise. As does the evidence of anthropologists working in places such as the barren Kalahari desert, where the native inhabitants persist in smearing precious animal fats on their skin – even through times of famine – simply because they find shiny skin attractive.

Similarly, if less dramatically, many British punks will spend half their unemployment money on buying cosmetics and endless cans of hair spray, even if it means that their next meal is only a bag of chips. Throughout the world and throughout history, human beings have put up with hunger, continual discomfort and even agonizing pain for the sake of decorating themselves – a situation which, in the words of *Star Trek*'s Vulcan officer Mr Spock, surely seems 'highly illogical'?

Yet I am confident that after just a brief look at the facts even Mr Spock would find body decoration to be an extremely logical activity. Like Vulcans, human beings do things for good reasons and no universal human activity would have evolved if it did not serve some practical purpose. But to appreciate this it is necessary to re-examine the word 'practical'.

Common usage today gives this word a very limited meaning. A practical coat is one which keeps you warm. A practical car is one which gets you from A to B without breaking down or using a lot of petrol. And, like Sanchez Labrodor, the Jesuit priest who criticized the Caduveo Indians for painting their bodies instead of going hunting, we tend to label anything to do with body decoration and adornment as frivolous, unimportant and impractical. Yet in doing so we reveal a serious lack of understanding of human needs.

It is said that man does not live by bread alone and it is certainly true that people have always had and will always have needs other than food, warmth and efficient transportation. People really do pine away and die from unhappiness and lack of affection or purpose, and the fulfilment of such needs is a logical and practical concern. Body decoration has a part to play in this: recent studies of a wide range of treatments given to mental patients have found that workshops in grooming and make-up are amongst the most effective means of overcoming depression and lack of self-respect. Looking after and experimenting with one's appearance obviously has many psychological benefits.

But it is sociological rather than psychological functions of adornment which I wish to explore here. Human beings are social animals; our ancestors became the dominant life form on our planet because of group effort. Ten men in palaeolithic Siberia could fell a giant mammoth whereas one working alone would have gone hungry. Furthermore, by living in tribal units, our ancestors could learn from the trial and error experiences of previous generations. In this way human knowledge became cumulative. But living in tightly knit social groups has never been easy and it is within this context that body decoration has made its most important practical contribution to humankind.

Let us return to 24,000 BC. *Homo sapiens* is emerging as the dominant species largely because they are organized into tribal groups. These tribal groups must, however, have some means whereby they can distinguish the members of one group from the members of another group and, for obvious reasons, these distinctions must be visible and immediately recognizable.

So our ancestors began to adorn themselves in distinctive ways in order to advertise which tribe they belonged to. Thus everyone in one group might have red streaks painted on their faces, while everyone in a neighbouring tribe might wear a bone through his or her nose. In this way, the individual gained a sense of camaraderie and group solidarity through his or her distinctive adornment uniform while the society gained greater cohesiveness through the enforced conformity of appearance.

This helps to transform a loose collection of a few hundred or thousand people into a social unit which is more than the sum of its parts. A comparison could be made with the distinctive head scarfs of street gangs in Los Angeles (one group, the Crips, wear blue ones while another group, the Bloods, wear red ones) or with the team colours of football supporters whose adornment in the form of scarfs, hats, T-shirts, logos and so forth, not only serves to distinguish one group of fans from another, but also provides a visible symbolic focus of loyalty and helps to make a team more than just eleven men kicking a football around.

Important as it is, this is not the only way in which body decoration helps (and helped) *Homo sapiens* to live together in social groups: distinctions *within* a group can also be highlighted using adornment.

Japanese mannequins at a trade fair in the late '70s.

Mannequin used in Mary Quant exhibition in the early '70s from the collection of the Museum of London, Department of Costume.

Close-up of face and wig of early '80s mannequin by Adel Rootstein.

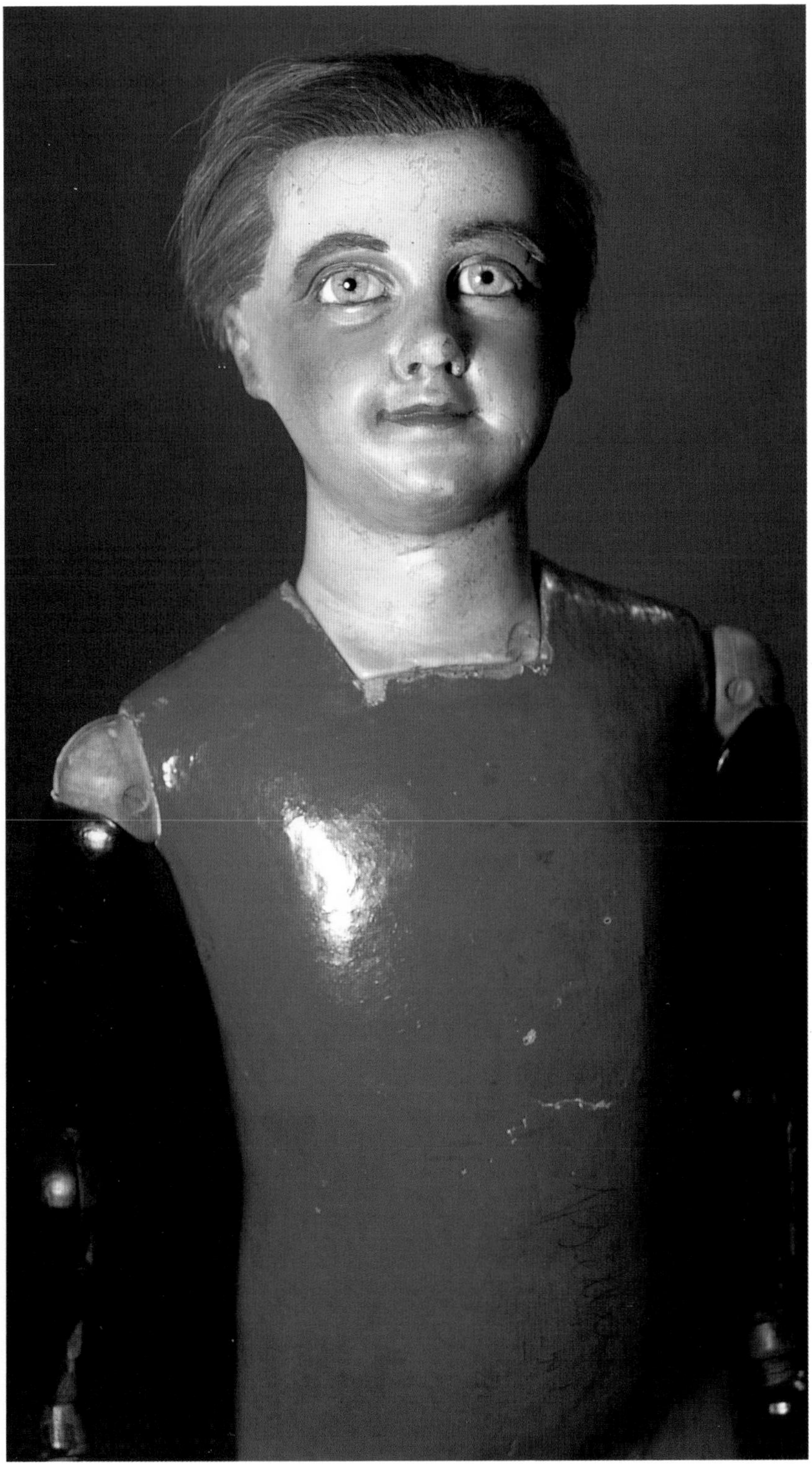

Wooden boy mannequin by Siegel and Stockman, circa 1929.

Although human flesh can rarely hope to compete with the eerie and unnatural perfection of artificial bodies, random genetic variation ensures that, for any given physical characteristic, some people will be born with bodies which approximate to the beauty ideals of their society or historical period. These 'freaks of nature' – if born in the right place at the right time – are celebrated as 'natural beauties'.

Men of the Fulani tribe of Niger participating in the gerewol 'beauty contest'.

'Miss Universe' fairground game.

Girl touching up her make-up in a London night club.

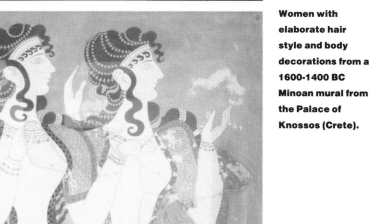

Women with elaborate hair style and body decorations from a 1600-1400 BC Minoan mural from the Palace of Knossos (Crete).

Man of the Melpa tribe of Papua New Guinea.

Cindy Cat, London
1979.

Jane Kahn (who now runs a shop called Kahnivirous in Hyper Hyper, London) and ex-partner Patti Bell, King's Road, 1980.

Elaborate or unique decorations can underline the authority of political and religious leaders. Likewise, differences of adornment can be used to indicate differences of social status. For example:

'A warrior of the Hidatsa, an Indian tribe of North America, signified his military exploits by decorating himself with feathers according to a closely defined code. The number of men he had killed could be calculated precisely from his appearance: a red feather with a few strands of horse hair attached to it signified that he had killed an enemy, a feather with one red bar signified that he was the second person to strike, and further bars indicated the strikers of succeeding blows. If he had been wounded in battle, he was entitled to wear a red feather: if he had killed a woman he wore a feather with a bound quill. (Ebin:p.56)

Differences of decoration styles can also be used to distinguish between various kinds of sub-groups within a tribe. Thus amongst the Arnhem Land aborigines of Australia, each clan has its own designs for body painting which are the sole property of that clan and which are passed down from generation to generation (and even retained after death, as skulls are – or at least were – painted with the deceased's clan designs). And even where a group has few other divisions of role, status or group identity, specialization according to gender is always reinforced by having men and women adopt different adornment styles.

Similarly, special occasions and ritual events such as festivals or religious ceremonies can be isolated from the daily routine and their ritual significance underlined by the especially elaborate adornments reserved only for such events.

But perhaps the most important contribution of body decoration to tribal life is the part it plays whenever new members are initiated into the group. There is little point in a social system which ceases to exist when its founding members die off, for only by surviving from generation to generation can a tribe become the depository of all the knowledge gained through daily experience.

For such a system to work, however, it is constantly necessary to effectively bring new members into the group, to replace those who have died. The young must be transformed into fully fledged members of the society and a great variety and number of tribes from all over the world have found that the most effective means of accomplishing this is through a rite of passage ritual which involves visibly changing the body of the initiate. By publicly and formally adorning an initiate's body with the decorations reserved for adult status, the significance of this transformation can be underlined. And if those markings or decorations are themselves semiologically meaningful and/or permanent (two subjects which will be dealt with in later chapters), so much the better.

In these and other ways, body decoration has always aided tribal groups in their day-to-day operations and in their survival over centuries. Differences and similarities of adornment serve as a means of mapping out the structure of relationships and the rules or oganization of a social system, just as the colour coding of wires and resistors in a stereo amplifier or TV set provides a guide to the electrical relationships of the components within the machine. And just as it would be extremely difficult to design, build or repair a stereo amplifier without such colour coding of parts, it would be extremely difficult (if not impossible) for tribal units to function smoothly without these visible differences and similarities of body decoration, which serve as daily reminders of the social order which a society must impose upon its members if it is to survive.

If adornment activities use precious time and resources and sometimes involve considerable pain and discomfort, it is simply because there is no easier alternative way of accomplishing the same things. It takes a special form of communication to express the limits, internal mechanisms and fundamental beliefs of a socio-cultural system and the 'language' of adornment is uniquely suited to this task. By means of streaks of pigment on flesh, the feathers of particular birds placed in the hair, tattoos or scars cut into the skin and bits of jewellery and clothing added on to the body, the patterns and structures of a way of life can be mapped out and made explicit.

But this isn't all that body decoration can accomplish for tribal men and women. High in any tribal person's list of the functions of body decoration would be its role in making them more attractive and sexually interesting. If we in the modern-day West fail to see any great practical purposes in this use of adornment, it is perhaps because our world is *over* rather than *under*populated. But for most of the world's tribal societies (and most certainly in the palaeolithic world of our ancestors) high infant and adult mortality means that anything which promotes procreation is clearly of great practical benefit. The definition of beauty inevitably differs from tribe to tribe, but according to their particular definition of beauty, the members of any society can make themselves more appealing to sexual partners by decorating and adorning themselves. Thus in the Mount Hagen area of New Guinea,

'For courting parties the girls are elaborately decorated, wearing, perhaps, a pearl-shell crescent and cowrie necklaces. They are said to mix love-magic with their pigments and the men mix it with their grease, the magic attracting the opposite sex by its perfume. On these occasions the painting of men and women is noticeably different. Women paint their faces in triangles, stipples and streaks of blue, yellow and red, ringing their eyes with white. The men normally use a black base; the designs which follow their facial features are commonly in white, while other colours are found on the cheeks, the chin and the forehead. The white areas are mostly superimposed on the black base, emphasizing

the blackness around them. The coloured designs are applied to charcoal-free areas. Blackness, or a combination of black and white, is peculiar to the men; by contrast the women wear a red base. Boys whose beards have not grown take women's patterns – in fact the charcoal base of the grown men is designed to emphasize the beard and the dark appearance which goes with it.'
(Brain:p.37)

Maori girls, on the other hand, tattoo their lips and chins to make themselves more attractive to would-be suitors. (They say that a 'naked face' is old and ugly-looking.) Polynesian women use cosmetics to darken their lips and their teeth for the same reason. Walbiri women of Australia paint their bodies with designs which are carefully chosen to make them look fatter – and especially to make their breasts appear larger. Likewise, Tobo women of South America paint their bodies with elaborate designs whenever they are in the mood for sex.[1] In the Disappearing World film *The Mehinacu*, as we watch a woman of that tribe carefully decorating her body, it is noted that it is only after decorating herself in this way that the men of the tribe will find her to be attractive and of interest sexually.

Many tribal peoples the world over also use body decoration to accomplish just the opposite – to make themselves as *un*attractive as possible. War paint and other horrific-looking decorations are rarely used in modern Western warfare but this is probably only because soldiers today have become so physically distanced that they rarely see the faces of their enemies. In hand to hand combat, on the other hand, a warrior's appearance can be a potent psychological weapon – whether he uses feathers and paint to make himself look horrible and larger than life, or whether he sports some adornment which must obviously have been acquired with great pain.

In the ethnographic film *Dead Birds* we see a fierce battle between two tribes of Dani warriors in the highlands of New Guinea. These men tend to fight until at least one of their number is dead or critically injured, unless (as in one of the instances we observe in this remarkable film) it starts to rain in the midst of a battle, in which case both groups of warriors will beat a hasty retreat. These renowned fighters are afraid of a little rain, but not because they are worried about catching a cold. They know that a frightening visage is at least as valuable a weapon as their spears and that if the rain should ruin their war paint or feathers they would be revealed as mere men and therefore far less intimidating to their enemies.

Just as adornment can be a useful weapon on the battle field against a human enemy, it can also be a valuable weapon against spirits and demons. A talisman can keep evil and misfortune at bay, a tattoo can cure a sick body by driving out a demon, a woman's breasts may be painted to prompt them to produce more milk, and chalk sprayed over the face and body can protect someone who is about to participate in a dangerous ritual.

In the West we may not believe in magic but we can nevertheless appreciate that the motives of wearing such body adornments are, for the people who do so, entirely logical and practical (according to their own beliefs of cause and effect). Besides, we in the supposedly sophisticated West wear rabbits' feet, crucifixes, St Christopher medals and even lucky charm bracelets to keep evil or misfortune at bay and to bring us good fortune. And have we not seen with our own eyes how, in countless Hammer horror movies, Count Dracula's hunger for blood can be overcome by his respectful fear of a crucifix strung from a dainty neck?

Other functions of adornment with which we Westerners might more readily identify include:

---

1. Adornment as a display of wealth (e.g., jewellery made of precious metals and stones, pearls and ivory, or adornments such as designer labels/logos which, while having no intrinsic value, indicate wealth symbolically).
2. Adornment as a token of a relationship (e.g., a wedding or engagement ring).
3. Adornment as an indicator of mood (e.g., the choice between a bright or a sombre shade of lipstick or eye shadow might not be something we normally think about, but most of us would consider brilliant red lipstick and vibrantly coloured eyeshadow to be inappropriate at a funeral).
4. Adornment as an indicator of sexual interest or inclination (e.g., the garish make-up of prostitutes or the visible key rings and bandanas of homosexuals which indicate either a dominant or submissive sexual orientation, depending upon on which side of the body they are worn).
5. And – most obvious of all – body decoration as an indicator of personal identity (a subject which will be dealt with in Chapter 11).

Clearly, the decoration of the body, far from being a frivolous and insignificant expenditure of time and resources, can be a highly practical, efficacious and necessary activity. Without it we would have great, perhaps insuperable, problems creating and maintaining those networks of social and cultural relationships which have always been and will always be the foundations of human accomplishment. As Mr Spock would put it, the Nuba man or the Western punk who both spend hours every day putting on make-up and adjusting their hair styles are engaging in a highly logical activity.

1. For further information and insights about tribal adornments on this and other subjects the reader is referred to Robert Brain's *The Decorated Body*, Andrew and Marilyn Strathern's *Self-Decoration in Mount Hagen*, James Farris' *Nuba Personal Art* and Victoria Ebin's *The Body Decorated*.

2 Adornment

8 Messages in Make-up

In 1977, the American space agency, NASA, sent a small planetary probe, *Voyager I*, hurtling into space. The purpose of this exercise was to learn more about Jupiter and Saturn. In 1980 *Voyager I* completed its highly successful mission and it is now in escape velocity from our solar system. In about one quarter of a million years, its batteries long since depleted, *Voyager I* will reach the stars.

Etched onto the side of *Voyager I* is a small plaque, the purpose of which is to tell any aliens who might chance upon it something about the life form which created *Voyager I*. Besides various diagrams, there is on this plaque a drawing of a typical human male and female. I will call these figures Adam and Eve.

I say 'typical' (and NASA clearly intended them to be just that), but Adam and Eve are, in point of fact, atypical in many ways. For example, they are depicted as caucasian (which leaves the majority of the world's population unrepresented), and neither figure has pubic hair. But the most atypical thing about this Adam and Eve is that they are neither clothed nor adorned.

The only human beings on our planet who display themselves publicly in such a state are Western naturists (and even they are known to sport the odd bit of jewellery or make-up). Certainly no human society has ever been found where people normally present themselves publicly in this way. Everywhere people are either adorned or clothed or, most commonly, both. My concern is that any aliens who might come across *Voyager I* will get the wrong idea about us *Homo sapiens*. And although this might seem a rather trivial point in the context of such a grand project, it is actually of considerable importance, for it raises the question of the relationship of intelligence, communication and body decoration.

Do intelligent life forms on other planets wear make-up and decorate their bodies? Judging from the portrayal of aliens in science fiction films, it is clear that *our* general assumption is that they do not. We presume that any life form intelligent enough to have mastered space travel would find no need for such a frivolous activity – that superior intelligence and body decoration are antithetical.

My own view, on the other hand, is that intelligence and communication skills are closely linked and that any creature capable of inter-galactic travel would have the wisdom to utilize all available channels and modes of communication – including body decoration. Indeed, if *I* were to make a science fiction film in which alien spacecraft landed on Earth, the aliens which emerged through pneumatic steel doors to greet us would be covered from head to toe with dazzling decorations which flashed out non-verbal messages as they lit up like pinball machines.

If this seems fanciful, consider an extraordinary creature which lives on the same planet as we do – the squid – which possesses an astonishing communication system based upon many contrasting colours which ripple in constantly changing patterns

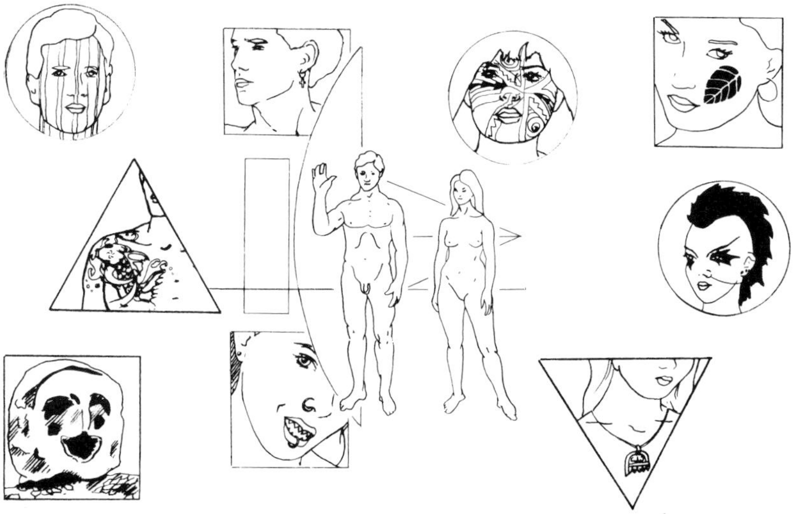

Centre: part of the plaque on the side of the Voyager I space probe. Symbolic body decoration clockwise from top right: Burmese facial decoration made from the imprint of a leaf of a pipal tree, Western punk adornment, Berber (Morocco) neck pendant in the form of a stylized hand, Dogon facial decorations with filed teeth and rings worn through piercings in nose and lip, Asoro (New Guinea) mud mask, Japanese tattoo in the shape of a carp, Moqui (North America) facial painting designed to bring rain, Western earing in the shape of a cross.

Modern Western erotic piercing.

Tattoos and piercings of British girls Froglet and Nikki.

across its body. Aside from superficially decoding the simplest and crudest messages transmitted by the squid (e.g., danger), we are at a loss to know just what these organisms are 'saying'. (Those who presume that a 'language' based upon a few contrasting colours could never be very sophisticated should consider that all the design information necessary to build any of us is communicated through the language of DNA, which has an alphabet of only four chemical components. Or that even a simple binary (+/–) system such as that which is found in computers can accommodate any known verbal language.)

My point is simply this: sophisticated communication can be expressed in a non-verbal medium. Bodily adornment is just such a medium of expression and no intelligent life form could afford to ignore it. Hence my vision of extraterrestrials gleaming with intricate decorations from head to toe – decorations which (although perhaps partly narcissistic) would be primarily intended as communication. *What* such creatures might be trying to 'say' in this way is anybody's guess, but *how* they would be 'saying' it (that is, the nature of the communication code itself) we can perhaps speculate upon.

Firstly, we can guess that it would compliment rather than replace some vocal mode of expression (why have but one channel of communication when you can have two?). Secondly, I would suggest that such a communication system would be based upon symbols rather than signs and therefore would not be linguistic in the sense in which we normally use this term.

The reader will recall from our discussion of semiotics in Chapter 2 that in a symbolic system of signification there exists some 'natural' linkage between a concept which is to be expressed – the signified – and the form of its expression – its signifier. This is a fundamentally different process of signification than that found in a sign system – a true language – where the relationship of signifier and signified is arbitrary and purely the product of lexicographic precedent.

Although neither of these systems of signification could be said to be better than the other (to do so would be like saying that novels are better than paintings), it is nevertheless true that there are differences in their effectiveness in various expressive situations. Language systems composed of arbitrary signs are very effective at the rapid transmission of most types of ordinary data – precisely because of their arbitrary nature, they are highly adaptable and flexible. Symbolic communication systems, on the other hand, are resistant to change and often cumbersome but they are capable of a power and immediacy – a compression and layering of meaning – a poignancy which linguistic systems can rarely achieve (great poetry constituting an exception which proves this rule). Generally, whereas signs can be depended upon to get a message across, it is symbols which succeed at driving a message home.

When we examine human adornment and body decoration as communication, it is clear that these generally signify symbolically rather than linguistically. There are exceptions. The word 'SKINHEADS' tattooed across a British teenager's forehead is a linguistic sign, as is an amulet bearing a passage from the Koran or an inscription on a ring.[1] However, looking around the world it is infinitely easier to find examples of body decoration which are symbolic in the sense that they have some 'natural' affinity with that which they signify:

* A crucifix or cross worn to identify its wearer as Christian is a symbol because it graphically represents the manner of Christ's death. (Likewise a Star of David is an appropriate rather than an arbitrary expression of the Jewish faith. These symbols are not 'naturally' interchangeable.)

* A traditional and popular Japanese tattoo design depicting a carp 'naturally' signifies bravery and masculinity because of the heroic way in which the carp climbs waterfalls and the fact that, if caught, it stoically awaits death without quivering. (A tattoo depicting, for example, a cherry blossom could not – at least in Japanese society – convey the same meaning.)

* Moqui Indians of the southern part of North America paint vertical lines on their faces as a plea to the gods to bring rain. When they want the direction of the wind to change they paint slanting lines across their faces. Both designs are 'natural' symbols in that they depict the meteorological phenomenon which they seek to invoke. Again, they are not arbitrary signs because they are not interchangeable.

* A Dogon (Somalia) woman's nose and lip rings and sharply filed teeth are symbols of the origins of speech. According to Dogon mythology, speech was created by the action of their ancestor Noomi weaving thread through his teeth. Instead of thread out came speech and the Dogon celebrate this by filing their teeth to resemble a weaving loom and wearing a ring through their nose and lower lip to represent the bobbin and shuttle used in that mythical weaving.[2]

* The imprint of a leaf from the pipal tree on the cheek of a Burmese woman is a symbolic adornment because this particular tree is sacred to the Buddha and its religious significance is represented in the form of this decoration. (The pattern of a leaf from any other type of tree would not be capable of conveying the same meaning.)

* The silver jewellery worn by Berber women (Morocco) which in stylized form represents the human hand (the function of which is to protect the wearer from the evil eye by means of the five fingers which can, symbolically, be thrust into the eye).

* An Asoro (New Guinea) man's slimy covering of mud is a symbolic reminder of an ancient criminal act and its consequence. The Asoro believe that their ancestor killed his brother and they ritualistically cover themselves in mud as a symbolic self-burial.

* The intricate arabesque designs which Caduveo (Amazon) women paint on their faces apparently have a 'natural', if complex meaning. The anthropologist Claude Lévi-Strauss has suggested that the juxtaposed symmetry and asymmetry of these designs is a symbol of Caduveo social structure. The Caduveo are the descendants of a huge and powerful civilization which was divided into three hierarchical groups each of which was itself divided into two matching kinship groups. Apparently, the symmetry in these distinctive designs represents the sociological symmetry of these paired kinship groups while the asymmetrical aspects of the designs represent the inherent asymmetry of the Caduveo's trinary hierarchical system.

* The adornment of punks is one of many examples of symbolic body decoration in the West. The artificiality and aggressiveness of this style of make-up, coiffure and jewellery is designed to portray an ideological opposition to the 'natural', 'love and peace' style of the hippies who preceded them.

Everywhere people use adornment as a powerful medium of symbolic communication. Symbols compress information and by employing them rather than signs, adornment communication drastically increases the amount of information which can be transmitted in an instant of visual recognition. Because such symbols are linked with all of the different strata of meaning in a culture, they are but the tip of the iceberg of signification and great power can explode through them.

Furthermore, whereas signs are digital (packaging information into discreetly quantified yes/no units), symbols convey information analogically (i.e., like a watch with hands as opposed to a digital one) and can, therefore, express minute gradations of

1. Note, however, that the *style* of such a tattoo, amulet or ring is more likely to signify symbolically – for example, the *shape* of a ring is often seen as a 'natural' expression of the continuity and unity of a relationship.
2. It is interesting that, like most people in the modern West, the Dogon place great emphasis on verbal language as a defining characteristic of human nature.

meaning. Thus a Punk's adornment and body decoration can be a bit aggressive, highly aggressive, *and anything in between*. A verbal description of the same person's appearance, on the other hand, could only use adjectives and their modifiers to label specific, discreet points in this cline. For these reasons, symbolic body adornment can possess both subtlety and enormous power simultaneously.

Finally, through the combination of different symbols, some of which might even, in their meanings, be contradictory to each other, another, even more complex level of signification – a meta system of meaning – can be achieved. We have seen that in Japanese tattooing the image of the carp is symbolic of that animal's bravery and stoicism. Another popular subject in Japanese tattooing is Kannon the Goddess of Mercy who feels pity and sorrow for the ways of men. If these two symbols should occur within the same tattoo, their specific meanings (which are actually much more complex than I have indicated here) would be sublimated into an overall meaning which, although difficult to define in words, would clearly revolve around a compassionate bravery or a brave compassion.

A Western example of this same phenomenon (and throughout the world this is a normal rather than an exceptional aspect of body decoration) might be a woman who wears 'tarty' make-up (to a certain extent *all* obvious make-up and body decoration in the West, according to the tenets of our Judeo-Christian heritage, has symbolic connotations of impurity) together with a crucifix. Here – even more so than in the Japanese example above – the separate adornment symbols cancel out each other's specific signifieds to generate an amazing complexity of meaning.

Amazing, at least, in the fact that such a lot of information can be transmitted *instantly* – the 'read out' process taking only as long as it takes the eye to scan the displaying subject. It is this characteristic of immediacy which makes symbolic adornment communication so very valuable in social interactions. A skilled writer of fiction may be able to translate such appearance information into words (arbitrary signs) and a true literary genius may succeed in compressing such data into a few salient phrases, but even in such extraordinary circumstances transmission can never be instantaneous and immediate the way it is with 'natural' adornment symbols which can detonate complex and powerful meanings in micro seconds.

Before moving on, further comment is needed about the 'natural' nature of adornment symbols. When Saussure first described symbols in this way he did not, as I have done, place quotation marks around the word 'natural'. Saussure's usage implied that such signification is 'real' in the sense that it is outside human jurisdiction. Today, however (primarily through the work of social anthropologists), we appreciate that even nature itself is perceived and defined differently – indeed, it *is* different – from one society to another.

Each and every culture has its own perceptional framework, its social construction of reality, which it imposes on the universe and 'nature'. Thus in one society the full moon may be seen as romantic, while in another it might be seen as sinister, and an item of adornment (e.g., an earring or a tattoo) which utilized the moon as a symbol would have different 'natural' meanings in these two situations. Yet as long as we keep quotation marks around the word 'natural' it is a useful description of symbolic signification. For something to be 'natural' it is only necessary that it fit in with all the levels of meaning within a culture. (Which is exactly what a symbol does and what a sign doesn't do – the latter being linked only horizontally to other aspects of the linguistic system, such as grammar and lexicographical precedent.)

That said, there are perhaps some adornment symbols which do qualify as natural without any need for inelegant quotation marks. These are universal symbols to which all human beings ascribe the same meaning. There are few such symbols but it has been suggested that three colours used in adornment throughout the world – red, white and black – may qualify as truly natural symbols. This is because all human beings have red blood, white milk or semen and brown/ black excreta and experience decay as a darkening process.

For these reasons the anthropologist Victor Turner has argued that anywhere in the world people adorning themselves with these colours will attribute similar natural meanings to them. Thus red is everywhere associated with war, hunting and/or life, vitality and the tie between mother and child. White is, according to this theory, everywhere associated with reproduction. And black is in every human society associated with defilement or death (or with the transition from one status to another, which is a kind of death).

I'm not entirely convinced. I keep thinking of Jean Shrimpton in the '60s in white lipstick. Is the signification of her lipstick really that of reproduction or is it artificiality? (Given that lips are naturally red, to paint them white is to defy nature.)[3]

And what about white confirmation and wedding dresses which are, at least in our culture, taken as referring to purity/virginity rather than reproduction? And, although it is true that a black tie is appropriate at a funeral, the usual meaning of 'black tie' in our society is social formality.

But it's all academic anyway. When those dazzlingly decorated aliens finally do arrive from outer space their lipstick may be green to match their blood, their hair dyed bright blue to match their milk and semen and their eyeshadow lime green as a symbol of death and the frailty of life. And in one instant these creatures will have shown us just how Earthist we are in presuming to have discovered *universal* symbols of adornment.

3. Or was this choice of white lipstick dictated purely by changing fashions and therefore meaningless?

2 Adornment

9 Tattoo

To make sense of body adornments and decorations it is necessary not only that we categorize them according to their social function, their process of signification and their meaning, but also that we categorize them according to their transcience or permanence. It is this final characteristic which dominates all the others – for whether an adornment is permanent or transient will always decide what particular social functions it is most suited to and will always provide an additional meaning (sometimes the primary one) to its signification. (A tattoo of the word 'MOTHER', for example, says much more about one's maternal relationship than would a transient decoration of the same design.)

Besides the body modifications which were discussed in Section 1 (tooth filing, cranial 'deformation', foot binding, etc.), methods of permanently altering the appearance of the human body include tattooing, piercing and scarification (only the latter two of which are generally found on dark-skinned peoples). We needn't concern ourselves here with the technical methodologies for the creation of these permanent body decorations, but it is important that we recognize their antiquity.

At excavations of Ice Age sites, discoveries of bowls of black and red pigments together with sharp-pointed flints and 'needles' made from bone splinters and reindeer antlers suggest that the art of tattooing was carried out at least 10,000 years ago. There is also evidence that the ancient Egyptians, the Mayans, the Oaxacans and the Aztecs used tattooing to permanently transform the appearance of their bodies. Of the latter, Fray Bernardino de Sahagũn, in his *General History of the Things of New Spain* (the *Codex Florentino*), commented that the women in particular were 'well scratched, well scarified, very green, bluish, very beautiful'. More spectacularly, the discovery in 1947 of the mummified body of a Sythian chief (preserved due to the constantly low temperature of the burial site) demonstrates the degree of sophistication achieved in tattooing prior to 2000 BC.

The ancient inhabitants of Britain also practised sophisticated tattooing and Julius Caesar, when he brought his armies North to conquer these people, remarked, 'The area is partly occupied by barbarians who bear on their bodies, from childhood, scars ingeniously formed in the likeness of various animals'. 'Barbarians' or not, Caesar's armies learned the tattooing art from these Britons (whose name, according to some sources, originally meant 'painted in various colours') and tattooing flourished in Rome until Constantine made Christianity the official religion of the Empire in AD 325, and the Church declared it a sin to disfigure that which was 'fashioned in God's image'.

This did not stop the Crusaders, many years later, from acquiring tattoos as souvenirs of their travels and exploits. It was, in fact, only in the late Middle Ages and the Renaissance, when Western society moved away from a traditionalist world view to embrace modernity, a love of change for its own sake, and fashion, that the permanent changes to appearance produced by tattooing really fell from favour.

Although we will delay discussing fashion until Section 5, it should be obvious that its celebration of constant style change ('this year's look') would have made any permanent changes to the body's appearance undesirable. Because fashion and the progressive world view which sponsored it became a cornerstone of Western culture, the permanent body arts – since the Renaissance – have been practised by only a small minority of people in the West. (The reasons why this minority should defy the majority view and continue to permanently alter their appearance will be considered in a moment.)

Outside the West, in traditional societies, the permanent body arts have always played an important part in expressing and reinforcing social relationships, values and 'society' itself. Like transitory body decorations such as coiffure, body painting, jewellery, etc., tattoos, scars and piercings can help to define the boundaries of a social group, identify subgroups within a community, mark differences of status and

A drawing by a Maori (New Zealand) chief of his own facial tattoo.

role, etc. However, the very permanence of these forms of adornment allows them to perform functions which transitory adornments and decorations cannot.

From the earliest prehistoric times up to the present day, tribal socio-cultural systems have been highly traditional: always trying to preserve the status quo, and to ward off change. And it makes good sense that they should be so conservative. If the social body should not be preserved, if it should be destablized by outside forces or by the failure of a new generation to 'fall into line', then the very survival of all those individuals who constitute the membership of that society would be put into jeopardy. *The permanent*

body arts are the most effective devices ever created for preserving the status quo and vouchsafing the continuing of the social unit.

Because tattoos, scars and piercings are permanent decorations, they are a perfect means of demonstrating and reinforcing permanent social relationships. For tribal peoples, the most important such relationship is that between the individual and his or her society. Thus when a young man or woman reaches the age when he or she is ready to become an adult and fully fledged member of society, the most effective method of ensuring the permanence of this relationship is to permanently alter their bodies in some symbolic way in a rite of passage ritual.

For this reason, throughout the world and throughout human history, tattooing, sacrification, piercing, tooth filing or removal etc., have been utilized as a means of ensuring that the act of becoming an adult member of a tribe is a permanent social transformation. At the same time, such permanent alterations of appearance serve to demonstrate the supreme commitment of the individual to his or her society. Aside from laying down your life, there is no more powerful means whereby an individual can confirm commitment to the community.

In the West, there are increasing numbers of 'tribes' (Bikers, Skinheads, Punks, Teddy Boys) which make use of the permanent body arts for precisely the same reasons that Third World tribal peoples do. The Biker's patch (a tattooed insignia of a motorcycle club or gang), the Punk's multiple piercings or 'ANARCHY' tattoo, and the skinhead's graffiti-like markings all demonstrate a supreme commitment of the individual to the group and thereby help their respective 'tribes' to survive the passage of time. (Contemporary 'tribes' or style groups are discussed more fully in Chapter 23.)

For anyone in the West to make such a commitment by permanently transforming his or her body is an act of faith which many would describe as lunacy. Ours is the most unstable and fastest changing social environment of all time. As well as the perpetual fluctuations of fashion, we in the West are periodically subjected to technology, social, economic and political change. To make a lifetime, irrevocable commitment to a would-be stable social group within this maelstrom is to risk a great deal.

While not wishing to appear to be encouraging anyone to go out and get a tattoo which celebrates allegiance to a group, I do not, on the other hand, wish to condemn such practices.[1] A great many people in the modern West (maybe most of us if we were to be honest about it) feel themselves to be 'lost in the crowd' and 'just a number'. For millions of years our ancestors enjoyed the comforting and practical security of belonging to tightly knit, small-scale social groups but now, suddenly, we are expected to get by on our own without such communities

Western example of tattoo used to celebrate group membership; skinheads, Livingstone, Scotland.

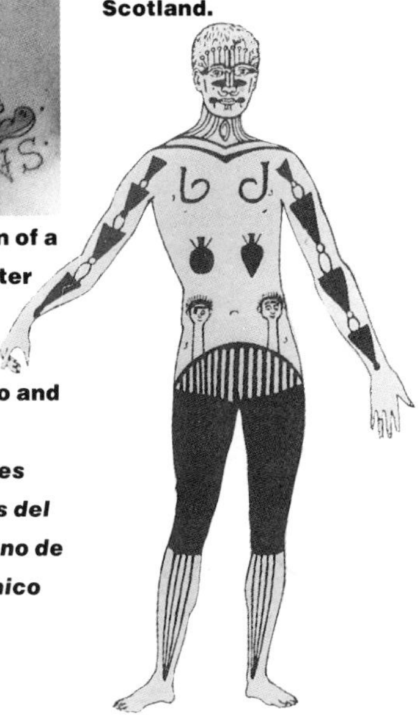

Tattoo design of a native of Easter Island as illustrated in Adolfo Dembo and J. Imbelloni, *Deformaciones Intencionales del Crerpo Humano de Cara cter E tnico* (1938).

to provide emotional, cultural and practical support. Recently – at a British tattoo convention – I watched as a young man named Dave was tattooed with the 'patch' of the National Chopper Club. On the one hand I found myself fretting that he (like some skinheads and punk acquaintances of mine) would regret such an action for the rest of his life. On the other hand, however, I felt a tinge of jealousy that here was someone who, unlike myself, enjoyed a sense of belonging to a tightly-knit community.

And let us also remember that – now that almost all the traditional tribes of the Third World are living under the threat of Westernization – Dave and his friends are not alone in making a leap into the dark when they permanently transform their bodies in the interests of demonstrating their commitment to their group. What remains to be seen (both in the Third World and in the West) is whether such permanent adornments of group allegiance are, simply by virtue of their immutability, a sufficient force to hold back the forces of change and individualization which are the hallmarks of the modern world.

Ironically, while the battle seems to be being lost throughout the Third World as the younger generations of ancient, tribal communities increasingly refuse to get their bodies permanently decorated with the adornment styles of their ancestors, it is only in the West that more and more people are submitting their bodies to the tattooist's needle or the piercer's gun as a sign of permanent commitment to their new found 'tribe'. Perhaps, in time, it will only be in the West that this ancient and effective device for safeguarding socio-cultural continuity will survive.

In Section 5 we will explore more fully the phenomenon and the future of the new, Western 'tribes'. For now let us consider some other reasons why the permanent body arts of tattooing and piercing are gaining in popularity in the West. Clearly the most important reason is the precise opposite of the need to demonstrate commitment to a social group – the expression of individuality.

While most body decorations and adornments in tribal societies are designed to *decrease* social differences so as visibly to demonstrate conformity, most adornment in the West is designed to *increase*, and emphasize, our individual differences of personality and world view. The reasons and functions of adorning and dressing ourselves to stand out from the crowd will be considered in Chapter 11. For now, let us note only that, in our society, permanent body decorations are the most effective means of emphasizing personal uniqueness.

Because of the fashion-conscious, pro-change nature of most of the West since the Renaissance, ours is a world where to have permanent body decoration such as a tattoo or a collection of facial piercings is, *ipso facto*, to be different from the norm. Therefore the Western man or woman who feels a strong need to emphasize his or her personal uniqueness will find that *any* permanent adornments will instantly and automatically go a long way towards fulfilling this need.

And if a tattoo design (by virtue of its subject matters, its artistic style or its placement on the body) is itself unique, so much the better. Only a decade or so ago anyone in the West who wanted a tattoo would have had to choose a blue-bird or a traditionally scrolled 'MOTHER' from sheets of 'flash' (the boards which tattooists nearly always relied on to show off their designs) and would know full well that thousands of other people would be walking around with identical designs. Today's new generation of Western tattooists, on the other hand, are eager to make each tattoo design that they execute unique. New colours, more creative designs and skills acquired from Japanese masters have all gone some way toward making tattooing in the West a vibrant and flourishing artform which offers those who want it a chance to transform their bodies into unique masterpieces.

Besides individualistic or 'tribal' motives, there is one further reason why people in our society might get a tattoo: *exhibitionism*. Although the urge to make a display of oneself is found throughout humankind, men in Western society are generally prohibited from indulging their exhibitionistic needs. This is the subject of the next chapter and we will note here only that there are two principal exceptions to this rule: *body building and tattooing*. Both of these activities, while not completely exempt from allegations of narcissism, to a certain extent allow Western males a chance to show off their bodies while avoiding criticism of their masculinity. Presumably this is because both of these activities are painful, requiring macho stoicism.

Each year, in Britain, the USA, Holland, Italy, Japan and Australia, tattoo conventions are held to celebrate this artform. Thousands attend each of these get-togethers where the latest books, magazines and videos on the subject are sold, a lot of beer is drunk, bands play and, in the middle of it all, dozens of tattooists from around the world can be observed at work hunched over a body, electrically-powered tattooing needles in their hands reverberating at over ten strokes per second.

The highlight of these events is a contest in which people exhibit their tattoos for which they are awarded prizes by a panel of judges. There is a women-only section in this contest and the predominantly male audience is always eager and pleased to see their 'pieces'. There are, however, always only a fraction of as many females competing as there are males.

When it is their turn, literally hundreds of men come out one by one to stand on a stage under a spotlight to display their tattoos. Cameras go off like fireworks in the audience as each man gets a chance to display his body in a way which most men in our society rarely can. And if anyone should question their masculinity in exhibiting themselves so narcissistically, there is always, in the background, the steady buzz of the tattooist's needles to remind them of long agonies stoically endured for this fleeting moment of exhibitionistic ecstasy.

1. I would, however, strongly urge anyone contemplating being tattooed to visit only a reputable tattooist who sterilizes all equipment before use, and to avoid being tattooed on his or her face or hands – the most often regretted sites.

Modern British tattoo design.

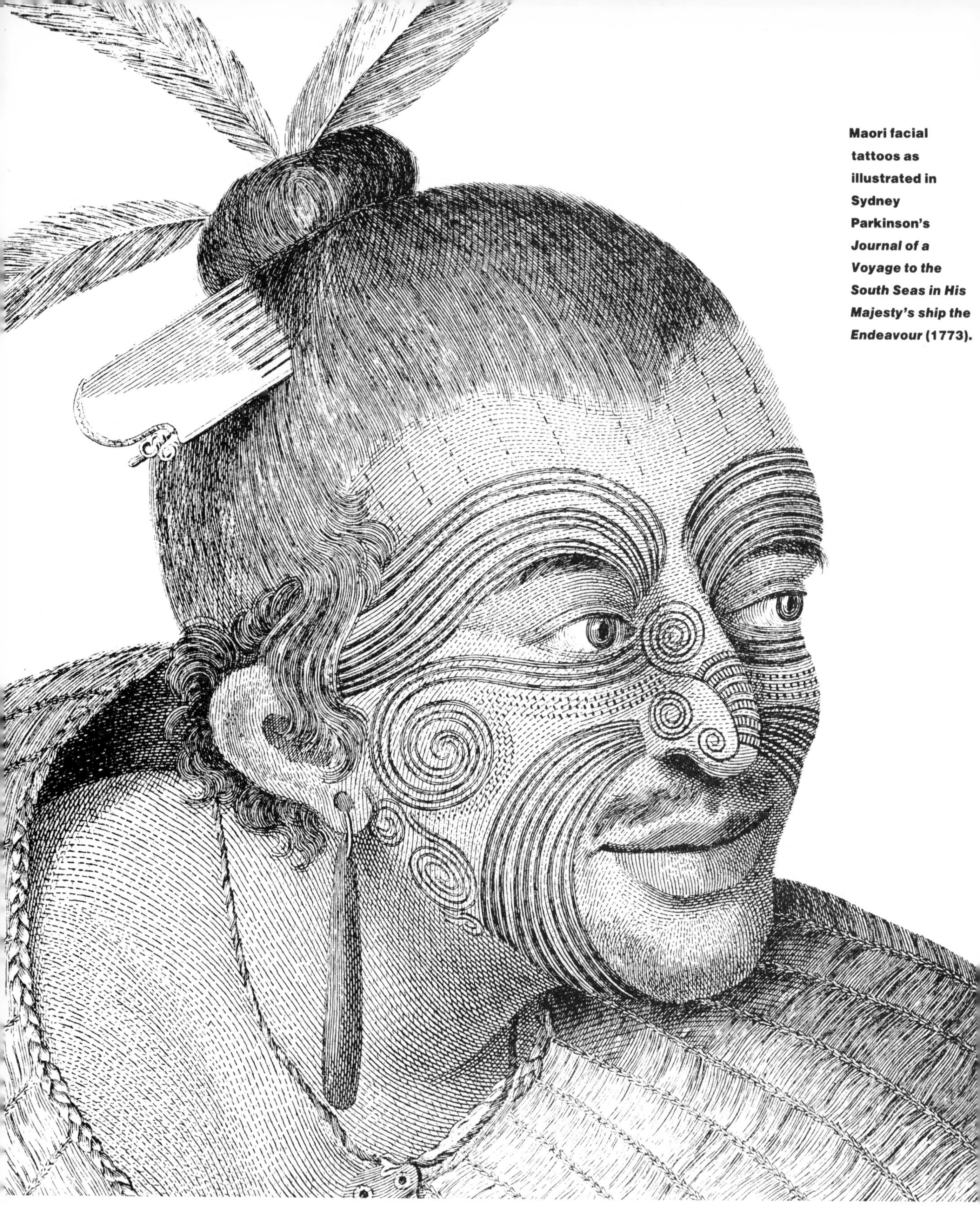

Maori facial tattoos as illustrated in Sydney Parkinson's *Journal of a Voyage to the South Seas in His Majesty's ship the Endeavour* (1773).

Traditional Japanese tattoo design.

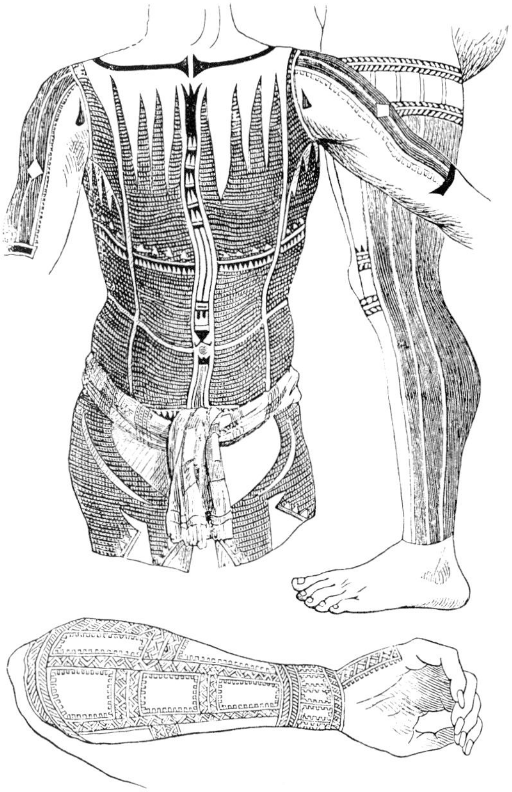

Tattoo design by England.

Tattoo designs of natives of Ponape (Caroline Islands).

Mura Indian man (South America) with lip tusks worn through facial piercings.

2
Adornment

10 Peacock Power

In the animal world it is typical for the male to be more visually exciting than the female. Excavations at late palaeolithic burial sites suggest that it was human males rather than females who first began decorating their bodies. Amongst those tribal communities which survive today it is rare to find one in which the men are not at least as adorned as the women, and not at all uncommon to find societies where men exercise a virtual monopoly over the adornment arts.

For example, amongst the Nuba of the Sudan, young men may spend more than an hour a day – every day – painting their bodies and fixing their hair, while young Nuba women usually take only a few minutes to smear their bodies with a mixture of animal fats and ochre. So concerned are Nuba men that they might ruin their elaborate hair styles while sleeping that they regularly lie with their heads stuck over the edge of their specially designed bed platforms.

Men of the Australian aboriginal tribe the Waligigi, in addition to their complicated body painting for ritual and spiritual occasions, regularly paint themselves so that they will be irresistible to women. They believe that, if drawn properly, the designs on their bodies will (literally) exert a sort of gravitational pull on women who – feeling 'sick with desire' – will find their bodies being pulled irresistibly towards them.

In Mount Hagen in the highlands of New Guinea, the best and most striking decorative feathers are always saved for the men. On special occasions the men also wear huge wigs which are made from human hair cuttings mounted on a frame of cane bound with lianas. And whether at a courting party or taking part in an inter-tribal work contest (where tribal groups compete to see who can, for example, construct a section of road in record time), Hagen men paint their faces and wear their 'second-best' feathers. Women also adorn themselves on such occasions but, as always, it is the men who are the real centre of attention.

Now that gold has been discovered on their land, men of the Kayapo tribe in Brazil must often travel to the Brazilian capital to negotiate with government leaders. For these expeditions they usually put on Western style clothes and wear little or no paint but as soon as they return to their tribal homeland they strip off their clothes and their wives paint bright patterns on their bodies. As the Kayapo men put it, 'We rub our culture into our skin'.

As we saw in Chapter 4, it is the male youths of the Fulani tribe of central Niger who compete in the 'beauty contest' of the *gerewol*, for which they spend hours decorating themselves and even longer standing on tip toe rolling their eyes and grimacing to attract the attention of the women.

Exotic hairstyle, Kings Road, London, 1981.

It is, in fact, almost impossible to find a tribal society where the men are not peacocks obsessed with their appearance. This may partly stem from the fact that it is usually men who are directly involved with ritual, magic, religion, warfare and politics – activities which in tribal societies usually demand the decoration of participants. But this isn't the whole story: when it comes to adorning and beautifying the body purely for purposes of attracting the opposite sex it is, in tribal societies, typically the men who take the most time and trouble with their appearance. From the Amazon to New Guinea one finds tribal men staring intently into hand mirrors, checking their paint and feathers and worrying if their hairstyles are just right.

Why then does modern Western man steer clear of the cosmetics counter? To answer this riddle it is necessary that we look back into Western history. Not too far back, however, as throughout most of European history men have decorated themselves as ostentatiously as have women.

'The Great Masculine Renunciation', as it was described by J.C. Flugel in *The Psychology of Clothes*, was a time when 'men may be said to have suffered a great defeat in the sudden reduction of male sartorial decoration'. This transformation from peacock to pigeon began at the end of the 18th century. In seeking to find some reason why men should have voluntarily renounced their right to 'all the brighter, gayer, more elaborate and varied forms of ornamentation', Flugel laid the blame on the French Revolution, arguing that prior to this event aristocratic men had been free to pursue a life of leisure which suited elaborate adornment.

Even in countries other than France, countries which had not themselves experienced revolution but which feared its spread, the aristocracy felt it prudent to curtail ostentatious display. The French revolution made *work* respectable. Whereas formerly, activities of an economic nature had been thought to be degrading to a gentleman, the changes in attitude fostered by the French Revolution meant that a man's place was in the workshop, the counting house or the office rather than in the drawing room. This change in life style, argues Flugel, called for sobriety and constraint in matters of appearance.

Or, to put it another way, whereas previously accepted styles of dress and adornment had reflected the lifestyle of the leisured aristocracy now, with the shadow of revolution hanging over Europe, the arbiters of taste and appearance became the established bourgeoisie. If not literally, at least ideologically, these were the descendants of the Puritans who, of course, were opposed to decoration and adornment in any form. Such anti-adornment principles were unisexual, with sartorial restraint demanded of both good men and good women. But, to return to Flugel's point, it was the *men* who went off to work and it was this environment which more than anything else curtailed showy decoration and promoted visual sobriety.

With the advent of the Industrial Revolution, these constraints on finery were further entrenched as technological and ideological developments changed the very nature of work itself. The fact that this revolution had been brought about by inventions such as the steam engine and the cotton loom, the fact that *mental* endeavours now brought the greatest rewards, had the effect of bringing into disrepute all physical activity (which, after all, would now be accomplished more efficiently by machines). In short, the New Man of the Industrial Age was ideally a brilliant brain bereft of an encumbering body and for a man to draw attention to his body through decoration was to disavow his own worth.

Thus was born, to borrow a phrase from H.G. Wells, The Invisible Man. This absurd creature might soon have become extinct, but the Empire followed in the wake of the Industrial Revolution and its effect was to give a new lease of life to Invisible Man.

When middle class European men – their adornment pared to the bone – found themselves (in the interests of extending their respective countries' empires) in the far corners of the globe, they generally encountered native males who adorned, decorated and exhibited themselves like peacocks. To distance themselves and to emphasize their presumed superiority over these 'primitives', the European male became even more sober, invisible and 'civilized' in his appearance. (Except, of course, for the military who – because of the macho and dangerous nature of their occupation – have always been exempt from the rule that real men don't decorate themselves.)

But as we have seen in previous chapters, the adornment and display of the body has been part of human nature since the origins of our species and one would not expect that such a universal human drive – perhaps even a biological instinct – could be easily sublimated. And indeed, it couldn't.

The 'solution' which the Invisible Man found to this problem was simply to conscript the females over whom he exercised control (his wife, daughters and servants) to serve as replacements for the body he himself had negated. If the Invisible Man, by his own choosing, could not decorate, adorn and proudly display his own body, then he would use these females' bodies as his surrogates. Thus was born the unpleasant situation which feminists have been protesting about ever since. (And to which men, if they'd had any sense, would have objected just as vociferously.) The slogan 'Our Bodies Ourselves' expresses the frustrations of Western women who since the Industrial Revolution – although encouraged to adorn and display themselves to their hearts' content – have lost control over the nature and style of their own body decoration.

Of course such a perverse situation has been unsatisfactory and frustrating for all concerned (even if men have rarely acknowledged, even to themselves, the source of this frustration). But the eventual feminist response which condemned *all* body decoration as demeaning was, I believe, a case of throwing the baby out with the bath water. Adornment isn't evil, as the Puritans thought, or inevitably sexist, as some feminists came to believe. It is a useful and necessary medium of expression and is not inherently sexist.

For feminists to denounce all body decoration as sexist nonsense and to follow Industrial Man into the sterile wastelands of sartorial sobriety and invisibility would have been a matter of two wrongs not making a right. That small but vociferous group of feminists who would condemn adornment *per se* should look beyond our crazy contemporary culture to re-discover how body decoration, even in its most outlandish and seemingly impractical forms, can be devoid of sexist connotations and manipulation.[1]

Happily, after a brief dark age in the 70s, this is precisely what has happened as most feminists in the 80s have come to realize that if body decoration – be it an outlandish hat, bleached or dyed hair, tons of jewellery, lashings of make-up or even a precarious pair of high heels – is *an expression of one's own self*, then it can be personally enhancing and liberating.

There is one more fallacy born of the foolishness of Industrial Man's renunciation of his body and its decoration which we ought to pause briefly to consider. Estranged from his body, Invisible Man attempted and largely succeeded in re-classifying anything pertaining to corporal adornment as not only un-masculine but (as one might expect) *insignificant*. One casualty of this attitude – our inability to perceive body decoration as a fundamental part of human nature – we have

Woman of the Melpa tribe of Papua New Guinea.

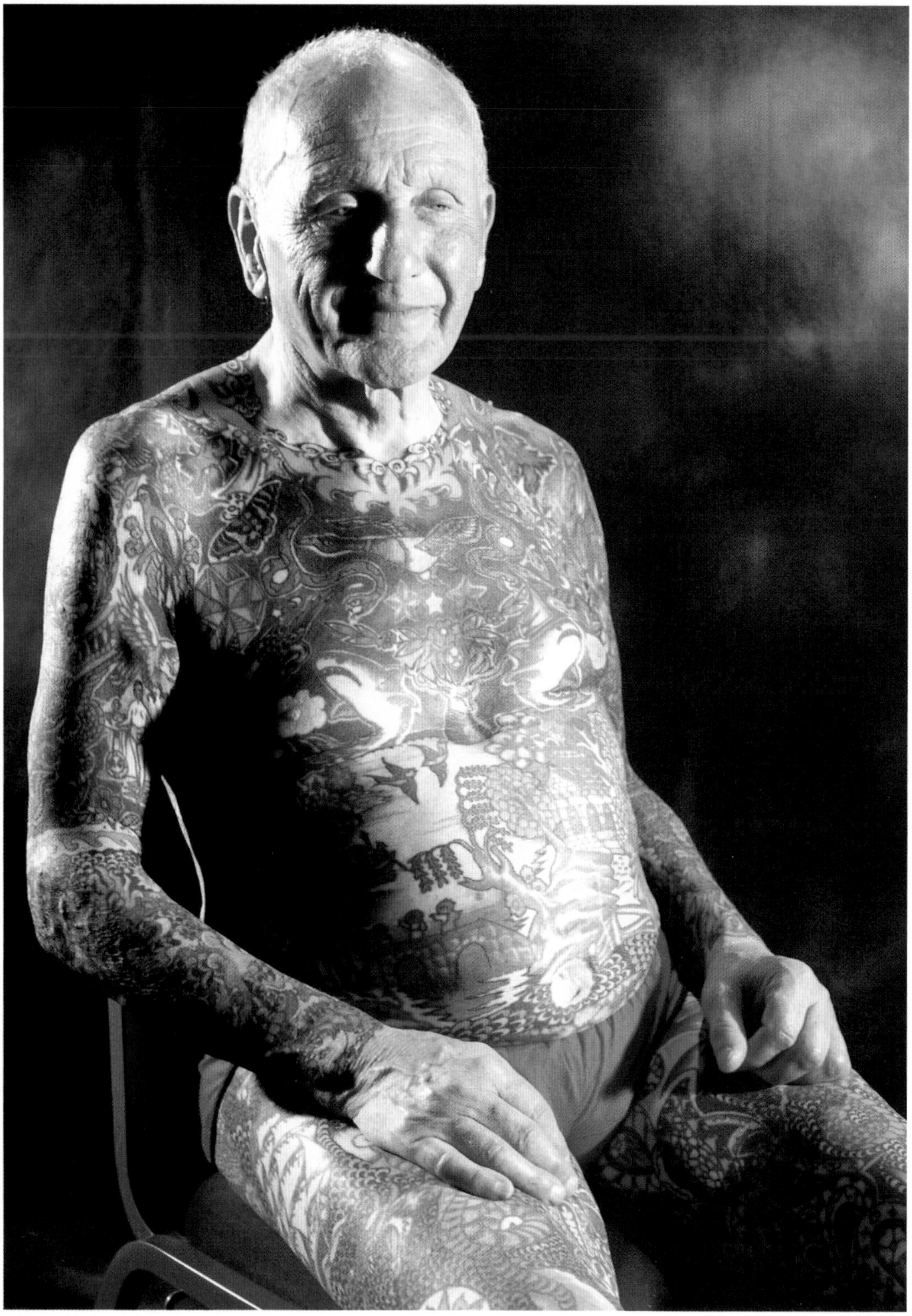

George Davies, who at the age of 63 began having himself tattooed and hasn't quit yet. Photographed at British Tattoo Expo, 1987.

'Picasso', photograph by Robyn Beeche, make-up by Philis Cohen, hair by Robert Lobetta. Photo courtesy of *The Observer.*

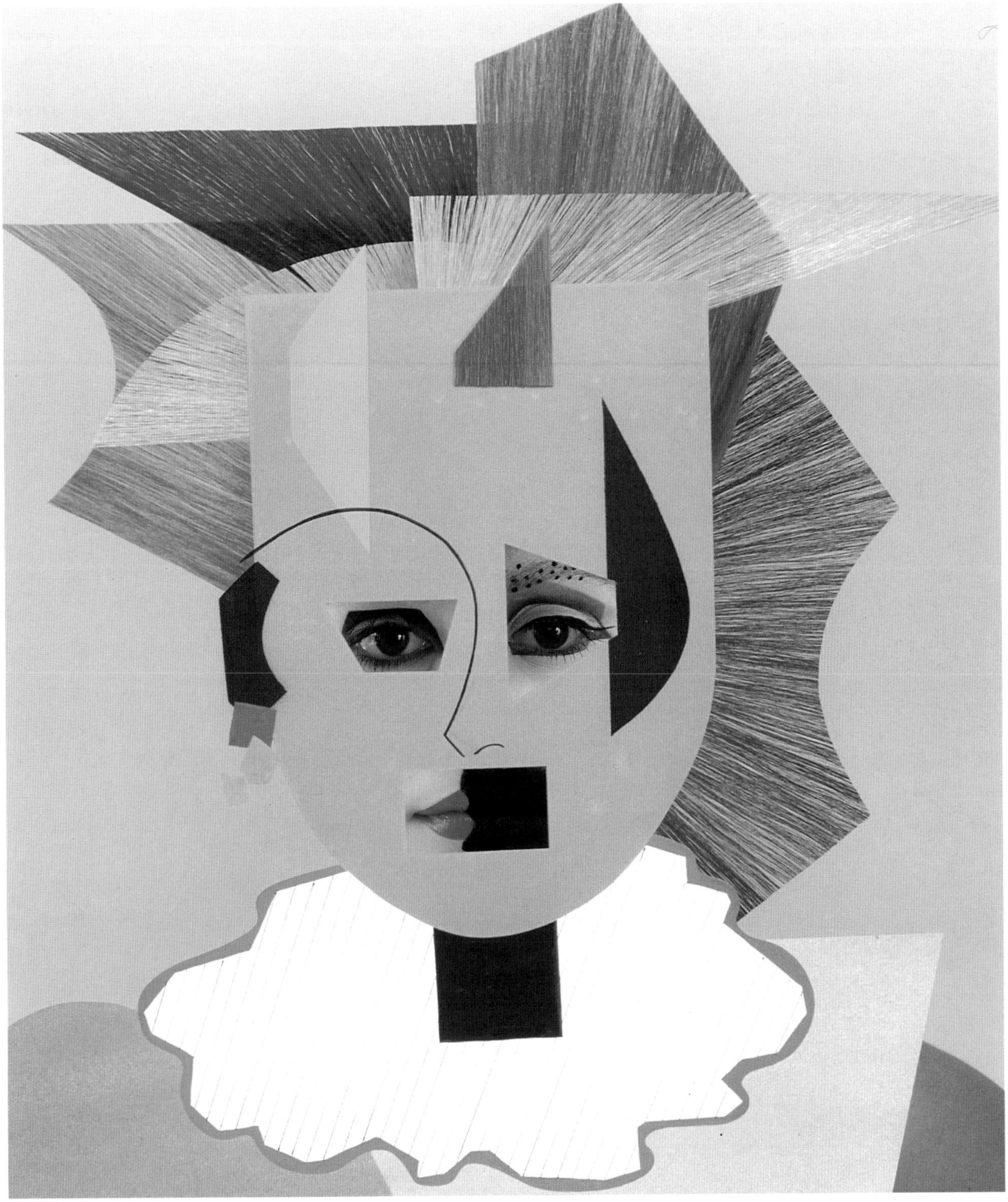

Top. Couple at the 1987 British Tattoo Expo, 1987.

Paula Kendrew with make-up by Tony Kendrew. (Photo courtesy of Tanta Fash.)

A modern reconstruction of the tattoo art of a 5th century B.C. Scythian chief whose body was preserved thanks to the constant cold of the Altai region of Southern Siberia.

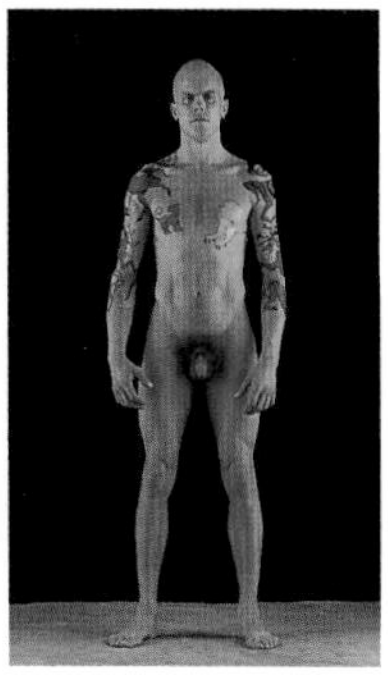

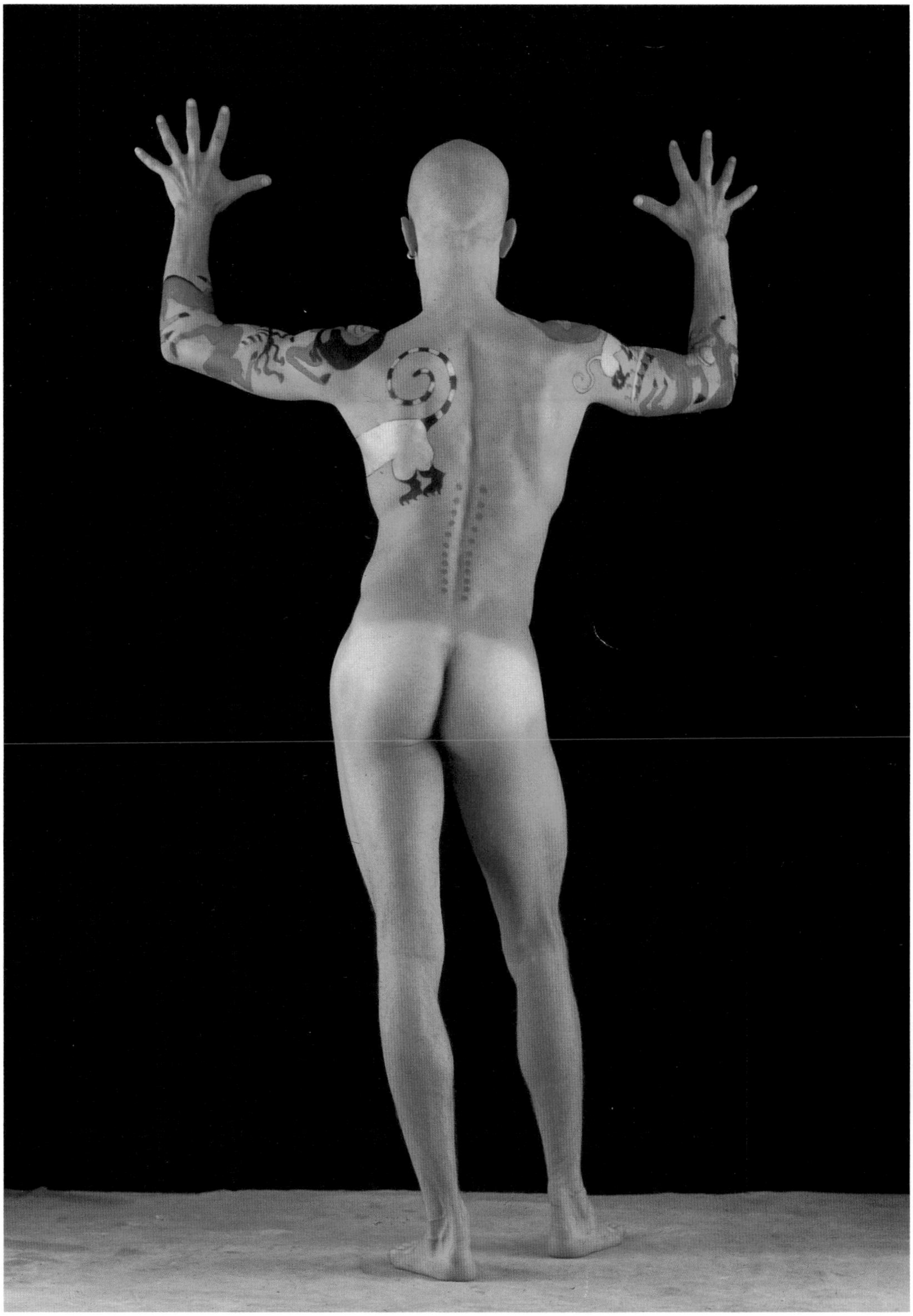

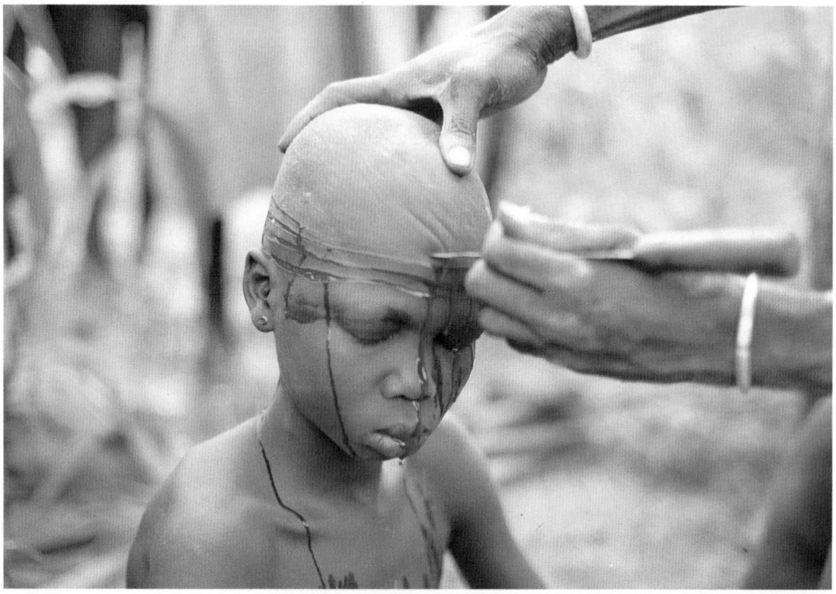

The forehead of a Dinka youth of the Sudan is scarred as a crucial part of the initiation rite which will make him an adult and full-fledged member of his tribe.

The tattooed 'patches' which members of the National Chopper Club of Great Britain acquire as part of their initiation rite.

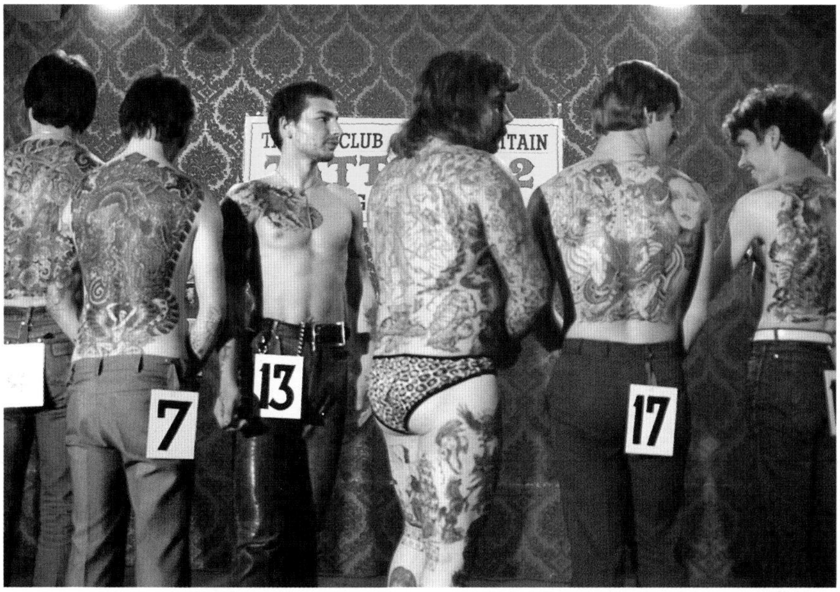

Line-up of a few of the contestants at the British Tattoo Convention which was held in Ramsgate in 1982.

Amazon man with a wooden plug worn in a stretched hole pierced in his lip.

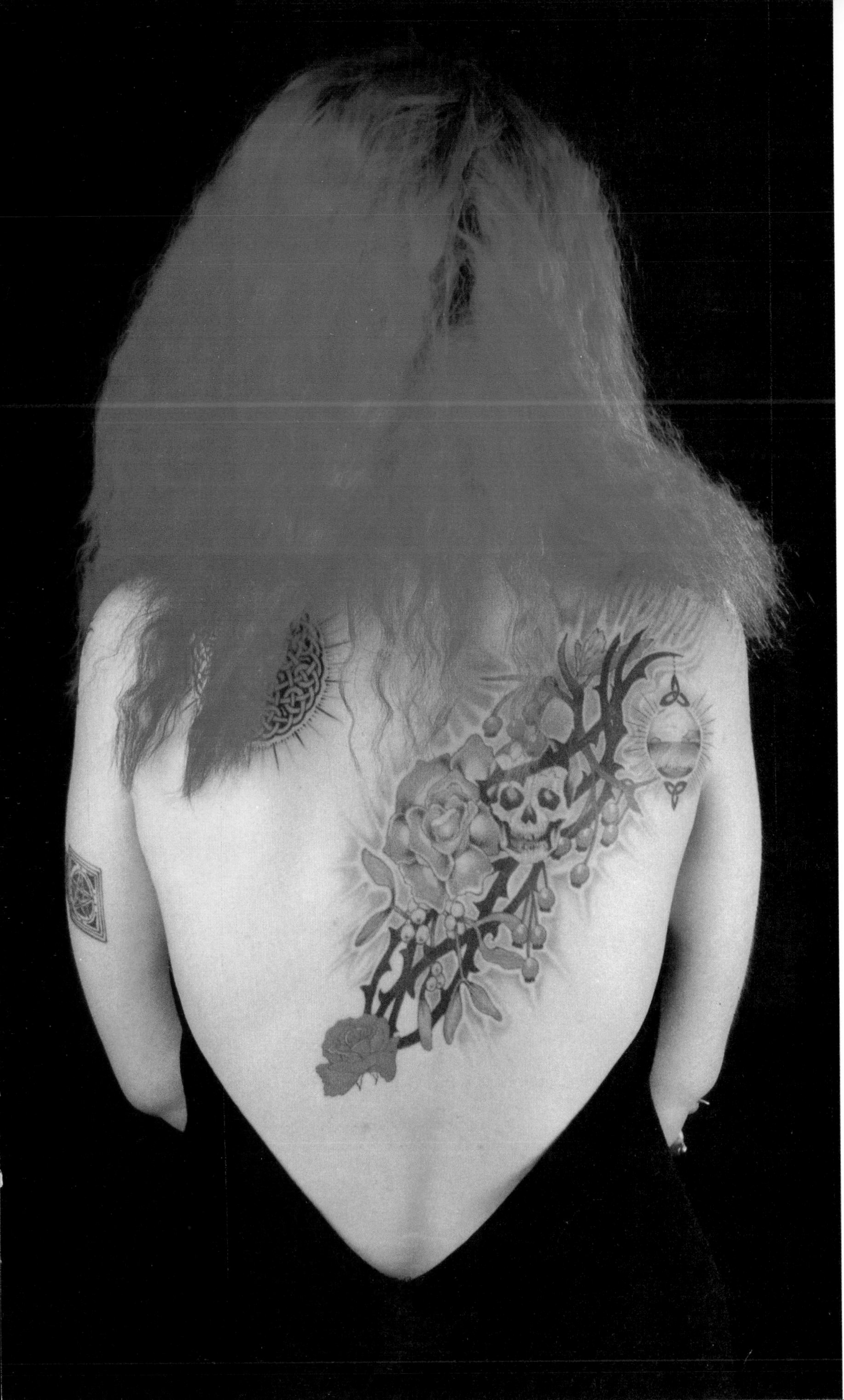

Distinctive back tattoo of British 'Rock poetess' Joolz.

considered in previous chapters. Another casualty of this attitude was that Art came to be seen only as paintings which hung on walls or sculpture which balanced on pedestals. For Invisible Man, adornment (and clothing), no matter how creative or magnificent, would never qualify as valid artistic endeavour.

In *The Obstacle Race*, Germaine Greer grapples with the question of why there have been so few female artists throughout Western history. It would be irrelevant here to comment on her interesting conclusions, but it is, it seems to me, necessary to chide her for founding her work upon Invisible Man's prejudiced assumption that any creative expression which uses the medium of the human body cannot be 'real art'.

If, as we should, we broaden the boundaries of 'art' to include body adornment and clothing, then we can readily appreciate the full extent to which women, over the centuries, have contributed to Western artistic traditions. Their creations in make-up, fashion design and coiffure may, in one sense, have been short-lived, but the great masterpieces and creative breakthroughs of each generation lived on in their influences upon the body art of future generations. Furthermore, advances in the arts of body decoration and dress have often had a direct and profound influence upon various non-corporeal forms of art (and, of course, architecture).

But we have, in this aside, strayed from the subject at hand. What about The Invisible Man? What future does he have now that many women have decided to re-gain control of their own bodies? Can the New Man of the post-industrial era break with the unhealthy attitudes of his forefathers, rediscover his body and delight in its decoration? For surely what is needed, instead of women rejecting adornment, is for men to start to rediscover it. The evidence from the streets, the pubs and the shops is both discouraging and encouraging.

First the bad news. The majority of Western men who grew up in an age when men were (invisible) men and women were bodies, seem unable to now renounce The Great Masculine Renunciation. The continued existence of these drab dinosaurs suggests that the attitudes towards one's body and its decoration which one acquires in one's youth are, as a general principle, fixed for life.

For such invisible men – and let us not forget that there are literally millions of these creatures still roaming the face of the earth – the closest they can ever get to creative self expression still seems to be DIY work on their homes or the customizing of their cars. (We could consider the car as a kind of 'clothing' but – although there may be some truth in this – to do so only begs the question of why modern man should have to extend his 'body' so far beyond its biological physicality.)

Now for the good news. A younger generation seems to have come along which considers that it is the privilege and the responsibility of both sexes to look after and decorate their bodies. Admittedly the styles adopted by this younger generation are often highly traditional – even conservative – but the penny does seem to have dropped that success at work or at a nightclub depends upon not just what you do or how much money you make but also upon what you *look like*.

Whereas clothing manufacturers used to find that money was, by and large, only to be made from women's lines, today this is no longer the case. For example, Top Shop's flagship store in London's Oxford Circus used to handle only a few gift items for men: it has now given over most of its ground and first floor space to mens and boyswear. And on the Kings Road (or the Roman Road in London's East End) where, only a few years ago, it was only women's shops which were crowded with customers, the situation today is the opposite.

Finally, hairdressers who once found it difficult to interest men in anything other than a quick, easy, cheap and standardized 'short, back and sides' are increasingly finding that it is their male customers who lash out on expensive perms and streaking.

Similar changes in all forms of body decoration are going on in Europe, America, Australia and Japan. But if, in a sense, the age of the dandy may be returning, the present day adornment of 'normal' men is still far removed from the flamboyant decorations of either tribal or Western peacocks before the 18th century . . . Except, of course, for the Punks, Gothics, Rockabillies, New Psychedelics and all the other modern-day style groups within which one finds exotic adornment indulged in equally by both sexes.

Amongst such groups of young people there is a refreshing assumption that what is good for one gender is good for the other. Here are girls who wouldn't think of going out with a boy who wasn't as completely, creatively and outlandishly adorned as themselves. And here are males who courageously defy the sober, anti-adornment definition of masculinity which was born of the industrial revolution and the work place. For ironically, it has taken the spectre of mass unemployment to free this generation from those constraints of the work place which first produced that drab dinosaur The Invisible Man.[2]

1. Which is not, of course, to suggest that the sexist manipulation of body decoration does not occur in tribal societies. It does, but the prime manipulator of body decoration is the socio-cultural system to which the members of *both* sexes must submit.

2. Another irony. Those male Hippies or Mods who, a generation ago, began to liberate men from the sartorial constraints of the work place were able to do so for precisely the opposite reason – the *lack* of unemployment which, coupled with a general prosperity, meant that they could thumb their noses at the demands of visual sobriety which boring jobs demanded. The important thing is that the end result is the same (the return of the peacock) and that its cause is, one way or another, contingent upon changing economic circumstances.

Decorated man from the central district of New Guinea.

Male and female attire from France in the second half of the 15th century.

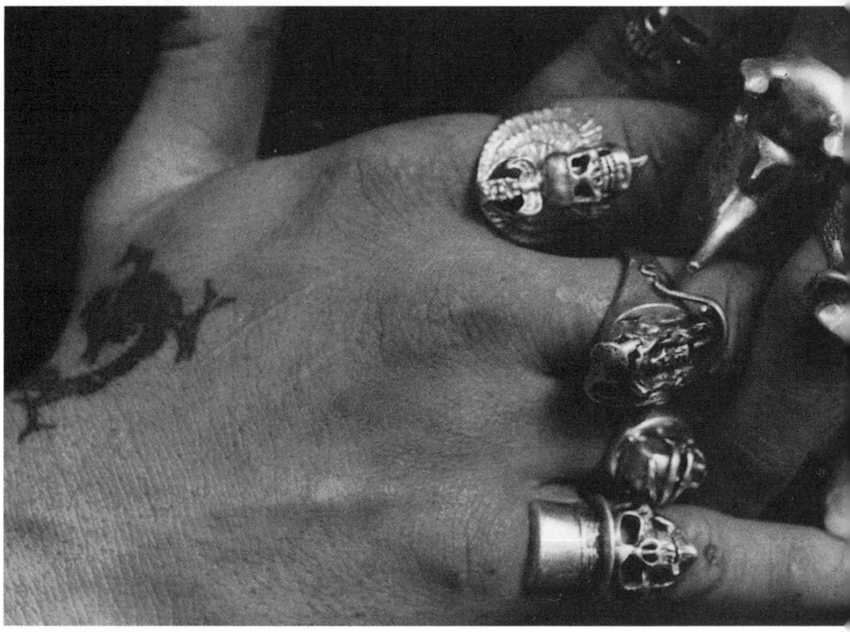

British musician Johnny Slut (clothes by Theresa Colburn, London).

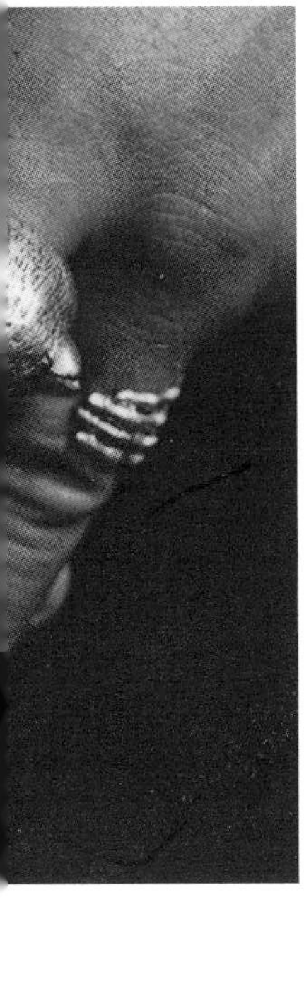

Boy George in a London club, 1980.

Male jewellery and tattoos, London.

The attire of Swiss soldiers in the 16th century.

2
Adornment

11 First Impressions

For members of a tribe in the middle of the Amazon or a peasant community in Tibet, even today, the appearance of a stranger is an exceptional event. For those of us who live or work in cities, on the other hand, to *not* find ourselves in the course of the day in the company of strangers is exceptional. These contrasting lifestyles demand very different things from body decoration.

In tribal and peasant communities, differences and similarities of adornment styles underline what is already known – they are a means of formalizing roles and relationships and expressing the structure of the group.

In urban or suburban environments, on the other hand, body decoration, together with clothing, gesture and posture, is a semaphore system which allows even complete strangers a means of relating to one another. For us, adornment is a form of self-advertisement – how we tell people at a glance 'where we are coming from'.

Just as rural people develop extraordinary skills in the perception of their physical environment, those of us who live in a world of strangers have developed extraordinary skills in the management of our own image and in 'reading' and interpreting the signals which other people project in their appearance. These skills are as necessary for our survival as the ability to read the tracks of an animal is for a tribal hunter.

Let us first consider the subject of image management – what the sociologist Irving Goffman has called *The Presentation of Self in Everyday Life*. Whenever we are in public our bodies and the way in which we choose to adorn and clothe[1] them are our calling cards – sandwich boards advertising our personalities, social situations and aspirations. In the West we have a wide variety of props (different styles of clothing, colours of make-up, types of jewellery, badges, hairstyles, perfumes, etc.) from which we select a set which we hope will communicate the 'right' things about us to others when we go out in public.

I put the word 'right' in quotation marks because this display is never an objective résumé of who we are. This is in contrast to tribal communities, where everyone knows just about everything that there is to know about everyone else and the honesty of self presentation is rigorously controlled.

For example, in the Mount Hagen area of New Guinea, 'Big Men' wear about their necks an item of decoration known as a *tale*, which is made of differing numbers of bamboo sticks of equal length. The greater the length of a man's *tale*, the greater his wealth (which in New Guinea refers to how much an individual has managed to give away in exchange rituals). The *tale* is a very effective use of adornment as a symbol of status and wealth, but the important thing about this decoration for our present discussion is that no New Guinea 'Big Man' could possibly add a few pieces of bamboo on to his *tale* on the sly without being caught out and thereby losing all credibility.

In our urban society on the other hand, cheating in our presentation of self is all part of the game of life. A man who is about to go bankrupt might wear an expensive-looking watch to impress those with whom he hopes to do business. Or a woman considered 'past her prime' might skilfully apply make-up to affect a younger appearance, just as a man in the same situation might use a lotion to get rid of grey hairs. In our society such dishonesty of presentation is the norm. Through image management we create a fictional character – a person we might *like* to be, or at least a person we would like other people to *think* we are.

Furthermore, a person's image often changes with reference to the particular other s/he is presenting to. For this reason most people possess a repertoire of prop sets for different occasions: for a job interview a man might wear a dignified and respectable style of tie whereas at a party he might choose something more flashy. Complications arise whenever we have to attend different types of social events within the same day and it is not unknown, therefore, for people to take along a change of props in their bags, briefcases or the back of their cars.

Props such as style of hair cut, however, can rarely be changed with alacrity and this is one of the reasons why hair is an important clue for catching other people at presentational deceptions. For example, in the late '60s a hippy's long hair would have caused problems at job interviews but if he cut it off he would have had difficulty at rock concerts where, despite possessing an otherwise full set of hippy presentation props, he could be dismissed as a 'weekend hippy'. Punks in the '80s, of course, can face similar problems.

Another sort of problem occurs when the self which we wish to project changes over time. Unless we continually reassess our personality and our prop sets, a time lag can develop between that which we want other people to think we are and the character which we actually project. For the young these changes are particularly rapid and continuous but it is often the middle-aged who, having long ago dispensed with periodic personality/prop reviews, suddenly discover that their image no longer fits with who they think they are.

An interesting (and frustrating) aspect of the presentational time lag problem occurs whenever friends, lovers or relatives give us presentational props as gifts. Some of these end up at Oxfam, but frequently men end up wearing ties and sweaters or women jewellery and scarfs which correspond only to an out-of-date version of who they would like to be. (This, of course, is the great problem with relationships. People change at different rates and in different ways over the course of a relationship and yet each party may keep trying to hold on to the person they first met. Thus he says: 'I remember how nice you looked with your hair permed when we first met', and she thinks: 'How could anyone have liked that hair style/person? He doesn't know who I *am*'.)

In summary, let us reiterate that in the presentation of self, everyone (or at least everyone in our society) is a con man/woman. Of course, some are better at this game than others (which might suggest careers in espionage, the theatre, undercover police work, private detection, crime or politics). But we *all* need some such skills for everyday survival.

Such presentational skills have only a little to do with technical proficiency in the acquisition of props (e.g., knowledge of clothing or adornment styles and shopping skills) and a great deal to do with being able to sort out in our mind's eye who we really are. Each of us, at any point in time, is a collection of characters in search of an author. The trick is in knowing which of these facets of self is the 'real' me. Various forms of mental illness can interfere in this process, which is why severely mentally ill people may exhibit presentational confusion. (Or, of course, you can find the opposite: the mentally ill person who is *too* good at presentation and whose only reality of self is in its signification.)

There is obviously much more that could be said about the presentation of the self, but let us move on to consider the flip side of this phenomenon: checking out the Other. Let's say that you are walking down a street late at night. The street is deserted and the night resounds with the sound of your footsteps. Then suddenly you dimly perceive in the distance a figure approaching you. At 400 yards this is just a spectre but already you are running through your mind a programme of questions which attempt to size up this Other.

The complexity of such a situation can only be appreciated by carefully taking note of what is going on in your mind's eye with every step you take. Several important things can be learned from such an experiment.

---

* Firstly, the astounding speed at which all of us deal with such situations – this entire perceptual and evaluative process can be run through in an instant.
* Secondly, I want to remind us just how sophisticated are our perceptual skills in spotting distant and subtle clues within a short time frame. Just as Eskimos can recognize many different types of snow, so some people in our society can, for example, spot the difference between a pair of Levi 501s and a pair of Wranglers at 200 yards on a dark street. Perceptual skills are, in any society, focused upon what is most important to that society. In the urban jungle the rapid interpretation of presentation clues can literally be a matter of life and death and so those who are street wise become skilled at observing such phenomena.
* Thirdly, I would hope by this device to underline the prejudicial nature of the evaluative process whereby we assign meanings to such clues. Visual perception *per se* is only the first stage of any such interaction. Our response – to nod, smile, look away or stare into the distance, to move to the other side of the road, to reach for the MACE or personal alarm or to flee in the opposite direction – is always determined by our mental evaluation of what we see.

And like our own presentation of self, our evaluation of the presentation sets of others is always subjective and rooted in prejudice. Whenever we check out another's appearance we evaluate such visual data according to a store of information derived from our own previous encounters, from the experience of people we know and from the media. Thus if we have, for example, recently read newspaper accounts of a villain with tattoes or hooligans with punk hair-dos, we (usually without realizing it) draw upon such information in evaluating the others whom we personally encounter – who may, of course, be completely unlike the stereotype by which we have judged them.

Our assessments are, therefore, inevitably built upon stereotypes and unproven prejudices. Indeed, this is the *only way* for us to make sense of, and therefore cope with, our visual encounters with strangers. Nevertheless, the street-wise person is aware of his or her visual prejudices and constantly re-evaluates them in light of new first-hand experiences. Furthermore, such a person bases their assessment of others not upon a single item in a presentation set but upon the relationship of all the items within such a set. Most often it is the lack of fit – the fact that the shoes or the hair-do don't go with everything else – which gives the game away. (This is what happens in, for example, a TV crime programme when a police detective or a criminal under surveillance has a hunch about someone being 'wrong'.)

The most obvious function of such checking out procedures is to avoid trouble. It is the positive side of such interactions, however, which often has the most effect on our lives. In small-scale communities people tend to form relationships with people about whom they already possess a great deal of *a priori* information. Differences of adornment and other aspects of presentation can, of course, be important in such an environment in that they may provide clues about the inner

1. Because we are here concentrating on Western society where clothing as well as adornment is of great importance in self-presentation, it will be necessary to interpret the subject of 'adornment' more flexibly to include dress.

self (in that there are some things which can only be expressed in such a non-verbal and symbolic form). Nevertheless, such information in a small-scale society is always rigorously cross-indexed against what is already known about that person as common knowledge.

In urban life, on the other hand, social relationships are often built from scratch upon first impressions (on the basis of which we sort all those people with whom we come into contact into those we would like to get to know and those we would hope to avoid). Thus, in urban life, visual interactions constitute a sort of DNA of social networks and relationships (occasionally including even such long-term relationships as marriage, business partnerships, etc.). And, whatever other sources of information we may possess, we often find that our gut reactions based upon first impressions are the most reliable.

But there is another reason why, in urban life, first impressions (across a crowded room, and so forth) are so important. As we have seen in previous chapters, modern society is highly pluralistic. Whereas all the members of a tribe or a traditional peasant community are likely to share similar world views, attitudes, beliefs and ideologies, the inhabitants of modern cities and suburbs (and this applies almost as readily to Third World cities such as Nairobi or Belem as it does to New York or London) have little in common except the weather, the problems of public transport and long queues in the supermarket. Such heterogeneity of world view and 'personality' must be advertised 'up front' if like-minded people are to have any hope of finding each other in the metropolis.

Because our unadorned bodies cannot readily signal such ideological differences, we customize them using clothing, jewellery, hair styles, make-up and perfume, thus converting them into walking billboards designed to instantly show others where we are 'at'. The end result is that our urban populations are as visually heterogeneous as they are culturally and ideologically pluralistic.

It is an incredibly efficient system. Without it we would all be lost in the crowd and the business of finding people like ourselves – people with whom we might form satisfying relationships – would be almost impossible.

To see just how different such a situation would be we need only consider the frustrating limitations of computer dating or the 'Lonely Hearts' columns of magazines. I don't deny that people have sometimes found Mr or Ms Right in this way, but the lack of visual presentation clues in such situations clearly stacks the odds against such an occurrence. Thus verbally encoded information such as . . .

'Attractive, articulate lady (39), independent, successful'

'English bachelor, 42, lively, attractive, likes cinema, dining, music'

'Male (44) professional (arts), general interest, own house'

. . . do not really tell us what we need to know about a person with whom we might hope to spend the rest of our life. What kind of hair cut they have, however, might provide a more valuable clue.

Why this should be the case stems from the differences between signs and symbols which were discussed in Chapter 8. As I pointed out, although verbal signs are highly proficient at communicating certain kinds of information, they often fail us when it comes to expressing vague, subtle and complex ideas such as world views or personality. A severe crew cut, a respectable short back and sides or a fluffy blow-dry style of coiffure, on the other hand, can symbolize and thereby publicly express subtle gradations of complex information about personality and lifestyle – things which are often impossible to put into words. Such adornment symbols allow us not only to 'say' the unsayable, but to compress such information into immediately recognizable and 'readable' form.

The importance of such visual presentation clues is demonstrated in the TV programme *Blind Date*. Here one person has

Imported Brazilian natives perform for party guests on the banks of the Seine in a *Fête Bresilienne*, Rouen, 1550.

to choose which of three members of the opposite sex to take on a date. The choice is, as the name of the programme implies, 'blind', owing to the fact that a screen separates the chooser from the would-be chosen. After three questions the screen is rolled back and then the real fun begins as the facial expressions of most contestants reveal their surprise at the lack of fit between what they can now see and what they had blindly heard. As entertainment, such programmes are highly effective but as a means of serious partner selection they have a poor track record with, apparently, more viable relationships being formed backstage in the hospitality room where face-to-face (and presentation prop set to presentation prop set) interaction is possible.

But that, of course, is the point. Without the visual clues of self presentation – no matter how dishonest their transmission or how prejudiced their interpretation – we are but strangers in a strange land.

From the urban to the tropical jungle, body adornment plays a vital part in creating and maintaining social relations. In tribal or peasant communities this takes the form of smoothing and reinforcing existing relationships by spelling out the boundaries of the group and differences of role, status and sub-group within the community.

In a modern urban/suburban context, on the other hand, in addition to assisting in such group dynamics, differences of adornment and presentation of self also serve as a device for separating out people 'like us'.

In either of these situations, if one were to strip away all the body decoration and adornments by which we advertise our similarities and differences – in other words, if we all were like poor Adam and Eve on the plaque of the *Voyager* space probe – then each of us would be bereft of visual meaning, signifying nothing and ill-equipped for any form of social interaction. It is our choice of hair cut, make-up, jewellery, clothing, perfume and posture which makes us more than a bunch of naked apes.

3
Modesty

12 Naked Savages

In 1550 a party was held in the French city of Rouen in honour of Henri II and his young queen Catherine de Medici. Guests arrived at what was surely one of the most extraordinary parties of all time, to discover that a portion of forest on the banks of the Seine had been arranged to look like a tropical jungle.

Trees had been painted, there were exotic birds and monkeys and in the midst of it all some 50 Brazilian tribesmen and women – recently brought from the New World by an explorer – hunted wild game, fought an inter-tribal battle with bows and arrows, smoked tobacco, rested in hammocks and danced. Many of these Brazilians wore ornaments through piercings in their ears, lips and cheeks. But what most fascinated and astounded the party guests was the fact that these visitors from the New World were naked.

The Europeans' shock at the sight of unclothed tribal peoples was not simply a product of prudishness: the discovery of 'naked savages' was a blow to the established European and world view on a par with Copernicus's disturbing revelation that the Earth was not the centre of the universe. Ever since Europe had embraced Christianity many thousands of years previously, our ancestors' understanding of human nature had been based on the story of Genesis. Adam and Eve had been created naked, but after tasting the fruit of the tree of the knowledge of good and evil they had 'seen that they were naked' and covered their embarrassment. According to Genesis, all human beings were descendants of Adam and Eve and therefore heirs to their sense of modesty. Thus humankind itself was defined by its concealment through clothing.

The discoveries of the Age of Exploration challenged practically every aspect of the cosy and stable world view of medieval Europe. The world itself was suddenly seen to be round and filled with such a proliferation of different creatures that Noah's ark must have been very cramped indeed. But the discovery of 'naked savages' was especially perplexing. Here were creatures who looked more like Europeans than like any known animal but who, in their nonchalant exposure of their bodies, showed no sign that they had inherited Adam and Eve's sense of modesty. Far from being a trivial matter, the discovery of such creatures threatened the very foundations of European religion and cosmology – they were disturbing anomalies at the very centre of what had previously been a tightly ordered framework of being.

While our ancestors were struggling with this dilemma, native peoples throughout the world must have been confronted with similar cosmological upheavals. Every tribal society which one day woke up to the sight of bizarrely attired European explorers would have had its own well ordered world view and presumptions about humankind suddenly thrown into turmoil. Ways of life which, for hundreds and thousands of years, had gone on virtually unchanged were now suddenly confronted by something so strange and alien that the only comparison which we could make in our own time would be the arrival of Martians in our midst – and very strange Martians at that.

For many tribal peoples, the arrival of European explorers proved to be too much of a culture shock. They were simply unable to accommodate such an experience within their world view and their culture and way of life never recovered. Other tribal peoples seem to have succeeded in simply incorporating such events into their cosmologies so that pale-faced explorers were cast in the role of mythical ancestors or gods returned to Earth.

European culture was obviously not so traumatized by the shock of the discovery of 'naked savages' that it collapsed altogether, but it was certainly the case that the medieval world view would never be quite the same again. Increasingly the Christian cosmological monopoly would be challenged by the rise of humanisim and other secular philosophies (eventually, even anthropological cultural relativity) and such developments clearly owed a great deal to this experience. But, like all societies throughout the world which reeled under the culture shock brought by the Age of Discovery, European society used every means at its disposal to safeguard its traditional world view.

If 'naked savages' were a classificatory anomaly and therefore a threat to the established order, the obvious solution was to simply classify them as creatures outside the boundaries of humanity. The logical device for accomplishing this was very straightforward: human beings are the descendants of Adam and Eve and as such possess a sense of modesty and shame. Tribal peoples who (regardless of their human-like physiognomy) do not cover their genitals in public cannot be children of God and are, therefore, animals. Besides safeguarding the European, medieval, Christian world view, this classification also had the practical advantage of ridding our Western ancestors of any guilt which they might have felt over the exploitation of such creatures. European governments could dispatch explorers and armies to the far corners of the Earth to found empires without any fear that in doing so they were violating any moral precepts.

While European kings grew wealthy and

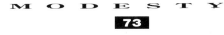

powerful as a result of such exploitation, the Church soon realized that it too could benefit and expand in light of the Age of Discovery. 'Naked savages' might not be descendants of Adam and Eve, but it was worth a try to see if missionaries could succeed in converting them to Christianity and humanity. Some argued, of course, that one might just as well attempt to convert creatures like the newly discovered apes, but it was more generally felt that one had a responsibility at least to try. (There were, apparently, even a few church leaders who proposed that attempts be made to convert the non-human primates.) And so missionaries equipped with the word of God and European clothing supplies were dispatched to follow in the footsteps of the *conquistadores*.

Today the success of these and subsequent missionaries is evident almost everywhere in the world. Tribal peoples from darkest Africa to the sunny shores of Polynesia have embraced Christianity, become children of God and learned to cover their bodies with Western-style clothing. Peoples who for thousands of years had gone 'naked' are today safely concealed behind second-hand Western garments (often to bizarre sartorial effect, with strange juxtapositions of styles and with undergarments such as bras worn as outwear). Indeed, anthropologists would be hard pressed to list more than a few dozen tribes throughout the entire world who persevere in their uninhibited display of genitals and breasts. It has taken hundreds of years but the world has indeed been made safe from the disturbing threat of naked savages (except, ironically, here in the West where, as we will see in the next chapter, the naturist movement has colonized beaches from the Mediterranean to Australia).

It would seem, then, that the missionaries have had extraordinary success in imbuing the world's 'naked savages' with a proper and decent sense of modesty and shame in the display of their bodies – if not in their bodies themselves. In one sense this is all too true – along with metal tools, glass beads and mirrors, shame is our principal export. But we have not succeeded in teaching the 'naked savages' a sense of modesty in one important regard: they all possessed such a thing long before our explorers showed up.

Neither we Europeans nor the semites of the Old Testament were the inventors of modesty. Our contribution (if that is the right word) was in specifically linking it with the act of covering the genitals and other parts of the body, such as the breasts and the backside, which we defined as obscene.

Because the formula:

modesty = genital + breast + backside concealment

is so entrenched in our culture and so deeply instilled in each of us from an early age, it is very difficult for us to appreciate that in other societies the same feelings and prohibitions can be associated with other parts of the body and even with decorations which do not (to our minds) qualify as 'coverings' at all.

It seems very strange to us that an Arab woman caught with her face uncovered might choose to fling her skirt over her head, thereby exposing her genitals. And perhaps even more peculiar to our way of thinking is

***'Two of the Natives of New Holland advancing to Combat'* illustration in Sydney Parkinson, A Journal of a Voyage to the South Seas in His Majesty's ship the Endeavour (1773).**

the belief of unclothed, tribal peoples that body paint, jewellery and other decorations can provide all that is necessary for modest attire.

Yet this is undoubtedly the case. For the Mehinacu of Brazil – to our eyes an unclothed people – the wearing of a tiny belt around the waist makes all the difference between unacceptable nakedness and respectable dress. Amongst the Nuba (a Nilotic tribe of the Sudan) proper attire for men is a covering of body paint while for Nuba women it is simply a thin layer of oil and ochre. Yet without these items of adornment a Nuba would feel acute embarrassment in public. Indeed, a Nuba girl who has no oil with which to cover herself will stay in her hut as if she were ill.

Botocudo tribesmen (Amazon) with lip and ear plugs.

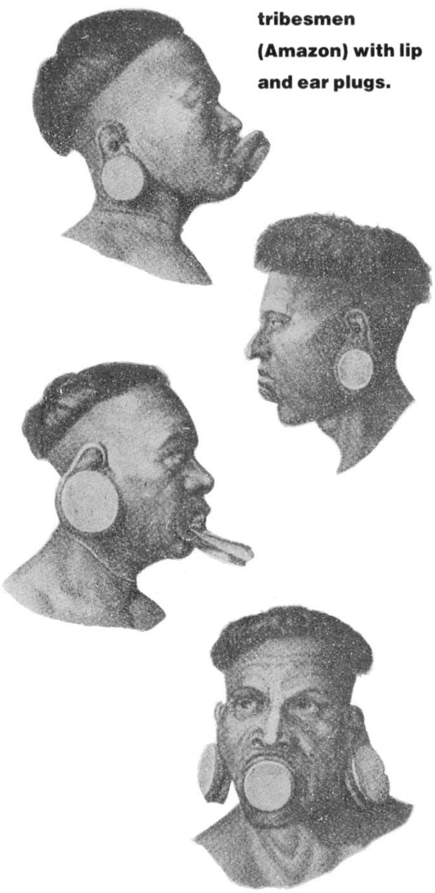

When the European explorer Baron von Nordenskiold encountered the Botocudo tribe deep in the Amazon jungle he was fascinated by the three to four-inch diameter wooden cylinders which the men and women of this tribe wore in stretched piercings in their ears and lower lips. But as he 'undertook to purchase the facial plugs of a Botocudo woman who stood all unabashed in customary nudity before him, only irresistible offers of trade goods at long last tempted her to remove and hand over her labrets. When thus stripped of her proper raiment, she fled in shame and confusion into the jungle'. (Hoebel:p.278)

To us such bits of wood would seem to provide no modest concealment whatsoever, but – and here we begin to broaden our understanding of the word 'modesty' – for such tribal peoples they are an essential component of public display without which they feel as naked as we would walking down a city street with our genitals exposed.

Just as the Caduveo Indians define their humanity by their body painting, so the Botocudo define theirs by their distinctive lip and ear plugs. Indeed, the word *Botocudo* itself means both the tribe which bears that name and the wooden ornaments worn by the members of that tribe. As the anthropologist E. Adamson Hoebel commented: 'The close identification between the Botocudo as a person and the *botocudo* as a plug is such that to become unplugged is most un-Botocudo'.

Throughout the world the definition of modesty and the definition of humankind derive from the same point: that which a group of people traditionally do to distinguish themselves from other animals. This may be burying the dead, defaecating, urinating or eating in private, etc., but always one component of this matrix of essential human characteristics includes something which is done to the human body to customize and 'clothe' it with culture.

In Judeo-Christian cultures we accomplish this primarily by covering our 'private parts' with clothing and we explain, justify and prescribe such behaviour through our mythical account of how our original ancestors, Adam and Eve, discovered the apple and the fig leaf in rapid succession. The Botocudo, no doubt, have some similar mythical justification for their customizing of their bodies by means of wearing lip plugs – and they go one step further by actually calling themselves by the same name as that which sets themselves apart physically from other animals and from other human beings. Is it any wonder that the poor woman bereft of not only her tribal but also her *human* identity should flee in shame into the jungle? (And, if offered some equivalent of what must have been to her astounding and extraordinary riches, how many of us would not compromise our dignity, as she did, by stripping off our clothing?)

Everywhere, as we have seen, human beings are either adorned or clothed (or both) and everywhere to appear in public without such essential components of human dignity is to risk defying the accepted definition of modesty.

The Brazilian natives who so shocked and amazed the party guests in Rouen in 1550 wore, we are told, ornaments in their facial piercings. Were they Botocudo tribesmen and women? Unfortunately we have no way of knowing. All that we know is that the Europeans who saw them exhibited on that occasion failed, like von Nordenskiold, to appreciate that such ornaments were an essential component of their armoury of modesty and of their definition of themselves as creatures unlike the other animals. Presumably those Brazilian natives, exposed to European diseases from which they would have had no immunity, must have soon died a very long way from home. Hopefully, they died with their ornaments, and therefore with their dignity.

No, these strange creatures were not animals, as many Europeans had originally presumed. Nor were they, at least in their own eyes, naked. And the savages, of course, were those who stole their land and kidnapped them to amuse a King and Queen.

3
Modesty

13 The Pursuit of an Innocent Eden

There were actually two very different strategies by which Europeans sought to accommodate the discovery of unclothed peoples within the traditional Western world view. The first – that they were not actually people at all – we have discussed in the previous chapter. The second – that they were innocents from Eden prior to the Fall – we will consider here.

'The First Steamer on the Orinoco' (Brazil) as illustrated in Robert Brown, *The Races of Mankind* (1873).

The 15th and 16th centuries were turbulent times. Not only had Europe been swept by the winds of war and plague, but the cosy and comfortable world view and way of life of the Middle Ages was increasingly under threat. Suddenly nothing seemed safe and secure and however hard the authorities might have tried to paper over the cracks, Europe was in the midst of what the philosopher T.S. Kuhn has termed a 'paradigm collapse'. That is to say, recent discoveries had so shaken the foundations of the accepted social construction of reality that a patch-work repair of this edifice would no longer suffice. In time a new framework for thinking and for behaving would emerge, but until it did, conceptual disorder would be what passed for normality.

For anyone living in such times, life must have been confusing and stressful and, like many before and since, Europeans in the 15th and 16th centuries reacted with a romantic yearning for a paradise 'where men still lived as they had in the Golden Age, happy, naked, free, without poverty, disease or melancholy, without the responsibilities of property or the need of government. The taste for a pastoral life was increasing and one motive for interest in Eden and the Arcadian theme in Greek literature was the desire to escape imaginatively from the harsh present'. (Hall:*A World Elsewhere*:p.339)

This mythical Eden would, of course, have bounteous riches with streets paved in gold, but it would also be a place of innocence and peace and the discovery of unclothed, technologically primitive peoples seemed to suggest just such a paradise. Therefore, although many were quick to label such people as 'naked savages', others (just as slanderous, but more humane) were quick to see them as alternative Adams and Eves who had somehow avoided eating of the tree of knowledge of good and evil. Exactly how this could be squared with the story of Genesis is something of a mystery, but the quest for Eden is never encumbered with too much logical baggage.

One such searcher after Eden was the Portuguese Pedro Vaz de Caminha who served as the official scribe on Cabral's expedition to the Far East which happened to discover Brazil *en route* in 1500. Sailing up the Buranhaem River from Porto Seguro on the coast, Caminha's party encountered the Tupi tribe.[1] In a long and fascinating letter to Manuel I, the King of Portugal, Caminha describes their first sighting of two Tupi men:

'They are a dark, rather reddish colour. They have good well-made faces and noses. They go naked, with no sort of covering. They attach no more importance to covering up their private parts or leaving them uncovered than they do to showing their faces. They are ingenuous in that matter. They both had holes in their lower lips and a bone in them as broad as the knuckles of a hand and as thick as a cotton spindle and sharp at one end like a bodkin.' (in Ley:p.43)

When the explorers erected a wooden cross and held a Mass, the not surprisingly curious Tupi came to watch:

'Only one woman came with those who were with us to-day . . . She was young and stayed through the Mass. We gave her a cloth to cover herself with and put it around her. But she did not pull it down to cover herself when she sat down. Thus Sire, the innocence of

Adam himself was not greater than these people's as concerns the shame of the body.' (*Ibid:*p.58)

Although Caminha was eager that Manuel should send priests to convert these peoples, there is no hint in his writing of moral censure of even their (to Western eyes) lack of modesty. Indeed, throughout his letter Caminha shows a fond respect and admiration for a way of life which was 'nude as in the first innocence, gentle and peaceable', and clearly implies that at least in this respect the Tupi were morally superior to prurient Europeans. Thus, far from being 'naked savages', to Caminha the natives of Brazil were Adams and Eves before the fall, inhabiting a much longed-for Eden.

Such an attitude set the stage for a school of thought which has surfaced periodically ever since in the West: Rousseau, Blake, Gauguin, Whitman and others (e.g., in films such as *Blue Lagoon* or amongst the hippies of Woodstock), while probably never having heard of the likes of Caminha, have developed this attitude into a fully fledged philosophy which has had a profound influence upon our culture and especially upon our reaction to unclothed tribal peoples. One tenet of this philosophy which is highly relevant to our present discussion is as follows: although the initial motivation of concealing the body behind clothing may have been modesty, its effect has been just the opposite – to increase our 'unnatural lusts'.

Clearly there is considerable logic in this view, for by covering up certain parts of the body we become fixated upon them. Surely unclothed tribal peoples or Adam and Eve before the fall would have seen little point in strip-tease, 'Girlie' magazines or topless waitresses. By covering the female breasts, for example, we have fetishized them: converting baby feeding devices into objects of desire has so estranged them from their biological function that the sight of a woman breastfeeding a baby in public can cause offence. As Walt Whitman put it:

'Sweet, sane, still nakedness in Nature! – ah if poor sick, prurient humanity in cities might really know you once more! Is not nakedness then indecent? No, not inherently. It is your thought, your sophistication, your fear, your responsibility, that is indecent. There come moods when those clothes of ours are not only too irksome to wear, but are themselves indecent. Perhaps indeed, he or she to whom the free exhilarating ecstasy of nakedness in Nature has never been eligible (and how many thousands there are!) has not really known what purity is – nor what faith or art or health really is.

(Probably the whole curriculum of first-class philosophy, beauty, heroism, form – the highest height and deepest depth known to civilization in those departments – come from their natural and religious idea of nakedness.)' (*Specimen Days*:p.101)

The tendency of clothing to eroticize the body is the underlying theme of the next section of this book. For now let us consider some of the difficulties and problems of a philosophy of innocence and purity through nakedness.

Firstly, it must be noted that Caminha and his followers made the same mistake as those who branded unclothed peoples as 'naked savages': they too assumed that the unclothed are without a sense of modesty. When Caminha describes the Tupi Indians of Brazil as 'nude as in the first innocence' he is not only saluting them for their lack of prurience (with which we would agree) but also, no doubt without realizing such implications, denuding them of a capacity to distinguish between the decent and the indecent. As we saw in the last chapter, unclothed peoples such as the Nuba, the Botocudo or the Tupi *do* make a distinction between modesty and immodesty on the basis of their body decoration. To ignore this fact is to fall into a disagreeable paternalism, the bottom line of which is to see the unclothed as not only innocent but child-like – and tribal peoples are no more children than they are animals.

Secondly, let us note the naivety of those who (like Whitman in the quote above) would suggest that by simply stripping off our clothing we can return to a pre-Fall state of innocence and purity. Thousands of years of prurience cannot be cast off as easily as a pair of Y-fronts.

Nor can we Westerners, simply by renouncing clothing, ever hope to become like tribal peoples. On the one hand there is the fact that Western society is much more than simply a clothed culture; our technologies, urban environments and scientific world view (for better or worse) set us apart from the rest of humanity. And, on the other hand, tribal societies such as the Tupi, the Botocudo, the Mehinacu, and the Nuba are much more than simply *un*clothed cultures. Each of these tribes is unique and it is only our Western preoccupation with their nakedness which causes us to think that this one aspect of their lifestyles justifies our lumping them all together into one Arcadian classification. Where we might see one common denominator – nakedness – the members of such cultures would see huge differences of lifestyle, history, economics, politics and belief. There are, if you will, many different Edens and in none of them do we really belong.

And yet the yearning after Eden persists. Our world, like that of the 15th and 16th centuries, is turbulent and in perpetual transition, but – now that the world has been charted and travelled not only by explorers and missionaries but also by untold package tourists – there is little prospect of our discovering Eden 'out there'. Indeed, if it was once located in some distant Pacific paradise or some remote African or South American jungle, we have long since destroyed it. Even outer space – that haven for would-be seekers of a science-fiction Eden in the '50s and '60s – is today deprived of its fantastic possibilities by the cold realities of scientific discovery.

So we have but one remaining option: to

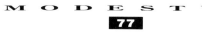

build our own Eden here and now. Which is exactly what the naturists ('nudists' in American) have been attempting to do throughout this century. Naturism emerged as a significant force in Germany between the two World Wars. If ever there was a time and a place which called out for escape to a tranquil Eden this was it. While debauchery

2e Année - No 20. Prix 3Fr 15 Octobre 1927

VIVRE

INTÉGRALEMENT

Culture physique & mentale
Hygiène - Sports. Arts & Sports

Primum vivere, deinde philosophari.

Direction
Rédaction
Publicité

2 bis, Rue de Logelbach
PARIS (XVIIe)

Paraît le 15 de chaque mois sous la direction de
M. K. de Mongeot

Téléphone :
Galvani 04-03
Chèques postaux 806.00 Paris

Une élève
de Mme VILLARD-LIRVA

Mme Geneviève IONE, de l'Opéra, est une fervente naturiste.
Clichés de Vivre.

Mme VILLARD-LIRVA
Professeur de Gymnastique
et de Danse, à Strasbourg.

Apprenez à vous nourrir, à respirer, à développer votre corps, à penser : A VIVRE !

***Vivre* French naturist magazine from 1927.**

Early German naturists in the sun.

and perversion held court in the cabarets of Berlin others sought escape into a pure, innocent, 'naturally naked' Eden.

Prior to World War I, a few German intellectuals had argued the benefits of naturism and had founded a nudist society, but it was between the wars and especially in the vicinity of turbulent and decadent Berlin that the movement struck a popular nerve. The man who became the driving force of this crusade was Major Hans Surén who, after being dismissed from the German army for organizing nude gymnastics sessions, wrote a book called *Der Mensch und die Sonne* (*Man and Sunlight*) which was reprinted some 61 times between 1924 and 1925.

1. Ironically, the Tupi peoples seem to have spent most of their own history migrating across South America in search of Eden in the form of the Land of the Sky God.

Surén's philosophy of naturism drew upon the work of the German intellectual Richard Ungewitter (who, prior to World War I, had argued that a world without clothes would be one without sexual neuroses) and the work of the Swiss Werner Zimmermann (who suggested that children raised in a naturist environment would grow up without feeling guilt about their bodies or their sexuality). But it was Surén's vivid prose and his vision of a pure and naked Eden in some distant Germania of old which captured the mood of the times:

'Up then, friends, to your holy work! Carry the torches high to show mankind the gate which leads out to Nature – to sunlight, for it opens the way to happiness and freedom.' (p.3)

'From the depths of its need mankind is raising itself to burst the bonds of this age. Amazed – overjoyed – freed, it realizes its true nature, and presses mightily forward to the paths which lead to joy, to Sunlight and Nature into true humanity. These paths lead upward – through the sunshine to light! In the glad distance of the future shines a wonderful edifice, invisible to earthly eyes. The splendour of its majestic beauty shines far and wide, blazing down the aeons of time. In the perfection of humanity – in harmony with the All, the Endless – rests the joy of sunlight!' (p.196)

Doggedly opposed to cigarettes, drink, 'degenerate civilization' and, most of all, clothing, Surén based his Utopian vision of a naked Eden upon the Olympic games of the

The author visits one of the supermarkets at Cap d'Agde (France).

ancient Greeks (a noble civilization who, according to Surén, were the descendents of ancient, unclothed Germans). He contrasted the 'obscene nakedness' of the cabarets and saloons of the modern world with the 'purity' and 'sacredness' of 'natural nakedness' and asked 'Is not the entirely naked body, when it has had some degree of culture and is governed by a moral sense, the best means for the upbringing and uplifting of man?' (p.36)

Despite the success of *Man and Sunlight*, rapid growth of *Nacktkultur* (three million practising nudists by 1930) and the blatant attempts by Surén and others to link this movement with German nationalism, Hitler (soon after becoming chancellor in 1933) banned naturism. Then came World War II and the Western world was preoccupied with other matters. But, unlike Hitler, naturism would survive to flower again – not just in Germany, but throughout the Western world.

In Britain a small group of devoted naturists (in publications such as *The New Statesman*) had argued for 'purity not prudery' since the '20s but it had always been an uphill struggle. Then in 1930 an angry mob of some 200 outraged citizens attacked a group of nudists sunning themselves on the bank of the Welsh Harp Pond in Kingsbury, north London. The tabloids had a field day at the expense of the naturists, but the police intervened to protect the sunbathers and the end result was to publicize the fact that people invited onto private property had a legal right to disrobe to their heart's content. Soon naturists were pooling together to buy up pieces of land on which to establish retreats for the unclothed.

In France, although there had initially been strong resistance to the naturist movement, two teetotal doctors, the brothers Gaston and André Durville, eventually managed to found a naturist resort which they called Heliopolis on the Ile du Levant. This grew and grew until by 1960 it had six hotels, nine restaurants and its own bus. Today there is also the Centre Hélio-Marin north west of

Bordeaux which accommodates some 80,000 naturists each year, and the huge naturist resort at Cap d'Agde which has some 59 shops, 20 restaurants, four bars, four swimming pools, three banks, three hairdressers, two night clubs, a bakery, supermarkets and even an open-air cinema.

In America nudists were prosecuted and sent to jail in some states but welcomed in others. The fact that the YMCA had always promoted single sex nude bathing helped some to appreciate the good intentions of the nudists but many more – in some areas whipped up by fundamentalist preachers – condemned nudists as the Devil's task force. When Hollywood produced the first naturist film (the inoffensive 'Elysia, Valley of the Nude') the judge who banned it commented: 'The picture might appeal to the gustatory appetites of very hungry cannibals; otherwise it is without any legitimate attraction, as far as I can see, even for the savage classes'. (K. Dennis, Chief Judge of the City of Baltimore)

Despite this sort of reaction, there are today many large nudist resorts dotted across America, just as there are in Australia and throughout Europe (including parts of the Eastern Block such as Yugoslavia). Such statistical success, however, does not tell us whether the original hope of the naturists – the creation of an innocent Eden – has been fulfilled. Or, to put it another way, what would Hans Surén have made of it all?

I suspect that much of what he would see today would horrify him. Especially in the larger resorts, there is no longer the puritanical fervour which he and most of the other early naturists advocated. Yet, writing as someone who has visited several naturists resorts, it seems to me that the basic tenet of the naturist/nudist movement – that prurience can be diminished by the innocent exposure of the body – has been proven correct. One sees this most clearly in the children of naturists who have grown up in an environment which is free of the sniggering innuendo of the tabloids.

At Cap d'Agde, where a small inlet separates the huge sprawling naturist resort from a 'textile' beach, one can make an interesting comparison. If you stand at the end of the jetty, on your right are thousands of people covered only in all-over tans while on your left are thousands dressed in all manner of swimming costumes. In many cases the only difference is a tiny triangle of fabric which covers the genitals, but the presence of this token concealment belies a very different mentality. Where there is concealment there is just enough mystery to arouse what Surén would have condemned as impure impulses. The 'textiles' are arguably sexier, but the naturists, mimicking Adam and Eve before the Fall, are perhaps just a little closer to Eden.

'You pays your money and you takes your choice': titillation or a taste of something approaching innocence. What is extraordinary is that, for the first time in human history, people should have such a choice.

3 Modesty

14 The Naked and the Nude

You're at the supermarket, at work or walking down the street. Suddenly you realize that you're completely naked. You've never been so embarrassed in your whole life. Then you wake up.

It's a common nightmare, and no wonder. We come into the world naked, spend our infancy and childhood learning that we must cover certain parts of our bodies in public, only to discover that on some occasions – such as a medical examination – we are expected instantly to switch off our inhibitions and operate according to a completely different set of rules of modesty. Modern life certainly is complicated!

In point of fact, however, life in even the most seemingly primitive society is governed by complex rules of situational propriety and impropriety. For example, in many tribal societies (including some where being unclothed is the norm) it is necessary to cover up when in the presence of certain categories of people. In Nuer society (the Sudan) men normally leave their genitals uncovered but 'a man must not appear naked before his parents-in-law, or even before those who possibly may become his parents-in-law'. This rule applies, though in a lesser degree, also to other in-laws and even to the wives of his wife's close kinsmen. 'I have seen,' writes Evans-Pritchard, 'a man's wife's paternal aunt make a great fuss when unintentionally he appeared naked before her. He knelt behind another man to hide his nakedness and received her reproaches when he became aware of his misdemeanour. On another occasion the fuss was made by a bride's paternal uncle's wife while the astonished bridegroom hastily retired into a hut'! (F Th. Fisher:p.185)

Although it may seem rather bizarre that a usually 'naked' Nuer man should hide in a hut because some distant in-law shows up, such behaviour actually makes a lot of sense. Like every other society, the Nuer have incest taboos which apply to both consanguines (one's biological family) and affines (one's in-laws).[1] The rules governing incest with consanguines are the same throughout a person's life, but the rules of incest with affines suddenly come into effect at the point of marriage and are, therefore, more problematic. The Nuer rules of situational propriety, whereby the genitals must be

Three cartoons by Tony Husband which reflect the tension most of us feel when confronted with sudden changes in the rules of modesty.

NUDIST CAMP
That wouldn't be a false beard would it Mr. Rose

ART ROOM
LIFE CLASS
She's a bit tense its her first sitting

I don't know why I feel embarrassed you doctors must have this sort of thing all the time

covered in the presence of affines, serve to remind any Nuer who has recently married or become betrothed that a new category of people are to be excluded from sexual relations, and to define the limits of this prohibition.

Likewise, in our own society, seemingly nonsensical rules of dress and undress generally make sense sociologically. For example, in modern Europe, a woman can (and, in some situations, it might be *de rigeur* to) go topless on a beach holiday. At the office, however, for a woman to reveal her breasts in this way might cost her her job. The breasts are the same in both circumstances, yet in the space of one or two weeks the rules governing their public exposure might change from no to yes and back to no.

As in the case of the Nuer, the logic of these fluctuations in the definition of propriety derives from different categories of relationships. On holiday we are usually in the company either of people we are closely related to, or people we don't know at all. The former are the same category of people with whom, in the privacy of our own homes, we may relax our public code of modesty. Complete strangers, on the other hand, are sort of non-persons and as such do not need to be worried about.

At the office, on the other hand, we are likely to be in the company of a third category of persons: those whom we know a little but not too well. People who fall into this category are neither intimates nor strangers and whether at work or at a dinner party we need to be guarded in how we deal with them. And, of course, it makes sense that we extend our guarded behaviour to our rules of physical exposure. (Or, looked at in another way, our degree of exposure, in each of these situations, provides a valuable guide to appropriate behaviour in a broader sense.)

But although this variable of modesty and propriety may be based on logic, this doesn't change the fact that such sudden alterations in what are incredibly deep-seated rules of behaviour can be difficult to deal with emotionally. (As I am sure they can be for the Nuer.) Every year, as Summer approaches, the mail bags of Agony Aunts and Uncles bulge with letters from women who are anxious about going topless on holiday. Some of these queries reflect concern about the size, shape or condition of the correspondent's breasts, but many stem simply from the fact that a lifetime of learning to cover up this part of the female anatomy is suddenly supposed to be nonchalantly cast aside.

Another situational variable of modesty which can be a cause of emotional trauma is disrobing in front of a doctor or nurse. Here two people who may be of opposite sexes and who, in different circumstances, might be interested in each other sexually, are expected to act as if such a thing was an impossibility.

By means of the uniform, surgery/hospital decor and 'professional manner' the doctor or nurse tries to advertise his or her status as a non-person (or at least a non-*sexual* person). The hope is that differences of role can negate differences of gender. Of course, we all know that this is something of a charade (doctors and nurses are 'only human', come in one of two genders, and possess sexual orientations and drives) but to reduce stress for both the patient and the medical examiner (indeed, to make the examination possible) we agree to participate in this fiction.

Many Arab women, however, after a lifetime of particularly stringent prohibitions against cross-gender exposure, find it impossible to subsume gender into role in this way and require medical attention from a doctor or nurse of their own sex. Tribal medical personnel, such as shamans, presumably face similar problems – even in unclothed societies where normal body 'covering' is provided by decorations which need to be removed for a curative ritual or examination.

One situational variable of decency which is perhaps unique to Western society is the artist's life class. Although artists and art historians have endeavoured to 'clothe' the

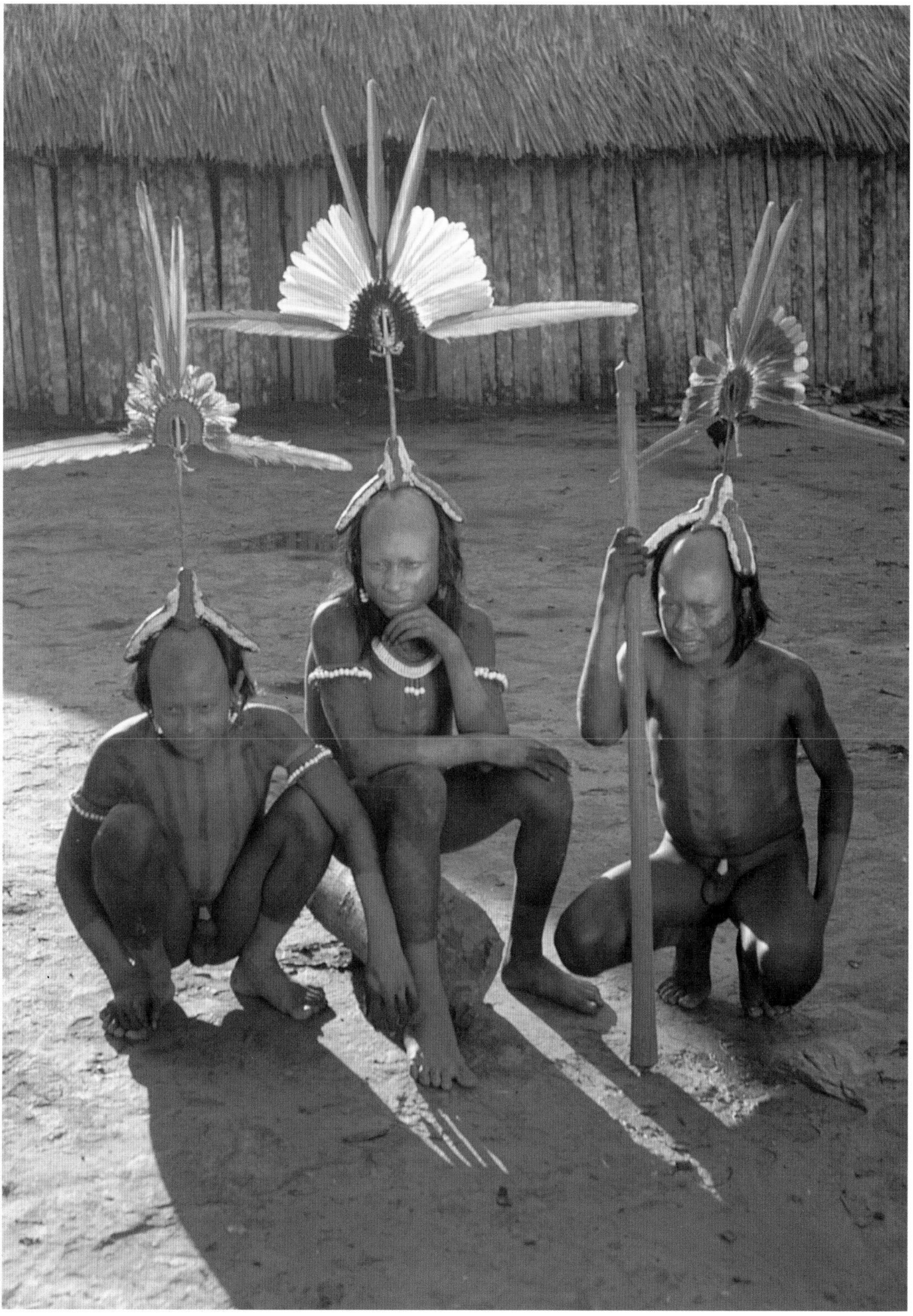

Three Kayapo Indian men of the Amazon with elaborate head decorations.

Western naturist on a beach in Formentera.

Indian women taking part in a ceremony of ritual purification in the holy waters of the Ganges at Benares (Varanasi).

When Western explorers in the Age of Discovery first encountered 'naked savages' they presumed that such unclothed tribal peoples were like animals and possessed no sense of modesty. Today, however, we know that – while every society defines modesty according to different criteria – even in the most (so called) 'primitive' society there are fixed rules of decency which are rigorously adhered to. It might be a belt worn around the waist, a decorative headpiece or a wooden plug worn in a stretched earlobe, but without this 'covering' a tribal man or woman feels the same embarrassment we would walking down a city street with our genitals exposed.

And just as all societies have rules governing the covering of certain parts of the body, so too, all societies recognize certain situations when the rules of modesty can or should be relaxed.

Rio Carnival attire.

British designer Babs Fotherby uses original '50s bras and corsets which she spruces up with colourful liquid latex. (Photo: Mal Stone)

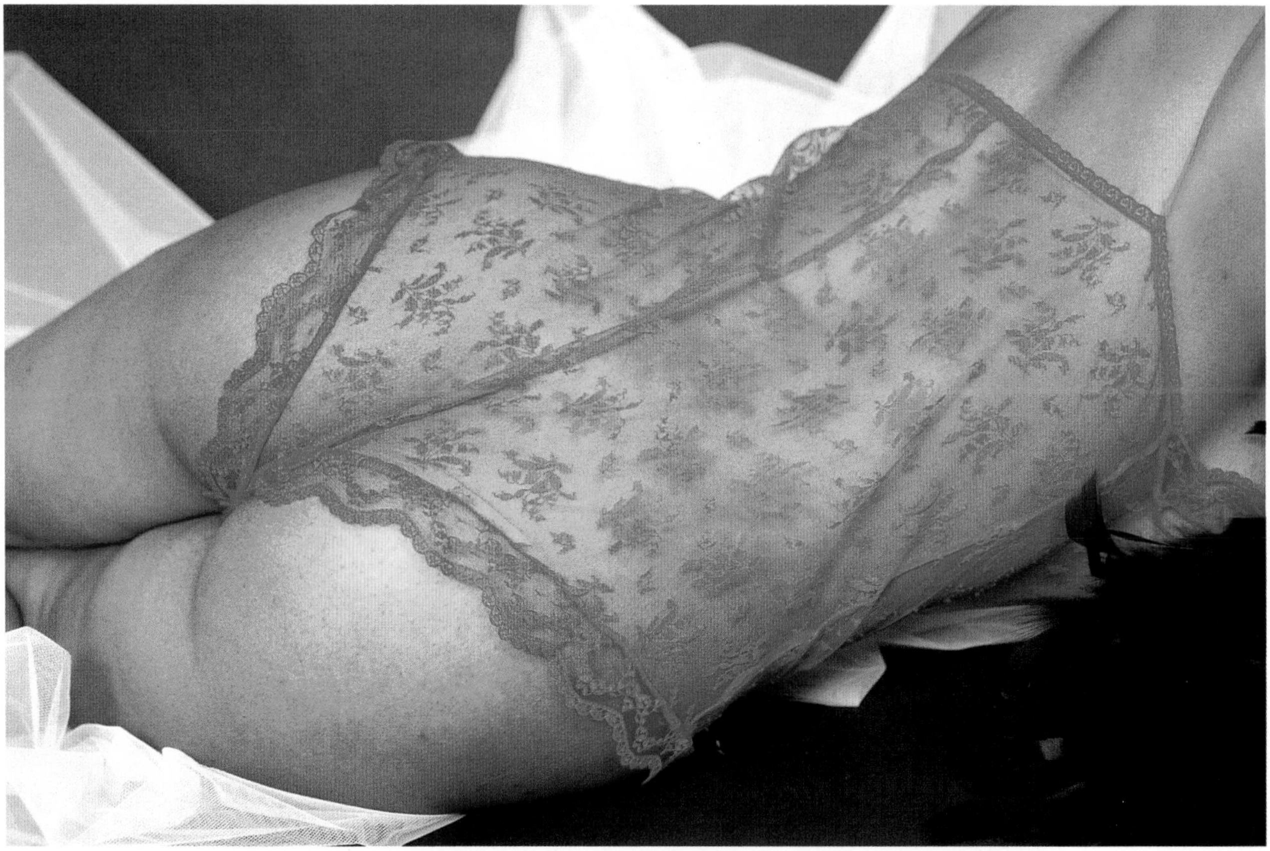

Red lace 'Teddy' by East of Eden, London.

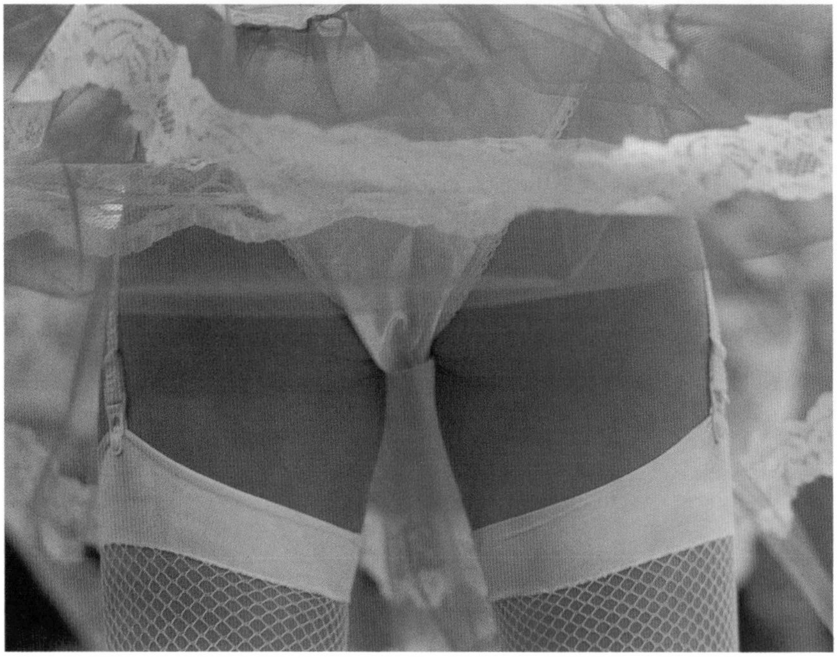

Underwear worn as outer-wear in London's Kings Road.

Girl in London's Taboo Club wearing underwear as outerwear.

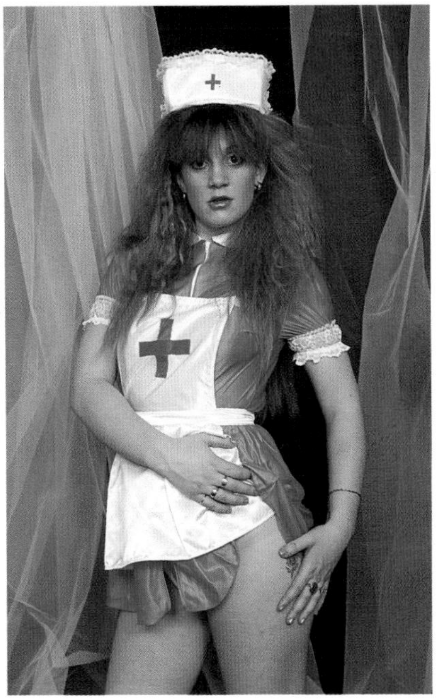

Erotic attire worn in a Japanese music hall entertainment.

'Fun Fashion' nurses outfit by Lady of Paris, Birmingham

Rubber garments by British designer Kim West. (Photo: Kevin Davies).

unclothed model in the respectability of Culture (with a capital 'C'), the public at large often seems unwilling or unable to fully accept this distinction between respectable nudity for artistic purposes and ordinary, inartistic, titillating nakedness. Yet although many or most people may harbour private doubts about the respectability of this phenomenon it is interesting how – at least publicly – the majority of us do try to accommodate ourselves to a distinction which to a certain extent defies common sense.

Kenneth Clark in his book *The Nude* tells us that 'To be naked is to be deprived of our clothes and the word implies some of the embarrassment which most of us feel in that condition. The word nude, on the other hand, carries, in educated usage, no uncomfortable overtones. The vague image it projects into the mind is not of a huddled and defenceless body, but of a balanced, prosperous and confident body: the body reformed'. (p.1)

At risk of sounding plebeian, I have to say that the way Clark explains it, this distinction seems meaningless. In *all art and in all pornography* (cf., Susan Sontag's or Roland Barthes' essays on photography) the body portrayed is always re-formed. And embarrassment (Clark's other distinguishing criterion) is inevitably subjective: there are people who feel embarrassment at the sight of Michelangelo's paintings in the Sistine Chapel and I would have thought that – like sociologists – art critics can not simply ignore such people and their reactions. To be blunt about it, all that Kenneth Clark seems to be saying is that *he* is not embarrassed by certain images which re-form and re-interpret the unclothed human form and that these images he will categorize as 'art' (and, therefore, respectable).

Anne Hollander's reworking of Clark's distinction in her book *Seeing Through Clothes* is perhaps more helpful. Here the naked is defined as 'an image of an unidealized individual bare body' while the nude is described as 'an idealized depersonalized image' (p.157). Yet there are clearly difficulties with this definition as well. Is there ever such a thing as an *un*idealized representation of the human body? And does not pornography also depersonalize its subjects to some degree? (Certainly the women depicted in 'nudie spreads' in men's magazines, as well as being highly idealized by the conventions of this form of photography, are depersonalized into stereotypes by the props they are shown with, the garments which they wear and the obviously fictitious names by which they are identified.)

Hollander then goes on, however, to explore many interesting aspects of the naked/nude in art. In particular, she shows how an artist's use of non-concealing contemporary clothing and decor can underline a model's nakedness, whereas drapery in a classical style can provide a historical and cultural gloss which renders an image respectably nude by distancing the viewer from its immediacy in the here and now. Thus many works of art which today seem to us to be artfully nude were originally seen as naked and erotically charged, even pornographic:

'The girls in magazine photographs seem sexier to modern eyes than those in Titian paintings, but his patrons undoubtedly saw Titian's nudes with Playboy eyes. Even Gulio Romano's pornographic *Sedici Modi* showing various coital positions, so shocking to his contemporaries, have a curiously unsexy look to modern eyes because everyone is 'wearing' the Renaissance figure now associated with idealized formal nudity.' (*Ibid.*:p.88)

Still, I must confess to a suspicion that the acceptability of the artistic nude in Western society since the time of the ancient Greeks is a situation akin to the emperor's new 'clothes'. When a child on a first visit to an art gallery turns to an adult in puzzlement at the fact that here, suddenly, society accepts and celebrates that which in other contexts it condemns as 'dirty', one is hard pressed to come up with a simple and sensible answer. Such a child – like the one who saw through the emperor's 'clothes' – is perhaps closer to the truth than the rest of us.

And when it comes to identifying particular paintings, sculptures or photographs as examples of acceptable nudity (especially as regards the contemporary art of any era) it must surely, at the end of the day, come down to the subjective assessments of art authorities in choosing that which they personally like and with which they feel comfortable. One cannot help but suspect that acceptable nudity, in this context, is that which is exhibited in art galleries and to which (because it represents the human form in a way which expresses the values of the dominant social body) the public and the media do not object too strongly.

Clearly our society's distinction between the distastefully naked and the respectably nude is much less clearly defined, more subjective and more problematic than, for example, the distinction between decent and indecent physical exposure which the Nuer make according to the more objective criteria of different categories of kinship relations.

The life class, the medical examination and topless or nudist sunbathing are all occasions when the rules of modesty which have been impressed upon us since childhood are suddenly relaxed and as such they are, for most people, a source of a certain degree of tension and stress. For this reason they have become the stock in trade of cartoonists and the creators of films such as the 'Carry On' series. The extraordinary popularity of such humour clearly reveals the deep-seated and all-pervasive nature of our unease at being expected to suddenly switch off our life-long education in modesty and adopt a different set of rules.

Needless to say, situations which require us to conceal *more* of our bodies than

1. Different societies, of course, differ in the extent to which such incest taboos apply to particular categories of relatives.

is normal do not generate so much emotional trauma. In our society, the head, face and hands are not generally covered; but our rules of propriety may demand that for certain formal occasions the definition of modesty is extended to include these parts of the body. For example, in some situations in the presence of Royalty, women were traditionally expected to cover their hands with gloves or their heads with a hat. Likewise, a bride on her wedding day is traditionally expected to conceal her face behind a veil. In such situations, a heightened definition of modesty serves to underline symbolically social formality and social barriers.

However, in modern society the principal occasions for an expanded definition of modesty are religious. In Catholic churches women are expected to cover their heads and in a Jewish synagogue all adult males and married females are required to do the same. Interestingly, in some other societies proximity to sacred forces requires just the opposite – the exposure of *more* rather than less of the human body. Amongst the Minanacho tribe of the Amazon, for example, the normal badge of modesty is a thin belt worn about the waist but during some religious or magical rituals this belt is removed so that the participants can confront the divine full frontally.

A similar approach was advocated by the Adamites (an African, Christian sect of the second and third centuries AD) who reasoned that, as clothing was born of the Fall, it – rather than the body – was an offence to God. Therefore, the Adamites (who in a sense were the first naturists) sought to re-discover Eden by stripping off their clothing. Their logical argument – that the body is pure because it was created by God, but concealing clothing is a product of evil and corruption – was rejected by the Church and in the West the idea that spiritual forces are best approached in one's birthday suit has fallen to the Satanists and devil worshippers. (Something which has no doubt been over-emphasized, but not invented, by horror movies.)

Two other situational variables of modesty deserve our attention: occasions of licence and life-threatening emergencies.

Throughout history, human beings have set aside certain times when the normal rules of behaviour can be ignored. In ancient Rome, the most important such period of licence was Saturnalia which took place on 17th of December and occasioned a complete reversal of social roles, with togaless senators serving a feast to their slaves. In Medieval times, the pagan rites of Saturnalia became the Christian Feast of Fools but lost none of the former's delight in role reversal or the relaxation of moral strictures. And in the 17th century, the carnivals of Rome, Naples and Venice became famous throughout Europe for their institutionalized debauchery.

The pressure cooker effect of tight social control which makes little provision for the release of our pent-up 'animal instincts', can sometimes become too much to bear and rather than risk total collapse from such pressures, prudent societies have always institutionalized times when rules and regulations can be inverted, perverted and mocked. Central to this, and the primary means by which such occasions can be marked, is always a relaxation of the rules of modesty.

And if, while parts of the body normally covered are exposed, parts normally uncovered are concealed, then a situational perversion of the rules of behaviour is further emphasized. This covering of the face is especially useful in that a person so concealed is distanced from his or her usual social roles and behavioural responsibilities. As the Italian dramatist Carlo Goldoni had one of his characters point out, the mask is 'the finest convenience in the world'. Certainly in the Venetian carnivals of the 17th century, the wearing of a mask was *de rigeur* and with the entire population in disguise, licence knew no bounds.

Ironically, therefore, occasions of behavioural licence such as carnivals, masques and balls can demand *both* increases *and* decreases in physical concealment. But although the increases involving masks,

A no doubt imaginary contemporary impression of a European bath house in the Middle Ages.

gloves, etc. may contribute to the success of such occasions, it is the removal of normal body coverings which is essential – for it is this stripping off of concealing clothing which symbolizes and condones the putting aside of broader rules of behaviour.

Today the spirit of carnival and the other occasions of licence live on in Rio, Bahia, Trinidad, New Orleans, Notting Hill and Venice. But whereas the majority might have once known periodic release from moral strictures and social constraints, today it would seem that – at least in an institutionalized sense – this is only to be enjoyed by a lucky minority.

Yet although most of us are not in a position to participate, except as observers, in the institutionalized carnivals of minority groups, we who belong to the 'straight-laced' middle classes do seem to be finding some degree of release in privately organized fancy dress parties and masked balls. In the last few years shops renting risqué party costumes and exotic masks have mushroomed in the most respectable middle class communities to cater for would-be French maids and Tarzans. By this means – if only for an evening – the specific rules of bodily exposure and the general rules of proper behaviour can be relaxed.

Finally, we should mention the rather obvious fact that the rules of decent attire can be swept aside in situations of life-threatening emergency. For example, in London during the Blitz, many of those who spent their nights camped out in the relative safety of the Underground relaxed their normal code of public attire and modesty to something like that which, in normal circumstances, would apply only to private life.

The same sort of thing is sometimes seen today in the shelters hastily set up to house those seeking refuge from natural disasters such as floods and hurricanes. I was once in Mexico City when a comparatively mild earthquake struck in the middle of the night and the lobby of the hotel in which I was staying was soon filled with normally scrupulously modest Mexicans suddenly attired only in their underwear, pyjamas and night gowns. While the hotel management served coffee, everyone bent over backwards to ignore the fact that here we all were in varying states of undress which, had it not been for the earthquake, might have got us arrested.

But the most fascinating and disturbing thing about this situational variable of modesty is the extent to which people have been known to refuse – even when it is a matter of life and death – to relax their rules of decency. Firemen report despairingly that far too often men and women are unwilling to leave a burning building simply because they are not sufficiently dressed for public scrutiny. Policemen tell of horrific road accidents in which a barely alive survivor's first concern was re-arranging his or her tattered clothing in order to preserve modesty. And lifeguards tell of occasions when people have risked drowning simply because their bathing costumes had fallen off.

That people might actually choose death over a little dishonour shows just how deep-seated are our prohibitions against immodesty. In the world envisaged by Hans Surén and the other naturists such problems would not arise.

3 Modesty

15 The Politics of Modesty

In 1968 the Tanzanian Government announced that members of the Masai tribe would, in the future, have to wear Western dress when visiting city centres such as the capital Arusha. One of the things which prompted this rather strange piece of legislation was the fact that, although the Masai traditionally wear robes and blankets draped around their bodies, these do not always provide concealment according to Western standards of decency. As the African historian Ali Mazrui has written in his thought-provoking essay 'The Robes of Rebellion: Sex, Dress and Politics in Africa':

'The authorities in Tanzania had decided that the Masai had been permitted naked indulgence for far too long; that their withdrawal from normal attire constituted a withdrawal from the mainstream of progress in their countries. It had therefore been decreed that no Masai men or women were to be allowed into the Arusha metropolis wearing limited skin clothing or a loose blanket. The Masailand Area Commissioner, Mr Iddi Sungura, kept on issuing a number of warnings to the Masai threatening retribution if they clung to awkward clothing and soiled pigtailed hair.

From prominent Masai across the border in Kenya came protest. A Kenyan Masai Member of Parliament holding a ministerial position, Mr Stanley Oloitipitip, asserted that Tanzania was denying the Masai the right to be themselves. Another Kenyan, Mr John Keen, threatened to turn up at Arusha, the new capital of the East African Community, dressed in his Masai attire and see what the authorities there would do to him.' (p.196)

The Masai elders replied to the Tanzanian authorities by posing the following, telling question: 'If the Almighty God could stomach seeing the entire anatomies of Adam and Eve in their complete nudity, is it not a little prudish for an African government to have fits by merely viewing a casually exhibited Masai buttock?' (The *Nairobi Reporter*: Feb 13 1968:p.4)

Throughout human history, political domination and, alternatively, rebellion have always found expression in the imposition or rejection of differing definitions of decency. As we saw in Chapter 12, the collision of cultures brought by the Age of Discovery focussed on the presumed nakedness of many tribal peoples. The suppression of these peoples' ways of life was, more often than not, entrusted to Christian missionaries who coaxed and cajoled them into accepting Western standards of modesty and rejecting their own traditional concealments of body decoration and adornment.

In time these tribes were organized into nation-states whose leaders often sought to inject themselves and their people into the Western sphere of influence. In the process these governments themselves frequently took up the crusade of the missionaries to stamp out un-Western body exposure. The end result of this historical process was legislation such as that of the Tanzanian government against the Masai's own complex and ancient code of modesty.

(The coda to this sad tale occurred when fashion, in the form of the mini-skirt, caused a change in Western standards of modesty which eventually spread to the Third World. In Africa, for example, Mazrui tells us that girls in mini-skirts were attacked in Dar-es-Salaam by members of the TANU Youth League and the police had to quell what amounted to a riot. Legislation to ban mini-skirts, wigs and tight trousers was proposed but, when it was slow in coming, further, more serious riots ensued and these had to be dealt with by armed police using tear-gas.)

Although extraordinary because of the world-wide nature of its success, the imposition of the Western definition of modesty onto the Third World is but one example of a general pattern throughout human history whereby one group which is dominant economically, politically and militarily has imposed its standards of dress

'LONG LEG' IS EVIL
Keep Yours Short
KILL CORRUPTION

An anti-mini skirt advertisement in the Nigerian magazine *The Bureaucrat* from the early 1970s.

and undress upon other groups which it has conquered. In point of fact, this is *always* the intended objective of the dominant group and it is only in exceptional circumstances that resistance to this ultimate act of suppression is persistent and successful. (An example of this is the Scottish kilt: banned as indecent by the English in an attempt to complete their conquest of the Gaelic peoples, it was never successfully eradicated.)

There are two reasons why this seemingly trival matter of modesty is a primary concern in the aftermath of any political conflict. Firstly, the requirements of physical decency are always a core component of any society's definition of its humanity. Secondly, it is only by the imposition of a new definition of 'proper dress' that conquest in its most fundamental sense – the imposition of the militarily, politically and economically dominant group's socio-physical reality – can be accomplished.

It would, in fact, be possible to outline all of human history and political conflict purely in terms of changing definitions of decency, and this is true not only of *European* history. Although I have emphasized the success of our Western/European/ Judeo-Christian culture in imposing its definition of modesty upon the rest of the world, it would be a mistake to assume that it has been the only one in recent history to succeed in such a project. Islam possesses its own rules of modesty which are in some ways more stringent than our own, and in, for example, vast parts of Africa this other political and religious power has left its mark, in the form of the veil, upon tribal peoples whose own, traditional definition of modesty was, in Islamic eyes, hopelessly inadequate.

Until 1492, of course, it looked as if Islam might sweep north through Spain and conquer all of Europe (as it had so successfully done throughout eastern Europe, the Middle East and North Africa). Perhaps, if Isabella I of Castile and Ferdinand II of Aragon had not captured Granada and re-Catholicized Spain, our own definition of decency might have come to include the covering of the face. But that was not the way things turned out and when Western control over the Middle East and North Africa grew in strength, it was *we* who sought to impose a 'civilized' definition of modesty upon the Islamic world.

Franz Fanon in *Algeria Unveiled* has shown the central role which the veil played in the French/Algerian conflict. Apparently the original French policy was that of assimilation through the gradual unveiling of the population, for the French had long recognized that the veil worn by Algerian women was an impediment to the colonization of this land and its people. And so, with a combination of persuasion and brute force, the colonial power attempted to strip off this badge of Arab identity. For a time they seemed to be succeeding as some Arab women came to see this item of their clothing as old-fashioned and totalitarian but, as open conflict intensified between the French and the Algerians, the veil became a symbol of the resolve of the suppressed people and a practical device for concealing and transporting weapons. As Fanon (who fought on the side of the Algerians) recorded:

'Three metres ahead of you the police challenge a veiled woman who does not look particularly suspect. From the anguished expression of the unit leader you have guessed that she is carrying a bomb, or a sack of grenades, bound to her body by a whole system of strings and straps. For the hands must be free, exhibited bare, humbly and abjectly presented to the soldiers so that they will look no further.' (Quoted in Mazrui:p.215)

Since the time of the Algerian/French conflict, the resurgence of Arab identity (supported economically by oil and politically by virtue of strategic geography) has lead to a re-veiling of much of the Middle East. Especially for Islamic fundamentalists, this has provided a powerful symbol of de-Westernization and as long as the forces of Islam control the price of oil and can play Russia and America against each other, the veil and the Chadra will taunt the West with an alternative definition of modesty which competes with its own. Should these practical circumstances change, however, there can be little doubt that Islamic societies, like the tribal societies of sub-Saharan Africa, South America, North America, Australia and the Pacific, will eventually adopt – in defeat – that standard of modesty which is both a product and a symbol of Judeo-Christian history. If this should happen the entire planet will have succumbed to Western proscriptions of physical exposure.

Just as there is always a politics of modesty between conflicting cultures, the same occurs *within* any social system. The hierarchy of ancient Egyptian society, for example, was clearly spelled out by differences of physical concealment. The very wealthy and powerful covered themselves with two layers of garments (which, even when almost transparent, still served an important symbolic purpose). People of mid-rank, on the other hand, wore one layer of clothing and slaves usually wore nothing at all. (Interestingly, in Egyptian tomb art slaves are often shown wearing garments but this was apparently just a device for increasing their master's apparent status in the afterlife.)

In fact, throughout the world, one finds a general rule of thumb to the effect that the more clothing is worn and the less flesh displayed, the higher a person's status. Even amongst the 'unclothed' Nuer peoples of the Sudan, the political and religious leader of a village can be easily identified by the leopard skin cloak which he drapes around his shoulders. To our eyes, given that this garment doesn't cover anything but the upper part of the body and leaves the genitals completely exposed, the issue of modest concealment seems quite irrelevant, but to the Nuer this is the significance of such apparel.

In a society such as ours, where the covering of most of the body is the norm, the 'clothing' of clothing in the form of added adornment and decoration can also signify a hierarchy of status. Thus military personnel wear various insignia and badges sewn onto their garments, and to 'strip' such a person of rank is to publicly remove such ornamentation (thereby leaving their clothing in a 'naked' state).

Although such a humiliation is only symbolic, we also demean individuals by ritually stripping away whole garments to reveal naked flesh. An obvious example of this is the forced stripping of prisoners or military recruits. Less obvious, but perhaps to similar effect, is strip-tease, nude modelling, topless waitressing and so forth. Part of the attraction (and indeed part of the sexuality – for let us not forget that sexual arousal also has a political dimension) of such situations seems to derive from the domination or superiority of the viewer as demonstrated by a hierarchy of decency.

But although some people can be encouraged or forced to disrobe by economic circumstances or political or physical impotence, there is another category of differential (im)modesty which is both self-imposed and an act of rebellion. One thinks here not of self-promoting, exhibitionist streakers, but rather of people like Ghandi who, though Churchill might have tried to dismiss him as a 'naked fakir', succeeded in his mission of protest partly by choosing to ignore the colonial oppressor's definition of modesty. Even when introduced to the British Queen, Ghandi wore only a *dhoti* which left him naked above the waist. In doing so, he forced the British Government and the world to respect his and his people's cultural heritage.

Since Ghandi, Western hippies have used self-imposed immodesty in the form of 'nude sit-ins'. Likewise some New Zealand Maoris recently threatened to bare their backsides to the visiting Queen of England in protest at their plight.

But far from being a purely modern phenomenon, protest by stripping goes back at least as far as Lady Godiva who disrobed publicly to force her husband to lower his taxation of an already impoverished population.

History has been most unkind to poor Lady Godiva, casting her in the role of a sex-crazed, exhibitionist trollop out on a joy ride. This is, however, hardly surprising given that our society seems unable to see any act of disrobing as anything other than erotically motivated. Such an attitude is the bitter fruit of centuries of prurience born of prudery and it has often robbed the human body of any signification other than the sexual. Not only does such an attitude do a disservice to dear Lady Godiva (and naturists, artist's models, etc.), it is also blatantly illogical.

Titillation was born not of natural, innocent nakedness but of the fig leaf and its legacy. It is concealment which puts the tease into strip-tease, and that is the subject of the next section.

'Tight Fit' photograph by Trevor Watson.

Revealing Rubber Dress.

Baby doll nightie.

4
Eroticism

16 Unnatural Desires

The intrinsic and psychologically deep seated association between clothing and modesty often leads us to forget the positive part which it and body decoration play in human sexual experience. As Robert Burton once wrote: 'The greatest provocations of our lust are from our apparel'. Throughout the world and throughout human history, there are and have always been many different ways in which clothing and adornment assist, amplify, define and, in some cases, create erotic experience.

Firstly, there is the role of physical concealment as an enticing gift wrapping. Just as a present is enhanced by being covered with concealing paper, so too the human body is made more intriguing and exciting by concealing garments and decorations. Familiarity can breed, if not contempt, at least indifference and by covering certain parts of the body these inevitably become more interesting and exciting.

Secondly, if concealment can enhance the erotic potential of the body it also makes the action of *un*dressing a potentially erotic act – as is highlighted by the art of striptease. Without the norm of concealing clothing we could never have discovered the *frisson* of what is one of the foremost erotic moments in our sexual experience: the point when a concealing garment is *about* to be removed. Although we share most other sexual experiences with the rest of the animal kingdom, the voyeuristic climax of the moment of disrobing is unique to humankind and as such is rightly celebrated in art and photography.

Thirdly, items of clothing and body decoration can serve as 'sexual flags' which draw attention to those parts of the body which are deemed to be erotic.

Fourthly, differences of clothing and decoration styles are the most effective means available to us for signalling and emphasizing gender differences. As well as straightforward identification of the sexes, these provide a symbolic reminder of a society's definitions of masculinity and femininity and thereby point the way towards 'normal' sexual roles and relationships. Likewise, by deliberately breaking the rules of gender identification, one can indicate to potential partners the fact that you are (or wish to be) out of step with society's presumptions about gender, and relationships can proceed accordingly.

Cartoon from *Le Rire* 'Dancing for Money'.

Fifthly, body decoration and clothing can signal sexual interest. In ancient Hawaiian society, if a girl or woman wore a flower behind her right ear this indicated that she was looking for a lover. A flower worn behind the left ear, on the other hand, indicated that she already had a lover.

Generally, in modern Western society, our system for signalling sexual interest is more subtle, complex and potentially confusing. Whereas the Hawaiian system employs a straightforward, arbitrary, linguistic sign and the message communicated is precise and digital:

looking for lover = flower on right
have lover = flower on left
not interested in lovers = no flower

our system is generally analogical and by degree.

For example, women in our society can wear make-up which is 'respectable', 'tarty' *or anything in between*. Although this system makes possible an infinite connotative subtlety, it can also be confusingly ambiguous. Adornment and clothing signals which in one context might carry (or be *perceived* as carrying) a message of sexual interest or availability – e.g., heavy make-up, tight dresses, micro-mini skirts, thin or tight trousers, stiletto heels, exotic wigs, fishnet stocking, etc. – in another context (e.g., in fashion or in the attire of style groups such as punks, where an ideological message is layered over a traditionally erotic one) may mean something entirely different (e.g., 'I am fashionable' or 'We are all prostitutes').

Presumably this ambiguity is deliberately built into our system of stylistic signification. We are perfectly capable of evolving a straightforward yes/no language of sexual interest but (with the exception of some prostitutes) we generally choose not to simply because we do not really want a direct answer to this particular question. This is because our society, unlike that of the ancient Hawaiians, is highly pluralistic, embracing many diametrically opposed sub-groups, and in such a situation even the highly promiscuous are generally only promiscuous within their own group.

For this reason, some sub-groups in the West have evolved separate erotic signalling systems – secret languages – which only the members of that particular group are likely to be able to decode (e.g., the homosexuals' system of key rings worn on either the right or left side of the body which indicate a dominant or submissive sexual orientation and which 'straights' might interpret as meaning only that men wearing such adornment work in some profession which requires them to keep their keys readily to hand).

Or, we might use dress and body decoration to frame an obvious signal of sexual interest within another signal of sub-group allegiance to indicate that the former only applies to those who are members of the latter (e.g., the highly made-up but also deliberately 'trashy' appearance of many female Punks, or the 'loose' but 'earthy' apparel of female Hippies).

Such narrow casting of sexual signals undoubtedly leads to further 'in-breeding' and social fragmentation but it is clearly necessary, given the pluralistic nature of our society. The *broad*casting of signals of sexual interest can never be a viable option in a complex society – except, of course, for those prostitutes whose only criterion for a sexual partner is financial reward.

Clothing and body decoration also provide us with a handy means of signalling not *if*, but *what kind* of sex we are interested in. Modern society is as erotically heterogeneous as it is culturally pluralistic (the former being, in part, an entailment of the latter) and every erotic inclination known to man (and woman) has its own vocabulary of presentation props. We will explore some of these in subsequent chapters.

Finally, and perhaps most importantly, body decoration and clothing play an invaluable part in the actualization of our ideals of beauty. As we saw earlier in this book:

---

* That which is deemed to be beautiful and attractive varies greatly from society to society and from historical period to historical period.
* Ideals of physical beauty are the expression of social values and beliefs.
* The origins of ideals of beauty are conceptual rather than corporal and there always exists a gap between the abstraction of ideal beauty and the reality of flesh.
* Body decoration and clothing are invaluable tools for helping to bridge this gap.
* Especially with the addition of adornment and clothing, the body has the potential to be – to signify – anything.
* In this way, the natural body is not only transformed, but its vocabulary of expression is infinitely expanded.
* In the process of making the body meaningful, we simultaneously make it attractive – provided that what it signifies is itself deemed to be *ideologically* attractive. For, ultimately, the object of our desire is the message (in semiotic terms, the signified) rather than the medium of its expression (the signifier).
* Conversely, if the message contained in the transformed body is undesirable then the body and its adornment/clothing is seen as unsexy, ugly, horrible or monstrous.

Even the naked human body is never devoid of meaning. In every society differences of body type, shape, skin tone, hair colour and so forth have a construction of meaning imposed on them. If, for example, we hold to the view that 'Blondes have more fun' this is because our society has imposed the semiotic construction [blonde hair = fun-loving = sexy] upon one shade of hair colour (presumably as an expression of white Anglo-Saxon Protestant hegemony).[1] Even if a person is a natural blonde their hair colour has, in a sense, been rendered unnatural by virtue of this signification. (And if it should be statistically proven that blondes indeed *do* have more fun and are sexier, then this would be a result of this presumption and not a cause.)

However, while blonde hair can signify 'fun', a tan can signify 'healthy' (quite incorrectly as we now know), rippling muscles can signify 'strong' and so forth, the possibilities for signification of the naked body are often limited.[2] Furthermore, the very fact that we are all 'stuck' with the particular body dictated by our genetic inheritance, means that most of us, if we were to leave our bodies in their naked, natural state, would also be stuck with bodies which 'say' things which might well be antithetical to our personalities or our cultural values (i.e., a natural blonde might not want to advertise him or herself as fun-loving and sexy preferring to be seen as serious and intelligent).

1. Yes, of course the immediate inspiration of the 'Blondes have more fun' signification is Hollywood's casting of women with naturally or artificially blonde hair. However, one has to pose the question of why Hollywood discovered that blondes were good box office and here I suspect that one would encounter an Anglo-Saxon domination of beauty ideals.

2. This is not, of course, in any cross-cultural, world-wide sense. Within a particular society, what the naked body can 'say' is limited by the area of overlap between the characteristics of that social body and its previous conceptualization of 'the body'.

Which is where body decoration and clothing come into the picture. With the aid of these presentation props, not only is the vocabulary of our physical expression infinitely increased but the possibility emerges that – whatever the characteristics of the body which we were born with – we can make ourselves attractive according to whatever definition of beauty might appeal to us as individuals or as a society.

To show how this works let us take one imaginary teenage girl and put her in two very different sets of presentation props. In the first case we will dress our subject as a punk with torn fish-net stockings, short PVC mini skirt, Dr Martin's 'bovver boots', bright blue crazy-coloured hair, a studded leather jacket and stiletto heels.

In her other guise we will dress our model as a 'Sloane Ranger' (in American, a 'preppy'). Here her presentation props include: a navy skirt with matching tights, Gucci shoes, a Cacharel wool jacket, a Hermés scarf knotted at the chin, a small patent shoulder bag on a gilt chain, short hair pulled back and 'natural look' make-up.[3]

Although she is the same girl with the same body, our model conveys radically different meanings depending upon her appearance. While it is impossible to produce a simple dictionary-style definition of the significance of each such appearance style (if that were possible people could just wear verbal badges instead of bothering with more complicated adornment and clothing) we can try to outline these semiological differences according to the parameters below, left.

(A) PUNK PRESENTATION SET

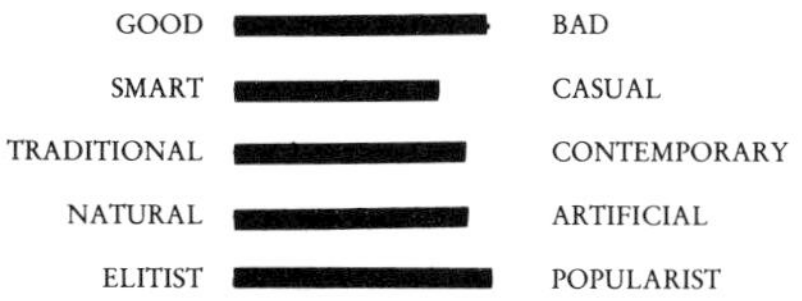
GOOD
BAD
SMART
CASUAL
TRADITIONAL
CONTEMPORARY
NATURAL
ARTIFICIAL
ELITIST
POPULARIST

(B) SLOANE/PREPPY PRESENTATION SET

GOOD
BAD
SMART
CASUAL
TRADITIONAL
CONTEMPORARY
NATURAL
ARTIFICIAL
ELITIST
POPULARIST

Of course, these meanings may or may not be what particular punks or Sloanes hope to express in their presentation of self, but they are nevertheless the sort of messages which we as a culture (allowing for some degree of subjective misinterpretation on my part) seem to attribute to these presentational signifiers. What is important for our present discussion is the fact that (1) some people would see our punk as more attractive and sexy than our Sloane – or vice versa, and (2) our sexual reactions would in each case be a product of how we feel about the messages conveyed by the different appearances.

If, for example, one is attracted to a egalitarian/left wing ideology then the sight of our model's bovver boots (an item of apparel which, whether or not it is statistically correct, has acquired working-class associations) would be a turn on. For someone who is ideologically elitist/right wing, on the other hand, the Sloane's Gucci shoes or Hermés scarf could have a similar effect. All of the parameters listed here (and these should not be seen as exhaustive) are important aspects of our contemporary, Western world views – they are all things which concern us fundamentally, ideologically and philosophically. (If it seems strange seeing them spelled out in this way, that is simply because these sorts of ideas are ill-suited to linguistic expression – which is precisely why we go to all the trouble of expressing them in appearance symbols.)

Without body decoration and clothing, neither we nor our model could hope to instantly express such complex ideas. And, if our model in either of her guises should trigger a spark of desire in any who might see her, this is because of the ideas embedded in and expressed through her appearance. In semiological terms our attraction derives from the signified (the ideas expressed) rather than the signifier (the adornments, garments and body which serve as the material of expression of these concepts) – even if it is the latter which appears to be the immediate object of our desire.[4]

Although I have illustrated this point with a modern, Western example, the phenomenon of meaningful attraction is hardly unique to our society. It is, in fact, universal. For all human beings everywhere and throughout history *physical attraction is always and has always been meaningful.* There is no such thing as a meaningless object of desire.

This assertion is diametrically opposed to what is, in our society, a widely held and deeply felt belief, namely that our lust and its provocations reside in our animal nature, miraculously insulated from our culture and cognitive processes.

Let us first of all be clear as to why such a belief is *itself* attractive to us. As civilization holds us even tighter in its inhibiting embrace, it is hardly surprising that we should yearn to discover some remnant of a free-range animal deep inside ourselves; an animal unemcumbered by rules, regulations and conceptual contortions. And so, in our sexuality, we seek another Eden – not, perhaps, an entirely innocent one, but one in which we can pursue the pleasures of simple beasts. Accordingly, to be described as 'an animal in bed' can be a supreme compliment and it is irritating (if ironic) to realize that even in this area of our lives we are all too human and un-animal-like.

Our model of ourselves as sexual animals proposes a direct path from the sight of the other's natural, beautiful body to our own instinctive arousal, without the intrusion of intellect and the social forces which shape it. In this view we would be like baboons who, at the sight of a bright pink backside, 'go ape' with sexual excitement. But, however appealing this 'Me Tarzan/You Jane' myth might be it doesn't fit the facts of human sexuality in two important ways.

Firstly, between the sight of a beautiful

backside and our sexual response there are always the machinations of the human brain which interrupts and re-creates that initial image. As Merleau Ponty has written in *The Phenomenology of Perception:*

'Sexual life is not a mere effect of the process having a seat in the genital organs, the libido is not an instinct, or an activity directed naturally towards definite ends, it is a general power, which the psychomatic subject enjoys, of taking root in different settings, of establishing himself through different experiences, of gaining structures of conduct. In so far as a man's sexual history provides a key to his life, it is because his sexuality is projected in his manner of being towards the world, that is, towards time and other men'. (p.158)

Or, as Michael Foucault has suggested in various works on this subject, human sexuality – instead of being defined by some universal, natural, biological given – is a social and historical construction. Far from being a simple matter of natural triggers and instinctive responses, human sexuality is an activity which involves all of our being – our social background and history, our personality and our culture. In other words, all those things which separate humankind from the rest of the animal world. Clearly, sexual arousal is an interpretive, cognitive, phenomenological process which is very different from a baboon's straightforward instinctive arousal at the sight of a pink bottom.

Secondly, let us consider the matter of the pink bottom itself. For the baboon, the object of desire is purely a product of nature. Try as we might to hold on to the idea that our own objects of desire are natural, objective realities beyond our influence, the fact is that we humans possess no equivalent to the baboon's pink bottom. The perfectly beautiful human body (or even backside) has yet to be found. Or, put another way, we have found *too many*, with every society and every age defining it differently.

In order to continue with our analogy (and for simplicity's sake) let us restrict ourselves to considering the human, female backside as an object of desire. Could we all agree on one particular shape, size and colour of this part of the anatomy which we might define as *the* ideal? I think not. A species of baboon, however, would have no problem doing just that. Nor perhaps would all the members of a small, homogeneous tribal society. But if we compared the criteria of perfection laid down by each such society throughout the world we would find no common denominator, no Platonic ideal of the female backside, upon which all the members of our species would agree.

Even within the few thousand years of Western history, the ideal bottom has undergone radical transformations. Judging by the 'Venuses' created in Palaeolithic times, our prehistoric ancestors must have been turned on by enormous expanses of quivering flesh. The Egyptians, however, seem to have preferred dainty backsides which preserved the straight lines of their tight gowns.

With the Greeks and the Romans we see a return to an ideal of voluptuousness (although constrained in comparison with pre-history). The ideal medieval rear-end was tucked in by an un-natural curvature of the spine so that the female belly could protrude. By the 16th century, however, huge contraptions called farthingales were created to pander to a craving for enormously wide hips. The Edwardians, on the other hand, used the bustle to extend the protuberance backwards. 1950s latex girdles sought to firm and tighten the posterior. Fashion in the '60s decreed that the ideal bottom was practically non-existent and it is only in recent years that wobbling flesh on this part of the anatomy has made something of a come-back.

And this is only the majority view of perfection in each era. With backsides, as with any other part of the human body, there is obviously no such thing as natural beauty. Our objects of desire and therefore our lusts are our own (i.e., our social group's) creations.

Individual bodies are, of course, the product of biological processes but these natural creations (even if they should happen to conform to our ideals) are merely the *occasion* of our desire. Ultimately – in and of themselves as natural objects – they are irrelevant to our passions. Not partly or mostly irrelevant, *completely* irrelevant – for if the body is to be a vehicle of desire, then it must always be recreated in our mind's eye as erotically and semiotically meaningful. Even Marilyn Monroe's bottom (which she wiggles so seductively as she walks to the train in *Some Like It Hot*) is only seductive by virtue of its cultural and historical context. In and of itself it is just so many pounds of excess fatty tissue and the ancient Egyptians, for example, would have found it a positively revolting sight.

How simple it would all be if our desires really were natural; if the naked flesh of our biological inheritance was devoid of connotation and meaning. But how boring this would be, and how soon we would tire of it. For the fact is that, whether we like it or not, we are sophisticated and intelligent creatures and as such are ill-suited to a life-time of pink bottoms openly displayed. If that was all there was to our sexuality, then we as a species would have died out long ago.

But if we have lost our capacity for straightforward, uncontrolled animal lust, then our consolation is an infinitely complex eroticism which prospers in the struggle between modesty, nakedness, passion and philosophy.

3. Like the label 'Sloane Ranger' itself, this description comes from Peter York's Oct. '75 *Harpers and Queen* article which has been reprinted in *Style Wars* and expanded in *The Official Sloane Ranger Handbook*.

4. Of course some adornments, garments and bodies can express the same ideas better than others and in this case (as long as the signifieds really are the same) we would be justified in a purely stylistic approach.

4
Eroticism

17 Fetishism

Another way of describing the unnaturalness of human attraction and desire is to say that it is fetishistic. Fetishism involves at least a temporary displacement away from the natural objective of genital intercourse and procreation. For most of us, this displacement is a detour which eventually arrives at a biologically effective conclusion and it may be that the longest way round is the sweetest (perhaps even the most efficient) way home. However, such an approach to sexuality is certainly unusual in the animal world.

When it comes to sex, our primate relatives, like all other animals, really are interested in only one thing. As we saw in the previous chapter, the natural object of a male baboon's desire is the female baboon's genitals which (because baboon's copulate in a rear entry position) is visually targeted by a brightly coloured backside. Although male baboons will fight to put themselves at the top of the pecking order to copulate with those females who are on heat, and whose backsides are therefore the right shade of pink, any other physical characteristics of the females (e.g., breast size, facial features, etc.) seem to be completely irrelevant.

We humans, on the other hand, exhibit a polymorphous perversity such that parts of the body (e.g., breasts, hair, lips, eyes, navel, back, feet) and items of adornment or clothing (e.g., stockings and suspenders, knickers, bras) which have no natural part to play in procreation may be important triggers of sexual arousal. Such displacement is a direct entailment of our human tendency (discussed in the previous chapter and in Section 1) to re-invent the body as a symbolic medium; to make of it an expression of values and beliefs which, at least initially, are cultural and ideological rather than corporal.

In this process the body is inevitably divorced from its natural, biological nature, therefore our arousal at the sight of it is also inevitably caught up in its semiotic rather than biological reality. In other words, if a culture (for some socio-symbolic reason) attaches a particular positive significance – some 'attractive' meaning – to large breasts, stretched ear lobes, hairiness, filed teeth or tiny feet, then these parts of the body become triggers of sexual desire which, if only temporarily, pull a member of that society away from concentrating on the only biologically natural object of desire, the genitals. Although such a situation would be completely unnatural for other animals, it is a natural part of human sexuality by virtue of its universality.

In anthropological usage, a fetish is an object which is thought to possess some special power which – purely as a 'real', non-symbolic object – it would not normally possess. In a tribal context this power is generally attributed to magical or supernatural forces. In suggesting that the 'unnatural' (non-biologically procreative) objects of our desires are fetishes I am – like the psychoanalysts and psychologists whose studies of this subject we will review in a moment – simply extending the principle of the magic power of the fetish to a sexual context.

For example, in ancient China, the dainty, compressed female foot (and its bindings) were fetish objects in that this part of the human anatomy possessed for these people a power and significance (and meaning is, of course, the root of such power) beyond its natural, objective capacities as an instrument of locomotion.

Likewise, in the West, the garter has acquired an erotic power and significance which exceeds its power and significance as an object which holds up stockings. We can see this power particularly clearly at a wedding when this object symbolically encapsulates the erotic component of the occasion.

Like the 'primitive' fetish, such objects are, in a sense, magical and supernatural. But we do not need to draw upon a spiritual vocabulary to appreciate that our own erotic fetishes possess a significance and power beyond that which derives from their objectness – nor to appreciate that this power is puissant.

I hope that in citing the two well-known examples of the Chinese foot and the Western garter I have not created the impression that the phenomenon of erotic fetishism is extraordinary or unusual. *All* objects of human desire, excepting perhaps the genitals themselves ('perhaps' because these too are subject, even in the mind's eye and certainly in artistic representation, to de-naturalisation), are fetishes because they all possess an erotic power which derives from cultural and semiologically imposed criteria rather than from any inherent natural, biological and procreative characteristics. For human beings, even the sex act itself (and clearly its provocation) is sponsored by an eroticism founded upon displacement and 'unnatural desires'.

The reader will have by now realized that my approach to fetishism is very difference from that of psychoanalysts and psychologists whose concern is with fetishism as a personal, neurotic disorder. Although some psychologists acknowledge a degree of fetishistic arousal in 'normal' human behaviour, most deal only with the question of why certain individuals become fixated on certain objects (usually parts of the body or items of clothing) to the extent that they are unable to experience sexual arousal without the presence of their particular fetish object.

Sigmund Freud was not the first to deal with this problem but his theoretical explanation of it has proved to be the most influential:

'This abnormality, which may be counted as one of the perversions, is, as is well known, based on the patient (who is almost always male) not recognizing the fact that females have no penis – a fact which is extremely undesirable to him since it is a proof of the possibility of his being castrated himself. He therefore disavows his own sense-perception which showed him that the female genitals lack a penis and holds fast to the contrary conviction. The disavowed perception does not, however, remain entirely without influence for, in spite of everything, he has not the courage to assert that he actually saw a penis. He takes hold of something else instead – a part of the body or some other object – and assigns it the role of the penis which he cannot do without. It is usually something that he in fact saw at the moment at which he saw the female genitals, or it is something that can suitably serve as a symbolic substitute for the penis.' (Vol 23:pp.202–3)

Freud also reasoned that, because the existence of people without penises is so threatening, the individual who suffers from this disorder develops an aversion to the sight of naked women and the symbolic penis, the fetish, 'saves the fetishist from becoming a homosexual by endowing women with a characteristic which makes them tolerable as sexual objects'. (Vol.21:p.154)

This theory, while perhaps explaining why fetishism seems to be found only in men (a subject to which we will return in a moment), leaves a lot of questions unanswered. Most importantly, why is exclusive fetishism (the inability to function sexually without one's particular object of desire) found only in a few unfortunate individuals?

Since Freud, many other psychoanalysts and psychologists have tried to answer this question by arguing that a susceptibility to exclusive fetishism is born of rejection by the mother and/or overly strict toilet training. In both instances the origins of adult fetishism are traced to very early experiences of infancy and childhood. The mother's inability or unwillingness to enter into a loving relationship with the infant forces it to form attachments to inanimite objects (eg a blanket, teddy bear, etc.) and this pattern is later reinforced by the traumas of (1) forced loss of 'self' (the stool) in toilet training, (2) the loss of the nipple at weaning, (3) the discovery of penis-less creatures, (4) the loss of baby teeth and, finally, (5) adolescent sexual development.

I find it very difficult to know how to react to such theories. Certainly I must admit to finding Freud's ideas about the fetish object as a replacement penis for the mother rather bizarre and unconvincing. (Especially as most fetish objects seem very un-penis like – a problem which Freud himself recognized but never resolved.) Nor does there seem to be any evidence that all or even most exclusive fetishists experienced premature or excessively authoritarian toilet training regimes.

What does seem to me to make sense is the more straightforward idea that infants and children who are thwarted in their relations with their parents and who therefore establish alternative 'relationships' with inanimate objects should in later life extend this anti-social pattern into the sphere of sexual relations. Or, to put it the other way round, if our infant and childhood experiences teach us that relationships with real people are dangerous or stressful and that the love of/for an object is safer, then it might follow that as adults we would seek to avoid human inter-dependence by employing the same 'successful' strategy of replacing people with objects.

Before moving on to consider the important problem of the 'choice' of love object, we should deal with the assertion of the psychoanalysts that only men are fetishists.

Although psychoanalysts and psychologists differ widely in their views as to the causes and possible treatments of fetishism (and, indeed, as to whether treatment is actually necessary), they all agree that women 'almost never' suffer from this complaint – or at least that women do not often come to them seeking treatment for exclusive fetishim. I personally suspect that this gender difference in perceiving fetishism to be a *problem* goes a long way toward explaining male/ female differences in seeking treatment and, furthermore, that it stems from the 'Great Masculine Renunciation' of adornment and flamboyant dressing, which began in our society in the aftermath of the French Revolution as men succumbed to the sobriety of the work place, and was reinforced by the Industrial Revolution and the Age of Empire (see Chapter 10).

Certainly in modern Western society a woman with an 'obsession' for fabrics or fashion is seen as normal whereas a man with similar interests would probably be seen as peculiar, or sexually perverted. For example, a man with a 'thing' about fur or silk would stick out like a perennial sore thumb whereas a woman with a similar inclination would be camouflaged by socially accepted gender conventions.

Secondly, one cannot help but suspect that our society's comparatively recent taboos governing male flamboyance in body decoration and dress have left a residue of a suppressed need for sartorial expressiveness and that this very suppression could be transferred to objects which, although a normal man would not dare wear them, can at least be desired as objects. This suggests that the taboo against 'cross-dressing' is stronger than the taboo against exclusive fetishism, and that the 'perversion' of fetishism could be seen to stem from the 'perversion' of The Great Masculine Renunciation which has caused most men in our society to suppress their need for self and social expression through the medium of the body.

But are there really no female fetishists amongst us? At London's fetish clubs such as

Shoes from Cover Girl (London).

Skin Two and Der Putsch, one sees plenty of women attired in leather, rubber and lingerie – items of apparel which are often seen in our society as fetishistic. And specialist magazines which cater for fetishists contain many letters purporting to be from women who are 'into' rubber, macs, leather, directoire knickers, and so forth. Of course, such letters could in reality be written by men and, of course, women who wear such clothes may be doing so to satisfy their husband's or boyfriend's inclinations (or, as we shall see, they may simply be following the dictates of fashion).

Whether there are any women in our society who are exclusive fetishists and always require the presence of their particular fetish to facilitate their arousal, I really cannot say. Unlike the psychoanalysts and psychologists, however, I suspect that there are such women and that their tendencies remain hidden by the differences of acceptable levels of interest in body decoration which are part and parcel of 'normal' society.

Let us bear in mind that (1) fetish objects need not necessarily be those items of clothing or materials which are generally presumed to be 'kinky' – silk, satin, wool, cotton, nylon, fur, lingerie, gloves, hair, lycra, make-up, ball gowns, swimming costumes and, indeed *any* item of clothing or even fashion itself can be fetish objects. And (2) the fetishist may be just as satisfied by *wearing* the fetish him or herself as by having a partner do so.

Yet, when all is said and done, I would certainly have to agree that exclusive fetishism does seem to be more frequently found in men than in women. Those of us who find little satisfaction in Freud's theory of the fetish as a substitute penis must, therefore, come up with some other explanation of this apparent statistical gender difference.

One theory is provided by Hendrick Ruitenbeek in *The New Sexuality*:

'We ask ourselves whether this peculiarity of fetishism may be derived from the fact that in the typical existential masculine pattern, the imaginary power plays a greater part than in the typically feminine pattern: and that a man perceives the world in a more universal spirit and conceives more abstract spiritual and perhaps fantastic connections and images, while female experiences of the world and love remain more bound to the concrete personal sphere. This could mean that men were still able to experience a certain existential and loving fullness transparent through the synonymous, peripheric, impersonal gestalt sector of a fetish though it is quite separated from the concrete body of a specific individual. Women who would reject love from the physical realm of the concrete partner to the same degree would react with total frigidity.' (p.109)

While this is an interesting idea it does, to my mind, raise too many old chestnuts about universal gender differences which are ideological and speculative. A much simpler and more logically defendable solution is suggested by Nancy Friday in her fascinating account of women's sexual fantasies entitled *My Secret Garden*. In trying to explain the lack of fetishistic fantasies amongst the thousands of erotic fantasies which she collected from women, she comes to the following hypothesis:

'. . . that since women were traditionally put into the passive role sexually, they never have had to have doubts about their ability. Inhibited or frigid, perhaps – but there is no word in the immense English vocabulary which is the exact female equivalent of *impotent*. On the other hand, the sexual distortions of society often force men to see every erotic encounter as a contest, in which the poor man has to compete, at least physically, with all the woman's previous lovers and those still to come – to say nothing of the imagined demands he may feel she herself is putting on him; perhaps it is to avoid these pressures that the fetishist sighs with relief when he can substitute the symbol for the substance, and settle down with a nice pair of fluffy, scuffed mules on a cold winter's night. Are they so different from Hollywood's favourite image of our soldiers and sailors as 'regular guys', who randily kiss their dream film star good night, when it is only her photo that is present on the wall above the bed, but who would be paralysed with embarrassment if that star should appear in the flesh in that bed?' (pp.171–2)

The key word here is *impotent* and Friday rightly puts it in italics. The need to achieve erection is an obvious requirement of male sexual experience which draws a firm dividing line between the sexes. *The fear then is not castration, as Freud would have it, but failure to perform. And the fetish, instead of being a replacement penis, is, in fact, a talisman to insure against failure.*

Finally, let us deal with the subject of the 'choice' of the fetish/ talisman. Freud argued that the nature of this object is dependent upon chance – it is that which the would-be fetishist happens to see just before the shock of the discovery of penis-less creatures. Others have argued that its character derives from the relationship objects of infancy (e.g., Teddy Bear→fur; 'dummy'→rubber garments).

Back in 1888 Alfred Binet – the man who first applied the concept of the fetish to sexual experience – proposed that the 'choice' of object was a learned response brought about by conditioning. This theory has much more recently been tested experimentally by Stanley Rachman and Ray Hodgson who showed male heterosexual subjects pictures of various kinds of boots immediately before showing them pictures of 'arousing nude females'. As a result of this conditioning Rachman and Hodgson found that their subjects experienced increased sexual arousal at the sight of boots (as monitored by a 'phallo-plethysmograph' – the mind boggles). In this way these psychologists apparently succeeded in adding five young men to the population of boot fetishists. (Interestingly, if the pictures of arousing nude females were shown *before* the boots it didn't work.)

Although I am amused by these antics and basically in agreement with Binet's theory, it seems to me that this matter can be put more prosaically. Sexual experiences – including, of course, masturbation – generate mental associations which in and of themselves can trigger erotic arousal at a later date. These associative triggers are not limited to the human body itself and frequently refer to garments, decor, perfume and so forth. All of us have a data bank of such associations and when, like Proust biting into his biscuit, we encounter them in later life, they detonate associations which can be erotic in nature.

Most people possess a large and varied repertoire of such erotic, associative triggers but the fetishist – either because of limited sexual experience or because his psychological history predisposes him to cling doggedly to the first handy inanimate object (thereby blanking out all other possible objects of association) – ends up possessing a much more limited set of arousal triggers.

But it may not be as simple as this. To explore how such a process might work, it is necessary to do what the psychoanalysts and psychologists so rarely do; return to the real world of cultural context. The potential fetishist, like the 'normal' person, lives in a world where all objects are semiologically loaded. Within this world, at least in modern, Western, post-Freudian society (Freud's work is itself of course part of our cultural context), some objects are labelled by society at large as 'fetishistic'. Leather, rubber, PVC, knickers, bras, stockings and suspenders are currently the most obvious examples. Popular entertainments such as strip-tease, television dance routines, art and photography leave us in no doubt about what is and what isn't sexy.

While the potential fetishist *may* arrive at the selection of his or her love object purely as a result of personal experience (and may therefore come up with something completely idiosyncratic), it seems probable that many potential fetishists who are, so to speak, in the market for a love object, might shop around at those counters labelled 'kinky' in our society's semiological hypermarket.

And not only does society label certain objects as fetishistic, it has also evolved a vocabulary of fetish symbols such that (in present usage) leather = aggressive/dominant, rubber = passive/submissive, PVC = futuristic/unnatural and so forth. This system of classification might well assist the fetishist in his-her selection.

To appreciate how the fetishist's choice of object might be influenced by our society's semiotics of fetishism, it is necessary to add one more point to our discussion. Because the 'choice' of fetish inevitably takes place in adolescence (if not before), the mature fetishist will usually be fixated upon some garment or fabric the erotic/semiotic significance of which is long out of date. Fashions, both in clothing and eroticism, keep changing for our society as a whole, but the fetishist remains locked into the fashions of his or her youth. Thus today's elderly fetishist often has as a love object an item such as directoire knickers or rubber macs which, in their day, were seen by society at large as 'hot' items and afforded a sexy signification but which a young person of today would probably see as un- or anti-erotic. Fifty years from now, fetishists who are adolescents today may be fixated on stone-washed denim jeans, lycra body stockings or 'funky disco' boots – items of dress which future generations might see as completely idiosyncratic fetishes, simply because our society's fashions in eroticism will have moved on. *Fetishism is always a museum of historic erotic signification.*

The relationship between *Fashion and Fetishism* goes further than this, however. In his massive book of that name, David Kunzle has shown how the complex history of the corset in Western society has alternatively seen that garment defined as either a 'normal' fashion or a 'perverted' fetish. Kunzle's point is not only terminological, but, more importantly, that changing fashions camouflage erotic fixations. In other words, some men of the late 18th or late 19th centuries might have been unable to experience arousal with women who were not wearing corsets (i.e., they were exclusive fetishists), but because this was the accepted fashion of the majority such displacement was not seen as deviant. While in, for example, the 1920s, the 1960s or the present day, on the other hand, to be aroused by women in corsets – and especially to have this as a prerequisite of arousal – might be grounds for psychological treatment. (This is something which I wish psychiatrists who treat fetishistic patients with electric shock and other 'negative reinforcements' would start to appreciate.)

But there is another aspect of the relationship between fashion and fetishism which is the cause of even greater confusion. As will be seen in the next section, fashion is a mechanism of perpetual style change which condemns this year's new look to next year's dustbin. In its hunger for anything new, fashion devours style ideas from every available source. Peruvian peasant costume, Chairman Mao jackets, previous fashions which are sufficiently dated that they have been forgotten, and sports clothing, are all fair game. And so is 'fetishistic' apparel.

In the '60s, when fashion change was so rapid that only those who shopped weekly at somewhere like Mary Quant's King's Road boutique could hope to keep up, fashion designers desperate for new ideas started introducing garments made of leather – a material which had previously held only pejorative fetishistic or boringly practical connotations. These styles were a great success and at the same time, the word 'kinky' entered the fashion vocabulary. But although this adjective might have been new, the phenomenon of fashion drawing upon taboo fetishes is probably almost as old as fashion itself, and is part of the reason why fashion history is littered with garments such as the corset which keep coming back like the un-dead in horror movies.

'60s fashion brought 'kinky' leather gear into the mainstream, but novelty soon wears off and by the '80s fashion was hungry for another fetishistic fix. So designers, first in Britain (and later in Tokyo, New York and Paris), hit upon the idea of making garments in rubber – a material which, unlike leather, still retained connotations of freakish minority perversity. As with leather (and as with the corset in its various sojourns in and out of fashion) rubber 'fetish fashions' were greeted at first with derision but rapidly achieved mainstream acceptability as publications such as *Vogue* featured them.

Today, in certain clubs in London one can witness the confusing spectacle of genuine rubber fetishists and followers of the latest fetish fashions bumping into each other on the same dance floor. However, both the outfits and the inclinations of these two groups are very different.

When fashion borrows an idea – especially from a risqué source such as fetishism – it will always re-style it in such a way that its original meaning is perverted. (Ironically, in the case of a garment made of rubber which originally carried a perverse meaning, since this re-contextualization must create a sort of double negative of signification.)

The message of the fashionalized fetish garment is (subtextually) 'I am outrageous and daring but I'm not actually a real fetishist. Isn't this fun!' and, most importantly, *'I'm fashionable'*. Without this meaning the whole exercise would not only be far too risqué for the would-be fashionable, it would be completely pointless.

For the fetishist who long ago locked his or her erotic future in the medium of rubber this is at once a blessing (there's a lot of it about) and a curse (the erotic currency has been devalued by those who have reduced it to the status of 'just a fashion'). Before long the fashionable will have moved on to plunder some other stylistic resource and the fetishist will be back where he or she started – except that the beloved fetish will have been semiologically abused and will not be quite the same ever again.

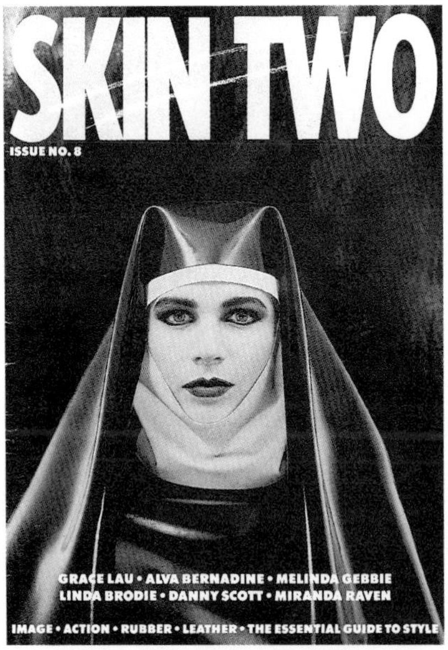
SKIN TWO

ISSUE NO. 8

GRACE LAU • ALVA BERNADINE • MELINDA GEBBIE
LINDA BRODIE • DANNY SCOTT • MIRANDA RAVEN

IMAGE • ACTION • RUBBER • LEATHER • THE ESSENTIAL GUIDE TO STYLE

Cover of *Skin Two* magazine.

Cartoon affectionately depicting some of the people involved in the London 'fetish scene' by Melinda Gebbie, featured in *Skin Two* magazine.

Ad for She-and-Me (London).

Leather catsuit by Atomage (London) modelled at car show.

Inflatable rubber suit by Atomage (London).

Clothing comes in two fundamentally different forms – costume and fashion – which are distinguished by completely antithetical relationships to time and history. Costume is traditional, backward looking and 'timeless'; its function is to mark social boundaries and to preserve the status quo. Fashion, on the other hand, is a celebration of constant change and novelty and, as such, it is futuristic – always pointing towards some brave new world. Prior to the late Middle Ages and the Renaissance, everyone in the world wore some form of traditional costume, but with the advent of social mobility and the creation of a new, 'get ahead' social class – the rising bourgeoisie – those who had personally benefited from change came to reject traditionalism for modernism and to replace 'timeless' costume with ever changing fashion. Since the Renaissance, the clock-work mechanisms of fashion have continued to generate a steady stream of new, 'New Looks' and, with the Westernization of most of the third World, traditional folk costume is everywhere in decline. Everywhere, ironically, but the West where more and more people are choosing to get off the fashion tread mill and opt for 'timeless classics' and where teen-age and adult style groups are creating their own traditional costumes.

Japanese family in traditional costume.

The colourful traditional costumes which have been worn for centuries by the Andean Indian women of Peru.

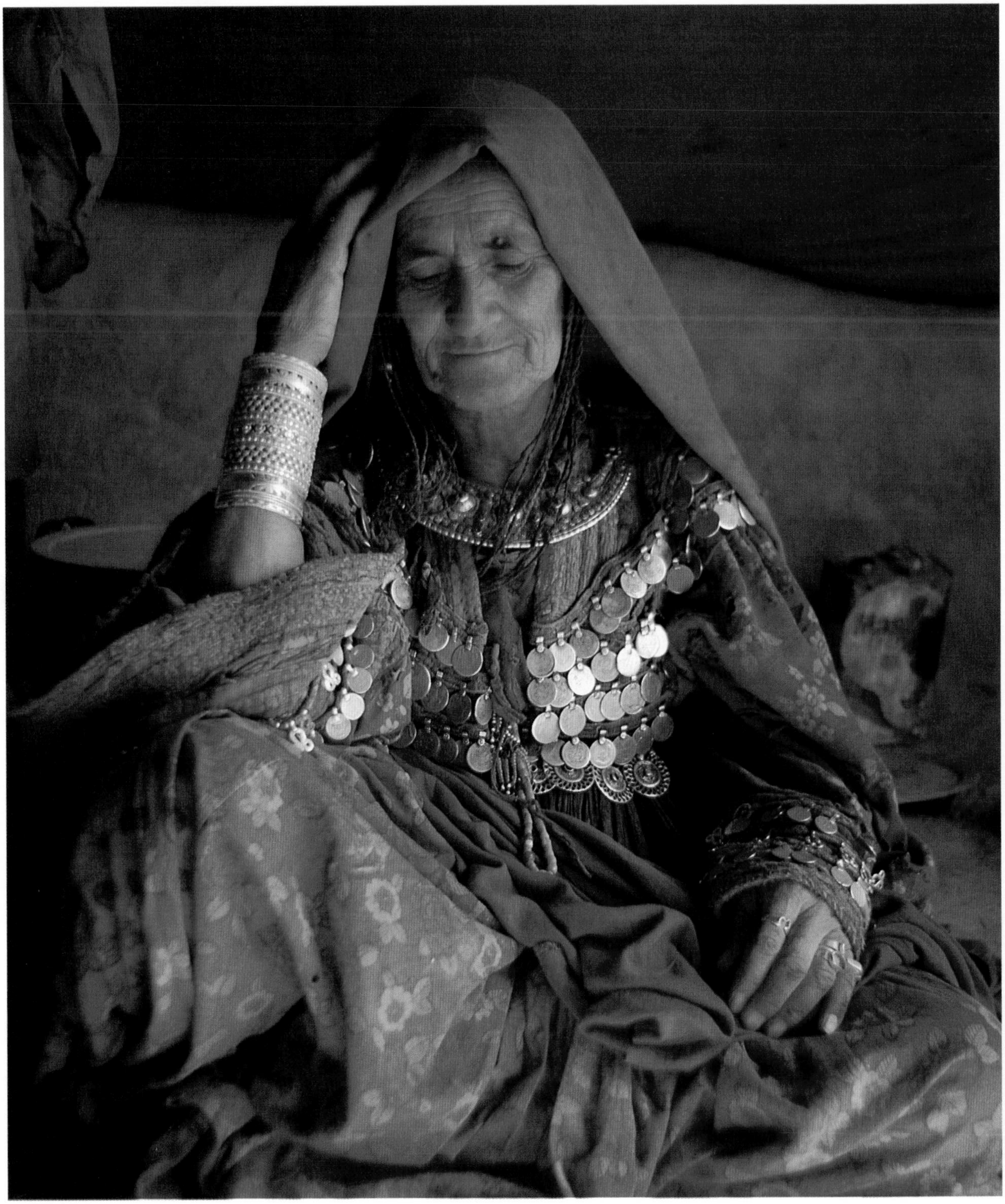

Woman wearing traditional Afghan costume.

Traditional costume worn by members of the Yellow Hat Sect of the Lamaist Buddhists (Tu people) who live in Huzhu county, Qinghai, China.

Traditional costume from Karpathos. (Greece)

Traditional costume of Western bikers as worn by members of the National Chopper Club of Great Britain.

Ingenious juxtaposition of two British costume classics: donkey jackets and Liberty prints. (photo courtesy of Liberty's)

Different strokes for different folks: Line up of British designer creations for 1987.

A few of the fashion innovations of British designer Vivienne Westwood, between 1980 and 1988.

Hip Hop costume worn on the streets of New York.

Even the photographers look stylish at a Westwood fashion show.

Rubber dress by Krystina Kitsis, Ectomorph, London, 1987 (Photo: Trevor Watson).

Gothic style corset dress by Symphony of Shadows (London), 1983.

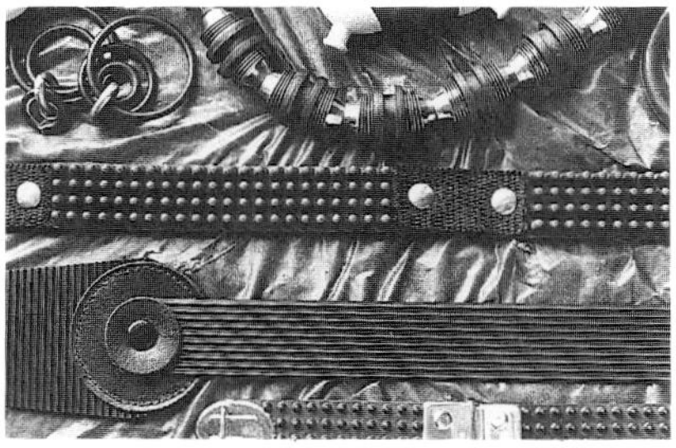

A selection of rubber jewellery from Detail (London), 1983.

Latex and lace camisole design by Kim West (London), 1988. (Photo: Kevin Davies).

Wasp waisted fashion from Paris by Felix as shown on 1898 cover of *Harper's Bazaar*.

4 Eroticism

18 Underwear

Underwear is the most obvious and the most understandable fetish. It incrues in erotic displacement because of its direct contact with those parts of the body which are defined as sexual and it enjoys connotations of intimacy because it is itself concealed by outer garments and therefore private. Undergarments cannot help but soak up an erotic charge from that which they are designed to cover, shape, protect and enhance.

It comes as no surprise, therefore, to learn that 'From the fetishistic point of view by far the most important and dramatic development in the history of clothing was the introduction of underwear. Of all forms of clothing fetishism that which focuses the sexual attention on undergarments is the most common.' (Brand:p.22)

A typical case history of an exclusive fetishist whose object of desire is an undergarment is 'Frederick C', (as related in Brand pp.25–32). Frederick first became obsessed with women's briefs when he was 15. His mother was a dressmaker and one day she was fitting a client while Frederick was lying on the floor reading a book.

'This dress had a flared skirt and the woman stood, quite unconsciously, where I could see right up her skirt. She didn't have a slip on and for the first time in my life I saw a woman's pants. I lay there, looking up her long, beautiful legs. She had pink suspenders which disappeared underneath her pants. They were white silk and I can clearly remember the way they hugged her bottom and showed off its shape. Around the legs was a deep froth of frilly lace. I got an erection at once. She stood talking to my mother for a long time and throughout I was staring and growing more and more excited. When she went back into the bedroom to change, I went to the bathroom and masturbated. Thereafter, I always conjured up the picture of her in her white, lace-trimmed panties whenever I masturbated.' (Brand:p.29)

A few years later Frederick – despite being chronically shy with the opposite sex – managed to get a date with a girl who was known to be 'easy'. However, as soon as she stripped off her briefs ('pale blue with little embroidered flowers on the side') he discovered that he 'just wasn't interested'. From then on Frederick decided to forget about trying to have sex with real women and to devote his life to watching women in short skirts as they boarded buses, to lingering outside lingerie shops and to visiting department stores where he would fondle the women's briefs which were on display. Eventually,

'I was on top of a bus and I was suddenly transfixed by a glimpse of a row of washing in a back garden. There were five pairs of pants, red, blue, black, all colours. I was so excited I couldn't stop trembling. I jumped off the bus at the next traffic lights and went back to the house. I must have walked up and down that road a hundred times just looking and growing more and more excited. I thought about the girl who must have worn them, and that only excited me more. At last I couldn't bear it any longer. I let myself into the garden and took the lot. I nearly had an orgasm as I pulled them from the line.' (Brand:pp.26–7)

Frederick C is an extreme (and extremely sad) case of exclusive fetishism, but in magnified and obsessional form his case reflects the feelings which, to a certain degree, we all have about undergarments.

Underwear is such a fact of life in our world that it is difficult to imagine living without it. However, no tribal society of which I am aware possessed (at least prior to Westernization) any garments which could rightfully be described as underwear (i.e., an intermediate layer of clothing which is worn between the skin and exterior clothing and which is not normally exhibited publicly). In such a world without underwear there is no insulating layer to mediate between the 'private parts' and that which is displayed publicly. Thus a single garment such as a loin cloth is on one side in direct contact with the genitals and on the other side usually exposed to public scrutiny. One would imagine that in such a situation there would have to be some degree of symbolic, erotic seepage which would have the effect of privatizing and sexualizing public encounters.

This is probably no great problem in small-scale communities where everyone knows everyone else and where a certain level of public intimacy is acceptable and inevitable. Modern life, on the other hand, could not tolerate such a level of public intimacy, and underwear affords us a double layer of protection which makes it possible for us to effect a highly public presentation of self.

For this reason, the wearing of undergarments as outer garments – even if one's 'private parts' might be completely concealed – is always shocking. The fashion designer Vivienne Westwood has produced brassières for wearing outside rather than inside clothing, and the pop singer Madonna has built a career on appearing on stage in lingerie which would normally only be worn in the bedroom, but the media attention which greeted these attempts to convert underwear into outerwear only serves to prove my point. (And even Superman's habit of wearing his underpants *outside* his other clothes makes him slightly suspect.)

Yet *historically*, the transformation of underwear into outerwear is a well established principle of clothing evolution. The chemise – which began life as an under-tunic in ancient Greece and which remained *the* undergarment of both sexes for many centuries – gradually became publicly visible in the second half of the 15th century as necklines fell, until it eventually became the male shirt and the female blouse. In a similar way, during the 19th century, drawers became bloomers and, together with a host of other ex-undergarments (such as corsets and leotards) eventually – at least in certain circumstances – became acceptable as outer wear. It is only with the passage of time and the introduction of new intermediate layers of undergarments that ex-undergarments may cool sufficiently to permit their public display.

This process takes a very long time. Undergarments have a radioactive half-life (to switch metaphors) of hundreds if not thousands of years. For example, the shirt/blouse (aka chemise) has had some 500 years to lose its erotic connotations.

Although all undergarments inevitably acquire an erotic signification, this does not mean that this was necessarily their original function. Underwear in the West was 'invented' by the ancient Egyptians who used two layers of transparent clothing as a symbol of wealth. In ancient Greece, on the other hand, although the bands of fabric which women wore to bind their breasts and buttocks had an erotic function in one sense (that by making their bodies more masculine women might lure their husbands away from their homosexual lovers) their immediate purpose was to alter body shape rather than to compete with the erotic appeal of the body itself.

In ancient Rome, undergarments were worn for modesty's sake (although courtesans – as we will see in the next chapter – soon hijacked them for erotic purposes). And throughout the Middle Ages, although the erotic appeal of undergarments was appreciated, their primary purpose was that of symbolically differentiating and defining gender differences.

Throughout Western history, underwear has continued to fulfil all these disparate functions (as well as that of hygiene, which we have not mentioned) and it continues to do so today. Silk underwear denotes wealth. Bras, corsets and girdles shape the female body. Vests and briefs provide hygienic protection and 'sexy undies' signal and heighten eroticism.

However, the importance of underwear as a means of altering body shape (its most important function throughout most of Western history) was severely curtailed in the late 1960s and is only now in the 1980s beginning to come back into favour. Modern bras may help breasts to defy gravity and some women may today wear elastic girdles to compress and firm the waist and buttocks, but such alterations of body shape are nothing compared to the complete re-creation of physical form made possible by the undergarments of other eras.

As has already been mentioned, the women of ancient Greece used undergarments (the *apodesme* which flattened the breasts and the *zona* which flattened the stomach) to masculinize their bodies. In the Middle Ages corsets forced a curvature of the spine so as to create a prominent female belly and abdomen while padding was stuck in pockets of the chemise to widen the hips.

In the Renaissance the farthingale (an amazing contraption of whalebone, iron wire, padding and sometimes wood) further extended the width of the hips until a woman was almost as wide as she was tall. And in the same period the *basquine* compressed the upper part of the female body into a 'V' shape which further emphasized the unnatural width of the hips.

In the mid-19th century the farthingale (by then known as a crinoline) was suddenly swept aside by the bustle which, by means of horse hair pads, greatly extended the backside. The post-revolutionary Directoire period in France, on the other hand, saw the disappearance of almost all shape-changing undergarments and, briefly, something close to the 'natural' shape of the human female reappeared.[1] This was, however, short-lived, as the Empire almost immediately brought back the compressed waist through the use of tightly laced corsetry and the crinoline – a huge structure which grew both in size and popularity as it spread through most of Europe.

The second half of the 19th century saw breathtakingly rapid fluctuations between the bell-like crinoline shape and the bustle. At one moment a fashionable woman would have great difficulty fitting through doorways and in the next she would have great difficulty sitting down unless she owned a spring-loaded bustle.

Then came the First World War and by 1915 the corset and the wasp waist had disappeared and – as in ancient Greece – women's undergarments served to compress and flatten the hips and breasts. By the 1930s, however, bras assisted the re-emergence of the breasts while elastic girdles flattened stomachs and backsides. Immediately after

Bustle dress from 1887 issue of *Harper's Bazaar.*

the Second World War the success of Dior's 'New Look' brought back the hour-glass figure, and bra, corset and petticoat manufacturers worked their miracles of transforming the female body yet again.

But, once more, it didn't last long. The late 1960s gave a thumbs down to all support garments and opted for an ideal which was 'natural' only for a handful of anorexic models. Then in the mid-1980s, curves came back and those corset makers who hadn't gone bust from lack of business suddenly found themselves back in demand. Today all sorts of structured undergarments have returned to the fashionable woman's wardrobe and even the crinoline has been revived by Vivienne Westwood in the form of the 'mini-crini', which has been copied all around the world.[2]

Why this preoccupation throughout Western history with using underwear to continually alter the shape of the human body? Three distinct causes might be cited.

Firstly, Western history has been peppered with social, political and economic upheavals which have continually altered the characteristics of the social body which the physical body always attempts to mimic. While traditional, tribal and peasant societies may achieve a 'timeless' stasis between social facts and physical ideals, our turbulent history has never permitted a particular socio-physical status quo to endure.

Secondly, since the late Middle Ages and the Renaissance (as we will explore more fully in the next section) Western clothing and body styles have been in the grip of the constant fluctuations of fashion change. This constant fluctuation of style which is the *raison d'être* of the fashion possesses a momentum of its own and the changes which it generates are often, if not always, independent of social or culture change.

Thirdly, as the fashion historian James Laver has suggested, those parts of the human body which are emphasized by exposure or structural elaboration (e.g., by means of undergarments) eventually lose their appeal and, in order to maintain erotic potency, it is necessary to emphasize other, different parts of the body. This mechanism of shifting erogenous zones, although often a factor in fashion change, appears to obey its own cycles of perpetual jadedness.

Although it is impossible to identify any one of these causal factors as more relevant than the others, their comparative importance is not itself unimportant.

Changes of underwear and body shape which are generated by either shifting erogenous zones or the fashion system cannot be expected to possess any intrinsic symbolic or social significance, as such fluctuations would be defined purely by their need to be different from that which existed prior to their introduction.

Shifting erogenous zones and fashion change are products of their own histories and as such are arbitrary semiologically and sociologically. Therefore, any alterations to body shape which they effected would be meaningless in and of themselves. Thus – according to this view – crinolines, corsets, cantilever bras, bustles and such like became popular simply because they change the body into that which it was not previously.

If, on the other hand, such undergarments became popular because they helped the physical body to mimic changes in the social body, then we would expect such changes to be meaningful and socio-culturally relevant – reflections of their socio-cultural requisites. Did tight-lacing reflect a perceived need or desire for social control? Did the unpopularity of all physically restricting and structuring undergarments in the period immediately after the French Revolution reflect an ideology of social liberation? Did the farthingale and the crinoline – undergarments which drastically extended the dimensions of the physical body – reflect and/or celebrate a philosophy of social, political or economic expansionism?

I cannot pretend to know the answers to these questions. At the end of the day, it might well be that the ideal body of each historical era constitutes the *only* viable means of expressing the true spirit of that age; its symbolism impenetrable because there is no possibility of translation.

Because of these difficulties, it is tempting to fall back on the view that the re-creations of body shape made possible by the crinoline, the basque, the bra, the girdle, the bustle and so forth are simply products of fashion's hunger for constant change, or our tendency to keep shifting our erogenous zones as a palliative of boredom.

Yet, although I believe that these factors do go a long way towards explaining why we in the West keep changing our undergarments and, therefore, our bodies, I cannot completely suppress my suspicions that such drastic alterations of the ideal body must have been born of changing social and cultural circumstances and that they must therefore have expressed some, albeit obscure, meaning. The women of the French Directorate who threw away their panniers (boned underskirts), or the feminists of the 1960s who purportedly burned their bras, must have shared this view that undergarments express and convey some symbolic significance which is social and ideological.

For if undergarments are nothing but the arbitrary and meaningless products of the fluctuations of fashion and shifting erogenous zones, then why should they be treated with such contempt or, in other circumstances, with such reverence?

1. The word 'natural' must be used in single quotes because, even without re-structuring undergarments, the shape of the body must have been altered by clothing styles, learned postures and the fact that the physical body is always perceived in light of artificial representations of the human form.
2. Although I have not had space to deal with this subject, throughout many periods of Western history, male undergarments have been at least as important in altering body shape.

4
Eroticism

19 Dressing for Sex

Every garment and every style of body decoration has some positive or negative erotic charge. It is impossible for anything which is worn on or applied to the human body to escape this sphere of connotation. There are, however, a few garments and adornments which have been created for no other purpose than to signal sexual interest, intent and orientation. Such exclusively erotic presentation props are quite common in our society but very rare in tribal or peasant societies.

In many tribal societies throughout the world men wear penis sheaths and one would have thought that such decorations – especially those made from large gourds which exaggerate the size of the penis and give the impression of a permanent erection – are obvious examples of specially erotic attire. Almost always, however, the primary reason for wearing penis sheaths is actually quite unrelated to eroticism. As Peter Ucko has shown in his comprehensive and amazingly detailed work *Penis Sheaths: A Comparative Study*, close investigation by anthropologists has shown that this garment has a wide range of functions or meanings, only a minority of which seem to be erotic:

* To distinguish one tribe from another
* To distinguish various sub-groups within a tribe (eg kinship groups)
* To distinguish various age grades within a tribe
* To mark a young man's coming of age
* To ensure against the violation of sexual taboos
* To prevent sexual activity
* To provide modest concealment
* To provide somewhere to put things (eg dry tinder for making fires, tobacco, food, etc.)
* To give protection against natural hazards (eg insects, fish, ants)
* To give protection against spiritual forces
* To signify society's control over the individual (especially control over his sexual freedom)
* To frighten an enemy on the battlefield

Although penis sheaths may in some societies be worn partly for reasons of sexual display, Ucko finds little evidence (especially from the statements of native informants themselves) that this constitutes their primary function and he concludes:

'From our review we see that penis sheaths in most societies have remarkably few phallic connotations and are, rather, symbols of modesty and decorum. This is perhaps not as surprising as it might at first sight seem to be, when we remember that most societies first adopt the penis sheath at or near puberty. The sheath is, in many of these cases, not simply a symbol of sexual maturity but one of social control of that sexuality. The penis sheath, in many instances, is not primarily a sexual symbol in itself but a visible sign of sexual restriction.' (p.60)

Likewise in peasant societies the only item of clothing or decoration which might be seen as specifically erotic – the wedding gown – on closer inspection is clearly primarily intended to signal the wealth of the bride and her family rather than to heighten her erotic potential.

In the West, on the other hand, we have created a whole range of garments the sole function of which is to eroticize the wearer and to designate certain occasions as sexual. It was perhaps during the Roman Empire that clothing and decoration were first used in this specifically and exclusively erotic capacity.

Cecil Saint-Laurent writes in his delightful *History of Women's Underwear:*

'Custom required that a man should not desire his wife and should not involve her in a sensual affair . . . To satisfy their sexual appetites the men turned to courtesans, having less inclination to homosexuality than the Greeks.

At first the courtesans were dirty, badly dressed little creatures, usually slaves, who lived in the gutter, offering themselves in their see-through tunics from half-open doorways. By the end of the second century they were an élite of elegant, perfumed, cultivated and ambitious adventuresses, whose insolent liberty contrasted with the docility and ignorance of the well-bred women.' (p.37)

These courtesans, whose prosperity and power depended upon their ability to titillate and satisfy the men of ancient Rome, equipped themselves with all manner of garments and adornments, the sole function of which was sexual stimulation. Then, as now, the erotic was often the exotic and the courtesans of Rome – mimicking the Empire itself – plundered garments from throughout the known world.

Garments from distant lands such as the scarfs and bands of Greece, the crinolines of Crete and the tunics and underskirts of Egypt were all part of a Roman courtesan's erotic arsenal. Thus garments which had originally served very different and not specifically erotic purposes were now worn purely as a sexual turn-on. (Their capacity to excite no doubt partly stemming from their symbolic connotations of Roman domination over the lands of their origin.)

To these exotic imports the courtesans added sexier versions of the underwear and other garments worn by respectable women as modest concealment. And, Cecil Saint-Laurent tells us, they may even have invented some completely new garments such as the garter which (especially given that there was no such thing as stockings) was intended purely as a trigger of sexual arousal.

Needless to say, it wasn't long before the *respectable* women of Rome tried to arouse their husbands (or perhaps their lovers) by *themselves* adopting the garments which the courtesans had defined as specifically erotic. From that day on, a pattern was established – an evolutionary process which is still with us – whereby sexual professionals create items of attire and decoration which in due course end up in the bedrooms of the respectable.

Although the courtesans of Rome might have made some stylistic innovations to certain garments, and although it is possible that they actually invented a few items like the garter, their principal contribution was in re-contextualizing existing garments to provide them with an exclusively sexual significance. (A tendency to re-contextualize rather than to invent *ex nihil* is also, by the way, a characteristic of fashion design.)

The way in which members of the sexual professions have over the centuries re-defined certain garments as exclusively sexual is illustrated by the story of the 'drawers' which were worn by many Italian women during the Renaissance. According to legend, these garments were adapted from male use by Catherine de Medici in order to make it possible for women to ride on horseback without unduly exposing themselves. They became very popular in certain upper class circles for a time but by the end of the 16th century they had become solely the uniform of prostitutes.

No doubt these prostitutes effected some stylistic changes to the garments which had been worn by Catherine and her friends, but what really eroticized their signification was simply the fact that the prostitutes had decided to adopt them – without even the excuse of horseback riding which had previously provided some degree of modest justification.

For several hundred years drawers remained the uniform of prostitutes throughout Europe – which ensured that this intrinsically practical and modest garment could not be adopted by either the fashionable or by advocates of dress reform until this association was diminished. This was a problem which was exacerbated by the 'can-can', which specifically celebrated the erotic and disreputable connotations of this item of dress.

Although the explicitly erotic nature of garments such as drawers was and is ultimately decreed by context and usage rather than by style, it is true nevertheless that a slight but symbolically important stylistic modification is always necessary to announce such a garment's new function. No matter how minimal it may be, such stylistic transformation is always necessary in order to strip a garment of its previous meanings before a gloss of erotic signification can be applied. In the present day we can see this very clearly in the French maid or nurse outfits which are sold by mail order manufacturers of 'fun fashions'[1] and worn purely as a sexual turn-on. In each case – as no doubt with the prostitute's drawers – a slight stylistic alteration from the original, 'real' garment is necessary in order to signal that the wearers of these outfits are not actually French maids, nurses or equestriennes. A garment or adornment cannot achieve its new (erotic) meaning until it has been sufficiently distanced from its previous semiotic connotations.

Such items of dress or decoration must, therefore, instantly convey three separate meanings: firstly, they must signal a repudiation of their origins (I am not a real nurse). Secondly, they must proclaim loudly their exclusively erotic purpose (I am interested in sex). And thirdly they must give some indication as to what kind of sex is on offer (the patient will lie back and take his medicine, etc.)

I would imagine that in ancient Rome a courtesan dressed in an Egyptian tunic promised a different kind of sexual experience than a courtesan dressed in a Greek *apodesme* or a Cretan corset, but it is impossible to know for sure whether the exclusively erotic garments of previous eras possessed such extensive vocabularies of sexual inclination. It is, however, certainly clear that *modern* garments do.

Throughout the Western world, mail order companies offer an increasingly mind-boggling choice of 'fun fashions', each of which seems designed to signal some different and specific sexual inclination. From Adelaide to Bonn this is big business, with millions of units sold each year – mostly to couples of long standing who want to put some zest back into their relationship. Such garments allow people a means of advertising their continuing interest in sex, of identifying certain occasions as specifically erotic and of effecting a non-verbal communication of sexual interests and inclinations. (Something which sex therapists are always encouraging, but for which we possess a very limited or too clinical *verbal* vocabulary.)

Each of these male or female garments is a sort of semiotic 'key'. As in the case of a selection of house keys, if looked at closely, some have configurations of erotic meaning which are quite similar while others are very different. Investigation here clearly suggests that, at least in the contemporary West, that which 'turns us on' (our personal erotic lock) is fascinatingly complex. Clearly, sexual arousal is not a simple ON/OFF switch like that found on an electric light. A more suitable analogy is a colour television set with a battery of adjustments for volume, contrast, channel, brightness, colour intensity, etc.

The other thing which should be clear

1. These are not, of course, fashions in a proper sense of the term. Such mail order erotic 'gear' is, in fact, an excellent example of timeless, classic costumes. See Section 5.

from our analysis of contemporary 'fun fashions' is their importance in our society. Garments such as these are almost always ignored by 'serious' commentators of clothing and fashion, yet an enormous number are purchased year in and year out throughout the West and despite the seemingly absurd nature of many of them, they obviously perform many serious functions.

Firstly, exclusively erotic garments such as these provide a much needed medium for the expression of personal inclinations – a symbolic language which allows us to express our sexuality and therefore our inner selves. Verbal language is rarely capable of communicating such information as precisely or succinctly.

Secondly, such garments provide us with a means of identifying certain occasions as specifically sexual. Simply by putting on a baby doll nightie, a 'nurse's uniform' or a PVC 'posing pouch', we can announce to our partner that non-sexual matters should be put aside.

Thirdly, such garments allow us to experiment with aspects of ourselves which are suppressed in the course of our daily lives. In this way, they provide us with an opportunity to take a 'holiday' from that definition of self which all too often straight-jackets our multi-faceted personalities.

Finally, by allowing us to explore hidden parts of ourselves and to take a vacation from the daily grind 'fun fashions' may make it possible for us to incorporate some of the excitement of promiscuous sexual behaviour, within the context of a stable relationship. With the threat of AIDS hanging over us this is not, perhaps, such a bad idea.

Late 16th-century Venetian courtesan wearing drawers. After illustration in Pietro Bertelli's *Diversarum Nationum Habitus*.

5
Clothing

20 Stitches in Time

In this, the final section of *Body Styles*, we will focus on the relationship between clothing and time. I have chosen what might at first glance appear to be a rather obscure facet of the subject of clothing because it is exciting and topical; it is only through an exploration of clothing as a symbol of time that we can begin to understand the extraordinary changes which are going on today in the garment industry and in our own wardrobes.

Our ultimate objective is to provide a definition of that oft misused word 'fashion', to distinguish it from traditional costume and to show how both of these systems of dress serve the social systems which generate them by signifying and marking different concepts of time (and therefore of world view). Let us begin by comparing what are arguably the two single most famous garments/styles produced since the Second World War: Queen Elizabeth II's coronation gown and Dior's 'New Look'.

Neither the Queen's coronation gown (1952) nor Dior's 'New Look' (1947) was an 'off-the-peg' garment. Both were obviously outrageously expensive by most standards and both were designed to be worn by women. But it is their differences which are important to us here. In particular we are interested in the way in which their respective styles permit them to express very different attitudes towards time and history.

Dior's 'New Look', as its name suggests, links the present (circa 1947) with the future. It was 'new' and 'progressive' because it marked a clean break with what had preceded it (both in terms of fashion style and the definition of femininity).[1] As the fashion historian James Laver has written, it was 'a deliberate attempt to break away from the short-skirted tubular appearance with its square-padded shoulders which had lasted since before the war. The new silhouette had narrow shoulders, the waist in the right place, a new emphasis on the bust and a longish skirt with a wide hem. This was a startling innovation.' (1969:pp.255–6)

Left, the Queen's 1947 coronation gown and right, Dior's 'New Look' circa 1952.

The Queen's coronation gown, although it too was a 'new' garment in the sense that it was created specifically for her coronation, was stylistically 'old' and thereby served to symbolically link the present to the past. It was designed to celebrate more than 1000 years of the British monarchy and its unchanging traditions. Although it was actually made in 1952 its design was deliberately intended to be 'timeless' because connotations of modernity or novelty would have undermined the Queen's authority. (It could not, for example, reflect the 'New Look' in fashion.) Its function was to support a perception of the status quo which safely and securely locates the present deep in the distant past.

To throw these two garments together in a single pile labelled either 'fashion' or 'costume' is to fail to see their separate meanings and functions. But before we can explore this point properly it is necessary to pause briefly and consider the phenomenon of time itself.

As in the case of the human body, we tend to presume that time is a fact of nature which is 'real' and unaffected by human experience – that if we human beings should succeed in obliterating ourselves in an atomic holocaust, time would go on as it always has, oblivious to our demise. In actual fact, however, time is always the creation of he or she who perceives it (or, more accurately, of that person's social environment). We 'make time' (speed it up, slow it down, take it off, lose it and so forth) exactly as we make other tools (and 'the body') with which to control and make sense of our environment.

That time is a product of human experience is evident from a host of different sources. For example, Sidney Cohen, reporting on the effects of the drug LSD, comments in his book *Drugs of Hallucination*:

> 'Change in time perception is one of the notable features that intrigue most subjects. One of them kept remarking on 'the eternal present', and another said that the second hand of the clock never moved. The slow-down in time is reminiscent of mental activity during certain moments of personal danger when a large series of memories is recalled within seconds . . . Subjective time normally varies with the metabolic rate, mental activity, the level of alertness and other factors. Clock time is arbitrarily divided into immutable units and does not ordinarily expand or contract. The slowing of subjective time under LSD cannot be demonstrated with a stop watch.' (pp.41–2)

A similar distortion and perversion of 'real time' is the stock in trade of astrophysics which, at least since Einstein, has argued that the rest of the universe does not function according to that perception of time which we identify as 'natural'. (In a black hole, for example, time apparently moves backwards.)

Finally, ethnographers who have investigated how time is perceived in other societies concur in the relativity of this phenomenon. Since the publication of E.E. Evans Pritchard's pioneering work on the Nuer of the Sudan, it has been apparent that not only do different societies mark and record time differently, but that each society's structure of temporal experience is so different as to make 'translation' between systems (e.g., Nuer time → Western time) impossible.

As we found with regard to 'the body', time is an expression and product of particular patterns of social organization. Thus, even though a tribe such as the Nuer might frequently mark time according to natural events such as the rising and setting of the sun and the waning and waxing of the moon . . . , there is, however, a point at which we can say that time concepts cease to be determined by ecological factors and become more determined by [social] structural inter-relations, being no longer a reflection of man's dependence on nature, but a reflection on the interaction of social groups . . . [Temporal] distance between events ceases to be reckoned in time concepts as we understand them and is reckoned in terms of [social] structural distance, being the relation between groups of persons. It is therefore entirely relative to the social structure.' (pp.78–9). Therefore: 'The distance between the beginning of the world and the present day remains unalterable. Time is thus not a continuum, but a constant structural relationship between two points, the first and last persons in a line of agnatic [male-based] descent.' (p.81)

There are, then, as many kinds of time as there are social systems. However, it is possible to classify perceptions of time into genera. For our present purposes the two most important categories of time perception are steady-state and linear-progressive. In the former, the passage of time is perceived in cycles, oscillations, etc., which (as Andy Warhol put it in the title of his autobiography) go *From A to B and Back Again*. In the linear-progressive system, on the other hand, time goes from A to B *and then on to C, D, E, ad infinitum*.

Traditional societies tend to perceive time as a steady-state. It may take a millennium, but eventually things are presumed to return to what they once were and always will be. People may come and go, one year of famine may be followed by another of plenty, but this is not seen as leading to some future era which is fundamentally different from the status quo. And in such a system, the present-day status quo is always a part of the past. As Evans Pritchard concludes his remarks about the Nuer perception of time:

> 'It is less a means of coordinating events than of coordinating relationships and is therefore mainly a look-backwards, since relationships must be explained in terms of the past.' (p.81)

Within the confines of such a steady-state system there is obviously no place for history as we usually understand it (a linear, progressive continuum which is forever looking forward to a new tomorrow). In a traditional, steady-state system there may be change from day to day, month to month, season to season and even millenium to millenium (as in the Indian system which is based on endless repeating cycles or *mahayuga*, the shortest of which, *kaliyuga* – 'the time in which men live' – is 432,000 years in length), but the presumption is always that stasis will eventually be achieved as one cycle gives way to another or as some cosmic pendulum swings back in the opposite direction.

It makes practical sense that traditional societies should perceive time and history in this way. Steady-state time is both a requisite and an entailment of a way of life in which an unchanging status quo provides the foundation of social authority. Within such a conceptual system each successive generation can be successfully slotted into a social construction of reality which presumes that the way things are is the way that they have always been and will always be. In other words, steady-state time is a machine for maintaining social and cultural stability, a device for keeping traditional societies traditional. (Or for keeping an institution such as the British monarchy 'old' and therefore inoculated against change.)

Generally in the West, however, we perceive time very differently. Our linear-progressive model of time enjoins us to 'put the past behind us' and 'build a better tomorrow'. We believe that (in the words of the American General Electric Company's advertisements of the 1960s) 'progress is our most important product' and we welcome

1. The irony that this definitive 'New Look' actually harked back stylistically to a bygone age of French elegance should only serve to remind us that fashion often achieves the effect of progress by excavating the past.

change as the mechanism of this never-ending journey into a new and improved future. (Or, at least, that was the view of the majority until very recently: the post-modern perception of time will be considered in Chapter 24.)

The idea of time as a succession of progressive changes – and the presumption that each of these is an improvement – is not only uniquely Western, it is also a comparatively recent phenomenon. As we will see in Chapter 22, this perception of time was born of certain social changes in the period immediately preceding the Renaissance and soon became a cornerstone of Western culture.

Besides simply pointing out the revolutionary uniqueness of this perception of time, it is important that we note that (like 'Nuer Time') linear-progressive-modern time is an expression of its social, rather than natural environment. The social substructural foundation of modern time is the phenomenon of social mobility, and the social group which parented it is the rising bourgeoisie. (A subject which we will also explore in Chapter 22.)

But what, you might well ask, does all this have to do with clothing? The answer, at its most basic level, is that *all* objects of human design (and all natural objects, through their perceptual and semiological categorization) participate in and express different concepts of time. A ceramic pot, a house or a garment – besides cooking food, sheltering a family and clothing a person – all function as signs of the times (or rather as signs of *time*).

For example, the traditional shape and ornamentation of an Amazon Indian's cooking pot, the style of a Bavarian peasant's home or Queen Elizabeth II's coronation gown all express and reify a steady-state system of time. Alternatively, a Dorothy Hafner ceramic bowl, Le Corbusier's Villa Stein, or Dior's 'New Look' all express and reify a linear-progressive system of time.

This is part of their job. Time, like the society from which it derives, is only a concept and, if it is to be shared within a community, it must therefore be embodied in some material of expression. (And, by the way, if some object's temporal signification matches our own ideology of time, then this is one of the things which causes us to find it attractive.) Like all artefacts, garments and other body decorations must point to, celebrate and reify one temporal system or the other. There is no way in which an object can abstain from participating in this sphere of meaning.[2]

And while this is true of all objects, it seems to be especially true of clothing and body decoration. This is probably because no other objects so readily lose their objectness and become 'part of ourselves'. A ceramic pot and a house are not-me, but a suit of clothes, if worn repeatedly, becomes an extension of my own body and myself (so much so that I might choose to be buried in it).

I have said that there is no such thing as *natural* time, but there is, of course, an exception to this rule: my own, personal, biological time. I am born, grow old and die, my heart beats, my lungs expand and contract and electrical impulses race through my nervous system all in their own time.[3]

For a social system to exist, however, it must always impose its own reality upon each and every individual person who, collectively, constitutes its membership. One of the primary ways in which it does this is by imposing its own, social time on to the biological time of the individual. This is most effectively accomplished by clothing the individual in garments or decorations which are semiologically pre-set to that society's temporal system. Thus clothing and decoration are the ultimate time pieces – ones which, even when we take them off, keep right on ticking because even in our nakedness we are defined by our *un*dress.

As we have seen, the Queen's coronation gown and Dior's 'New Look' express two completely antithetical systems of time. The former is pre-set for traditional time while the latter is pre-set for modern time. Each outfit serves as a vehicle for time travel – the one into the past, the other into the future. But they have something in common: the subjugation of the personal, biological time of those who wore them. At her coronation, the Queen *herself* became a symbol of traditional, steady-state time; an advertisement for the continuity of the monarchy. On the other hand, a customer of Dior's – simply by putting on the 'New Look' – would have had her own, biological time rendered semiologically insignificant by the imposition of Modern Time.

It is the same for the rest of us. Every day when we open the wardrobe door and select an outfit to wear, we are choosing between making ourselves advertisements of steady-state or linear-progressive-modern time. If we choose an outfit which is avant-garde then we will be advertising a concept of time which is progressive and which celebrates the future. And if, on the other hand, we choose a 'timeless classic' then we will be promoting a perception of time which is traditional and which celebrates the present as a manifestation of the past. Time is the most fundamental of all ideological systems and every human being in their choice of clothes or body decorations participates in this politics of reality.

2. Even a 'purely functional' object, if there is such a thing, is inevitably 'clothed' in such a temporal meaning by virtue of its purpose and history. Barthes has written, 'As soon as there is a society, every usage is converted into a sign of itself' which for present purposes I would paraphrase as follows: As soon as there is a society, every object/usage is converted into a sign (or symbol) of not only itself, but also the temporal system of those who physically made it or those who semiologically re-contextualized it.

3. To a certain extent even this body time (the time of my life, so to speak) is influenced by my social environment. Stress, love, sexual arousal and other, socially based situations can make my heart beat faster and so forth. Even death can be socio-somatic.

5
Clothing

21 Costume and Fashion

All of the principle themes explored in this book – beauty, adornment, modesty, titillation, costume and fashion – are also to be found in the Miss World Pageant. In the 'Parade of National Dress', for example, we can find folk costumes from around the world and, what is more important, a demonstration of the principal characteristics of costume itself: regional variation and 'timelessness'.

That costumes vary from area to area is obvious from watching only a few minutes of any year's parade of national dress. However, while the Miss World Contest divides our planet into some 80 costume regions, each of these – at least originally – was subdivided into hundreds or thousands of smaller ones. For example, Switzerland (whose national dress is such a cliché that the 1987 Miss Switzerland couldn't even bring herself to wear it, opting instead for an inappropriate contemporary and international style) was originally divided into innumerable costume regions many of which had strikingly different styles and many of which bore little resemblance to that style which we today accept as 'Swiss'. In the Braun and Schneider collection of engravings of costume and published between 1861 and 1871 there are illustrations of regional styles (Zurich, Solothurn, Lucerne, Zug, Schwyz, Valais, Aargau, Unterwalden, Fribourg, St Gallen, Berne, Schaffhausen and Appenzell) represented under the heading 'Late 18th century Switzerland'. Many of these regional costumes are so stylistically dissimilar that one might think that the people wearing them came from separate planets instead of a tiny area considerably smaller than the state of Texas.

Prior to the rise of modern nation states (and now the global village) our entire planet was differentiated into hundreds of thousands of such costume regions and therein lies one of the principal purposes and functions of this form of dress: to mark the boundaries of small-scale communities and to provide a focus of group identity for those who resided in these communities. Thus what I have termed regional differences are actually *social* rather than geographic markers.

The second characteristic and function of folk costume derives from the first. Each peasant group represented by a distinctive costume style ('Our Costume') was (or is) a community which sought to buttress itself against destabilizing change by means of a steady-state perception of time and by means of an unchanging and 'timeless' costume which was an expression of this perception of time and history.

Thus costume is a sort of time capsule which moves through history while denying its existence. By creating the illusion of the immuta-bility of the status quo costume helps traditional societies to nip in the bud the threat of change by denying it its reality.

In point of fact, however, neither traditional social systems nor their costume styles are completely immune to change. (Neither, obviously, could come into existence fully formed.) In *Folk Costume in Moravia Slovakia* (now part of Czechoslovakia), Peter Bogatrev comments:

'Folk costume is in many respects the antithesis of clothing which is subject to fashion changes. One of the chief tendencies of the latter is the ease with which it changes – the new fashion must not resemble the one it replaces. The tendency of folk costume is *not to change* – grandchildren must wear the costume of their grandfathers. [However] I am speaking here of the *tendencies* of urban fashion and of folk costume. Actually we know that even folk costume does not remain unchanged . . . ' (p.33)

Bogatrev goes on to tell how, in the course of his researches, he acquired evidence of some long-term historic fluctuations of the costume styles of Moravia Slovakia and how, when he pointed this out to the people whose costume he was studying, they not only refused to accept his evidence but came close to sending him packing.

While I am sure that Bogatrev's evidence was correct, it is also irrelevant. Because the function of costume is to deny change and because those who wear it participate in this fiction of 'timelessness' it is a 'fact' which, from the native's own perspective, achieves a kind of objective reality.

Within a traditional community, costume does not change simply because it cannot be perceived to have changed.

Certainly, even if viewed from the perspective of our linear-progressive time system, the rate of costume evolution is extraordinarily slow. The Miss World Contest, for example, would have to carry on for hundreds of years before one could reasonably expect that any of the costumes exhibited in its national parade of dress would reveal a discernible evolution. Miss Switzerland may one year choose not to wear her national costume, Miss New Zealand, Miss Australia or Miss USA may or may not choose to wear the costume of their countries' indigenous population. This doesn't alter the fact that any and all of these costumes (Swiss, Maori, Aboriginal, North American, Indian, etc) are 99.9% timeless. There is no such thing as 'this year's' Swiss, Maori, Aboriginal, North American or Indian costume.

This is not, of course, the case with fashion and this fact can be observed simply by viewing a video of an early Miss World Contest back to back with a contemporary one. While the clothing styles featured in the national parade of dress remain fundamentally unchanged from 1959 to the present, the styles of the evening gowns or swimsuits worn in the rest of the Miss World Pageant exhibit drastic changes between these years – and even from one year to the next. Hemlines and *décolletage* go up and down and up again, colours, fabrics, styles and decorations continually fluctuate as each year's batch of contestants from around the world demonstrate that they have one thing in common – they all read fashion magazines.

While the defining characteristics of costume are regional variability and 'timelessness', fashion is characterized by perpetual, restless change and by regional uniformity. If a costume could be described as an advertisement for the status quo, fashion is an advertisement for change and progress. By perpetually substituting this year's 'New Look' for last year's 'New Look' (which has become tarnished by time), fashion defines 'seasons' and thereby creates the impression of change. While costume aims to be fixed or frozen in time (and thereby to reify a steady-state system of time perception), fashion is a relentless march forward – of style and, by implication, of time itself. (Which is, of course, just as much a fiction as is costume's 'timeless' immutability.)

Both costume and fashion are systems of signification but, at least on one level of analysis, they each express very different kinds of information. Whereas costume says *where* an individual is located sociologically (eg in village A, in the upper class, in the category of widows, etc.), fashion says what a person's position is in linear-progressive time (behind the times/now/ahead of the times). However, because these meanings carry positive or negative social connotations for the would-be fashionable they also, by implication, define an individual's place in social space.

It is a mistake, however, to presume that the meanings generated by fashion (of which there are, at least in a pure fashion system, only the three identified above) have some fixed correlation with social stratigraphy as it is modelled by social scientists. Fashion always creates its *own* social structure and, although this system may appear to be rigid and uncompromising at any point in time, it is in fact always completely fluid.

Just as a costume system exists only in space and possesses no temporal dimension (all folk costumes are 'timeless') so a fashion system is located only in time and possess no spatiality (other than that which is defined and created in terms of its own temporal categories). This is true both geographically and sociologically. If London is deemed to be 'ahead' of Paris or if working class chic is deemed to be in the avant-garde, this is only the case within the time frame of one 'season'. In fashion all of geography and all of social space are compressed into one dimension – linear, progressive time – and there is no such thing as 'next to'. Thus, while costume might be described as a 'language' without tense, fashion is a 'language' consisting of nothing else.

Is it necessary to use the word 'language' in quotation marks in the sentence above? In the case of costume the answer is probably yes but in the case of fashion the answer is probably no.

As we saw in Section 1, a language is a system of signification composed of arbitrary signs which have no 'natural' affinity with that which they express. Thus, if (in English) the word 'cape' signifies a certain type of garment, this is only because this meaning is accepted usage. There is nothing cape-like about this word. A drawing of a cape, on the other hand, looks like (has some 'natural relationship' with) that which it signifies. In a linguistic system, meaning derives from the relationship of signifiers (cape ≠cope ≠code, etc.) and from historic usage.

This is in point of fact exactly how the fashion system functions semiologically. Each signifier (the 'New Look' of 1986, '87, '88, etc.) has no 'natural' symbolic meaning. Indeed, each such signifier *on its own* has no meaning at all. It is only when one 'look' is

contrasted with others which have come before or after it in fashion time that its meaning (behind the times/now/ahead of the times) becomes apparent. For example, if in 1988 black garments are out and flower print garments are in this cannot be taken to mean anything other than that this difference of colour and pattern is a device to signal change at a time when other parameters of style such as cut or skirt length have been 'used up' in order to effect style change in previous years. Flower prints do not, in the context of the fashion system, signify anything other than the fact of fashion change itself (of which they are an arbitrary sign).

Within the fashion system, differences of colour, pattern, cut, etc., have no more meaning than do the letters of a linguistic alphabet (e.g., the letter 'a' in 'cape' and the

1. See Chloë Sayer's *Mexican Costume*.

letter 'o' in 'cope' are only arbitrary devices of differentiation). In 1988 – within the fashion system – the only meaning which can be attached to a black blouse is old-fashioned and the only significance of a flower-print blouse is fashionable.

In a costume system it can happen that style differences are arbitrary signs which have no 'natural' meaning, but it is more typically the case that they are symbolic and meaningful – at least for the people who wear them (which is, of course, all that is relevant). For example, in Moravia Slovakia, young, unmarried girls and women wear brightly coloured – especially red – garments; married women wear black and white garments; and widows wear only black. Because the inhabitants of Moravian Slovakia equate these colours with certain culturally accepted meanings, they would find it completely unnatural to arbitrarily switch them around so that, for example, widows wore red and young girls wore black.

1971 Miss World contestants in rehearsal for 'Parade of National Dress'.

1971 Miss World contestants on a visit to the Tower of London.

The different characteristics of costume and fashion as semiotic systems are important because they point to the different kinds of relationship which each has to the society within which it operates. A costume system is always directly and symbolically linked to its socio-cultural environment such that social facts → culture → costume styles (→ denotes a 'natural' linkage and a generative process). Thus the social system expresses itself directly and 'naturally' in the style of its costume. In a sense, therefore, 'Our Costume' is a signifier of 'Our Society'.

In fashion, on the other hand, there is no immediate, intrinsic or 'natural' correlation between social history and fashion history. Flower prints do not signify that 1988 is *socio-culturally* a brighter, more colourful or flowery year than 1987. Their meaning is only that 1988 is a *different* year from 1987. The Chairman Mao jackets of the 1970s did not signify communistic trends in Western society.

The only 'natural' symbol to be found in fashion is that of the fashion system itself *taken as a whole*. Its unending stylistic changes – taken together – are a 'natural' symbol of time as change. (And, as we will see in the next chapter, this conceptualization of time is itself an expression of the phenomenon of social mobility.) It must be emphasized again, however, that this correspondence (social mobility → linear-progressive time → fashion) refers only to fashion as a *total system*: the individual phonemes of the fashion system ('this year's look') are meaningless pieces of a larger systemic jigsaw.

Just as fashion is a system, so too is costume. The difference is that while the former is a system unto itself, the latter is a shared system: costume is the signifier which symbolically expresses the signified of the socio-cultural system.

The fashion system, is always a law unto itself. For this reason social changes are rarely directly translated into fashion change.

In their monograph *Three Centuries of Women's Dress Fashions*, the anthropologists Jane Richardson and Alfred Kroeber statistically plotted fluctuations in women's fashion according to six separate parameters of dress (hemlength, height of waist, width of skirt, width of waist, depth of decolletage, width of decolletage). When they attempted to organize this data and, specifically when they attempted to cross-index between fashion change and general historical events, they found that:

'It may well be that unsettled times make for unsettled styles. Revolution, Napoleonic and World wars, struggles over the rights of man, Communism and Fascism, the motor car and jazz, may contribute to fashion's trying to stretch and disrupt its fundamental stylistic pattern. But while such an influence is easily conjectured, it is difficult to prove. In any event, there seems no clear reason for the specific fashion extremes which such a set of causes might be thought to produce. Social and political unsettledness as such might produce stylistic unsettledness and variability as such; but there is nothing to show that it would *per se* produce thick waists, ultra-high or low ones, short and tight skirts. If there is a connection here, it seems that it must be through alteration of the basic semi-unconscious pattern, through an urge to unsettle or disrupt this and that when increased fashion variability occurs, it is as a direct function of pattern stress, and only indirectly, and less certainly, of socio-political instability. In short, generic historic causes tending toward social and cultural instability may produce instability in dress styles also; but their effect on style is expressed in stress upon the existent long-range basic pattern of dress, and the changes effected *have meaning only in terms of the pattern*.

Concretely, it would be absurd to say that the Napoleonic wars, or the complex set of historic forces underlying them, specifically produced high-waisted dresses, and that World War I produced low-waisted ones.' (pp.147–8; my italics)

The point is that fashion change must always be in respect to the basic structure (pattern, programme) of the fashion system itself. Despite appearances, fashion change is never a random phenomenon caused by the whims of particular individuals. Style fluctuations are determined – as in a clock – by the internal mechanisms of that 'machine'. The designer who is hailed as a creative genius may indeed be a genius, but his or her talent is inevitably in understanding the basic internal arrangement of the fashion system and translating this into fabric.

Richardson and Kroeber suggest that within the fashion system there are two basic pattern components (we could think of them as cogged wheels in a clock). The movements of the smaller of these determines yearly fluctuations while the movement of a larger one determines major fluctuations of around a century in length. (I suspect, however, that this time span, indeed, time itself, has been drastically compressed since 1936.)

In theory one could, therefore, programme a computer to predict fashion changes and this would probably make someone very popular with the fashion designers, textile manufacturers, journalists and buyers whose job requires that they plan years in advance. It could also make someone very wealthy and could determine whether fashion time was calculated from Paris, London, New York, Milan or Tokyo. Unfortunately, however, I suspect that such a programme would be far, far too complicated to work out. Richardson and Kroeber identify six parameters of fashion change but I wouldn't be surprised if there were in fact hundreds. And anyway – as we will see in Chapter 24 – fashion today seems to be either out of control or no longer very important (or both).

Still, I wouldn't be all that surprised to learn that somewhere in one of the world's fashion capitals there is some top secret research laboratory where a special team of computer programmers are working night and day to beat the system. For now, however, we will have to go on relying on the intuition and hunches of our top designers. They usually get it right anyway – but then, given the fact that they need make only one major mistake to join the ranks of other ex top designers, they have to.

5 Clothing

22 The Bourgeoisie's New Clothes

Between the 14th and the 16th centuries a revolution occurred in Western Europe the like of which the world had never seen. Where previous eras may have witnessed the rise and fall of empires, this one saw the collapse of what, until then, had been a universal condition of humankind – traditionalism. Whereas, previously, steady-state time keeping had everywhere protected the status quo by safely wrapping the present in the past, suddenly everything – including even change itself – changed. In the future there would be such a thing as 'the future' and change would be seen as the road to progress rather than the road to ruin. The Modern Age had arrived.

It is often assumed that this revolution began in the Renaissance and that it came about because of intellectual and artistic developments. In fact, this revolution began in the latter part of the Middle Ages and changes in art and philosophy were an entailment rather than a requisite. The original cause was socio-economic: the advent of social mobility.

It is hard for us to appreciate that prior to this time the social order was completely fixed and rigid. If you were born a serf, you died a serf and if you were born an aristocrat, you died an aristocrat. There was no such thing as getting ahead. The steady-state perception of time, the traditional religious and philosophical systems, the 'timelessness' of the arts and the fixed nature of costume all underlined and reified this fact of life.

It was apparently the Crusades which set in motion the forces which lead to the modern revolution:

'One thing that can certainly be said for the Crusades is that they brought about the emergence of new conditions, aiding the development of international communications, the revival of economic exchanges, the strengthening of royal power and, in trading and industrial cities, the appearance of a system of compulsory corporations, and the emergence of a new social class composed of merchants and craftsmen. In the evolution of costume during this period the economic factors are of considerable importance.

The expansion of international exchanges resulting from the Crusades, the formation of important industries in Flanders, the south of France and the north of Italy contributed to the birth of a new capitalism, which provided a source of luxury in clothing and led to the constitution of organizations for the trades involved.' (Boucher:p.178)

This new social class – the rising bourgeoisie – not only broke down the steady-state world view which constituted the cornerstone of the feudal system (indeed, of *all* traditional socio-cultural systems), but having discovered for themselves personally that change could be beneficial rather than threatening, the members of this new class came to welcome change for its own sake. In the process, they created a new and entirely unique world view founded upon a perception of time as a continuum leading to a better tomorrow:

'It was the beginning of an era that concentrated on the notion of progress and the cult of anything new, so much so that great anxiety arose about the permanence of anything created, and religious art no longer dared seek inspiration in contemporary forms.' (Cecil Saint-Laurent:p.67)

This new way of seeing history opened the door on to a brave new world and brought radical innovations to the arts and, most of all, to the art of decorating and clothing the human body.

I am not here referring simply to particular new styles of dress, but rather to a system – a machine, if you will – for the perpetual production of new styles. Whereas in feudal and other traditional socio-cultural systems new styles of dress were suspect and devalued until they could be given a patina of 'oldness' and slowly be incorporated into traditional costume, fashion rejoiced in novelty. The social mobility of the rising bourgeoisie was replicated, expressed and celebrated in fashion's stylistic mobility and that which was new and different was afforded greater value *simply because it was new and different.*

As the social and cultural changes born in the late Middle Ages exploded into the Renaissance, the ever-expanding and increasingly influential Middle Class actively sought out fresh style ideas so that they could, as it were, wear their ideology of modernity on their sleeves. Artists such as Pisanello were conscripted into becoming the first fashion designers – sketching out new stylistic ideas to replace those that had become 'old hat'. The most valuable source of stylistic novelty, however, were the costumes of exotic, far away places such as Persia, China or Egypt. As the bourgeoisie of France and Italy incorporated such styles into their dress, there was born the process of fashionalization – whereby garment styles which in their native context are fixed costumes are plundered, semiologically re-contextualized and emerge (for a season) with a new, modernistic, fashionable meaning. (A process which is still a mainstay of fashion innovation, as the Mexican, African and Caribbean styles of '87 testify.)

Then as now, this plundering of the exotic and the previously 'timeless' helped to feed the fashion machine and for a time these costumes acquired a different meaning – that of progress and change. Then they were discarded and the fashionable moved on to 'borrow' other traditional peoples' costumes. Thus within a short period of time such styles were transformed from the past perfect to the future perfect – only to be discarded almost immediately on the scrap heap of the unfashionable.

In those parts of Europe which had first witnessed the rise of the bourgeoisie and in which general economic prosperity underlined the prospects of a new age, there grew a phenomenal hunger for new styles of dress. For the first time in history new clothing styles had more cachet than did traditional styles (which previously had been valued – as we would today an antique – simply because they were old). But an unfortunate characteristic of novelty is that it soon wears off and the search for new, new styles became a never ending task.

In cities like Florence, Venice or Genoa (where only a generation ago styles of dress were the same year in and year out – sometimes even century in and century out), fashions were here today and gone tomorrow. As Michael and Ariane Butterberry report in *Fashion: The Mirror of History:*

'In Venice, this northern craze [slashing], coupled with rising hemlines, caused concern in the senate, where the expense incurred by changing fashions was proclaimed a danger to the state. In Florence the mounting tyranny of fashion was noted by a diarist:
"In 1529 they stopped wearing hoods; in 1532 there was not one to be seen, for the usage had gone, and instead of hoods caps and hats were worn. At the same time they began to cut their hair short, where before everyone had worn it down to their shoulders without exception; and now beards began to be worn, where before no one could be found wearing a beard in Florence. Furthermore, at the same time, hose began to be made in two pieces, where before they were made in one, and without any slits; now they are slashed all over and they put taffeta underneath to come through all the slits."' (Michael and Ariane Butterberry; p.)

This same, peculiar phenomenon of constantly changing fashions in dress and adornment was also noted by Leonardo da Vinci in his *Codice Urbinate:*

'And I remember having seen, in my childhood, grown men and young boys going about with every single edge of their clothing dagged, from head to toe, and down right and left sides. At the time, it seemed such a wonderful invention that they even dagged the dags. In this way, they wore their hoods and shoes: and even the crowns of their heads looked like cockerel's combs. Such fashions appeared from all the tailors' shops, in a variety of colours. And afterwards I saw the shoes, caps and purses, the collars of gowns, the hems of their ankle-length doublets, each tail-end of clothing and even offensive weapons: in effect, everything I saw, right to the tips of the tongues of whosoever wished to appear beautiful, was forked in sharp points. In another era, sleeves began to grow and were so huge that each one of them on its own was larger than the main body of the garment. Then of course the clothes began to creep higher and higher up the neck until they finally smothered the whole head. Then collars began to peel away so that the clothes were no longer supported by the shoulders, because there was nothing left covering them. Then dress became so elongated that men had to bundle the excess textile into their arms to avoid trampling over the hems with their feet. Following this, the cut of the garments swung to the opposite extreme, and hems only reached down to the hips and the elbows: the clothes were so narrow that they suffered unbearably, and many split under the strain. And feet were so squeezed into slim-fitting shoes that the toes bunched up one over the next and developed corns.'

From Italy the mania for novelty spread to France, Spain and, in time, throughout Europe. However, nowhere – not even in places such as Florence and Venice – was this preoccupation with fashion and with the modern, progressive world view found in all strata of society. Indeed, for the vast majority of people life continued as it had always done, firmly embedded in tradition, and their clothing was inevitably a 'timeless' costume.

One group of people who liked it that way were the aristocrats. For those who had it made by virtue of birthright, spiralling social mobility and the steady advance of the rising bourgeoisie was a curse rather than a blessing. In an attempt to halt the changes which threatened their economic and political position, the aristocracy clung to their traditional costumes and passed sumptuary laws designed to keep the middle classes in their place sartorially.

These sumptuary laws were doubly doomed. Not only were they unenforceable but they failed to recognize the new phenomenon of fashion. Apart from those few members of the upper middle class who had risen to dizzy heights (who, like the aristocracy themselves, now hoped to put a stop to social mobility) those who belonged to the *rising* bourgeoisie craved novelty rather than simply a chance to wear the dowdy old costumes of an aristocracy who still thought it was yesterday. Of course, such people coveted the luxurious fabrics and the expensive craftsmanship of the aristocracy's costumes but their craving was for fresh fodder for the machine of fashion change rather than to get themselves stitched up for an eternity in the prestigious but traditional costume of the aristocracy. For those who embraced modernity, *anything* which was old fashioned and which could not be re-contextualized to give it a meaning of modernity would have been inappropriate.

Social mobility had broken the mould of the traditional view of reality and those who had tasted the fruit of this revolution (as long as they personally remained within the ranks of the *rising* bourgeoisie) would always hanker after the new, the progressive, the modern – the stylistic harbingers of a delicious tomorrow. For people such as these – people enamoured of change for its own sake – the past (even that enjoyed by the aristocracy) was now *passé*.

And this world view and the changing fashions which symbolized it were contagious. Although, at least originally, few in number, the rising bourgeoisie – in so far as their economic and social reality was the foundation of *everyone's* prosperity and in so far as they had considerable influence over what we would today call 'the media' – came to control the collective consciousness of Renaissance and post-Renaissance society.

So great was their influence that even some of the landed aristocracy found themselves eager to cast off their traditional, but now dated, costumes in order that they

Early 15th-century, Italian sketch by Pisanello who could be considered to be the world's first fashion designer.

might participate in fashionable society. For such people the new fads might have been a bit beneath their station and tainted by their *nouveau riche* associations, but in an age when the bourgeoisie controlled the definition of the beautiful and the desirable they would have been too sexy to ignore.[1]

Throughout the 16th, 17th, 18th, 19th and 20th centuries the socially mobile bourgeoisie continued to shape the Western world view. From era to era and from place to place their influence waxed and waned but, more often than not, it was their thoroughly modern philosophy of change for its own sake and their perception of time as a lineal and progressive continuum always pointing towards some futuristic Utopia which served as the foundation of the Western definition of reality.

1. Also, the social changes which the Crusades and, later, the Age of Discovery set in motion, blurred and decimated what had once been easily definable social divisions. Increasingly it became difficult to know where the aristocracy ended and the rising bourgeoisie began.

5
Clothing

23 Costume Today

The birth of fashion was not simultaneously the death of costume. From the Renaissance to the present day, even within the West there have always been some people for whom the modernistic, pro-change world view which fashion embodies is inappropriate and undesirable.

For example, the landed aristocracy who, by definition, have nothing to gain and everything to lose from social, economic and political change, have usually resisted the march of fashion, preferring, for obvious reasons, to use their clothing as an advertisement for the status quo and tradition. Such anti-fashion 'establishment' dressing is found today in Britain amongst the Sloane Rangers, the Hooray Henries and the Royals[1], and in the US amongst the preppies.

On the other hand, those who are socially, economically and politically disenfranchised and have little or no hope of benefiting from social change, while perhaps not adamantly anti-fashion, have always had little reason to embrace it enthusiastically. Today, the expansion of middle class social mobility into the lower and working classes has meant that the number of such 'serfs' has been drastically reduced, but such people still exist amongst the perennially unemployed and within the ranks of those caught in the 'poverty trap'. In so far as these people are 'stuck' at the bottom of the social system (and perceive themselves to be so) we would not expect them to celebrate social mobility via the medium of fashion change. Fashion has and will always be appropriate only for those who believe themselves to have 'prospects'.

Up-to-the-minute, fashionable attire has also always been inappropriate for those whose professional life demands a style of presentation rooted in the past and in tradition. Whereas a pop singer or a 'get-ahead' computer salesman/woman might benefit from dressing in clothes which advertise a 'with-it' approach to life, a barrister, judge, professor, nurse, priest, doctor, maître d'hotel, general, a conservative politician or even a 'traditional' butcher would be hampered by such a presentation of self.

By wearing a 'timeless' costume, such people not only identify which profession they belong to, they also instantly link themselves to their professions' long histories thereby increasing their own personal authority. Like a sign over a shop which announces 'Established in 1856', professional costumes suggest that someone is reliable, dependable and not 'fly by night'.

So effective is this function of costume that institutions may employ people simply to model outfits designed to confer a message of 'old fashioned tradition' upon the institution as a whole. Thus the relatively new Trump Tower in New York obliges its doormen to wear the uniform of some 'old' but difficult to define era. Likewise, Japanese department stores employ women in kimonos to greet customers and in Britain, palace guards and Beefeaters (and sometimes the Queen) model traditional costumes simply for their 'old' and 'timeless' connotations.

Occupational or professional costumes such as these have been important throughout Western history and will, I'm sure, always remain so. But it is a different type of costume – that which expresses and supports group solidarity – which (at least statistically) has done the most to limit the spread of fashion in the post-Renaissance West.

As we have seen, all social groups are inherently conservative and use some 'timeless', traditional style of adornment and/or dress ('Our Costume') to deny the possibility of change and thereby preserve the status quo. Previously we have discussed this phenomenon primarily with reference to non-Western social systems. Clearly, however, the same principle can be applied to, for example, a crofting community in Nova Scotia, an Indian immigrant community in London's East End, a Mennonite community in Pennsylvania, a Jewish Orthodox community in Manchester or even the entire traditional Working Class community of Great Britain (which took the cloth cap as its symbol of social identity).

Indeed, from the Renaissance until very recently, the *majority* of people in the West saw themselves as belonging to some sort of cohesive and 'timeless' social group, showed no interest in capricious fashions and throughout their lives wore some fixed costume as an expression of their social rootedness. (Exactly as everyone everywhere in the world did prior to the Renaissance and exactly as those inhabitants of the Third World who have not succumbed to Westernization continue to do today.)

However, especially since the Second World War, the number of such social groups and the extent of their memberships within the West (and the Westernized) has been drastically diminished. Although distinctive and 'timeless' traditional costumes may have helped, for a time, to keep such communities intact, their destruction was inevitable given the circumstances. The drastic increase in both social and geographic mobility, the rise of the nuclear family at the expense of the extended family, insensitive urban 'redevelopment' and the ever-growing importance of a homogenizing 'global village' media with a vested interest in broad rather than narrow casting, are just a few of the factors which have contributed to a collapse of our tight-knit, cohesive communities and the creation of a world in which 'there is no such thing as society, there are only individuals and their families' (to quote Margaret Thatcher again).

And as most of our regional, religious, class-based and other traditional communities have evaporated into the thin air of 'Western Society' and its ever-growing and ever more amorphous 'Middle Class', so too the costumes which identified these communities have disappeared except in travel brochures, nostalgic TV commercials and, occasionally (in recontextualized and semiologically meaningless form), in fashion.

For creatures like ourselves who are the product of millions of years of evolution based upon and prompted by communal life, an anti-society 'society' where there are only 'individuals and their families' cannot be entirely satisfying. Many people have found this brave new world to be unfulfilling, and from their disease has arisen a new 'tribalism' which seeks to create within the West new social groupings, each with its own form of 'our costume' to serve as a marker and symbol of socio-cultural identity.

Although we are generally inclined to dismiss Punks, Skinheads, Teddy Boys, Rockers, Bikers, Hippies, Psychedelics, Rockabillies, Gothics and their distinctive styles of dress and adornment as 'fads', this is a misinterpretation of the phenomenon. Each such 'cult' is, in fact, a viable social and cultural entity and the attire of each such group is a traditional costume rather than a capricious fashion.

There are, however, many things which distinguish these new Western 'tribes' from those of the Third World. While the latter possess a relatively fixed geographic territory and a membership linked together by intricate networks of kinship and economic relationships, the former are spread throughout 'the West' and are often actually strangers one to another. Thus the only thing which, for example, punks have in common is a world view and a costume style which serves as an expression of that world view. This is apparently enough, however, to provide them with a viable sense of group identity and membership.

Nor should the brief histories of these Western 'tribes' be seen as an important difference separating them from the tribes of the Third World, each of which possess a history of hundreds or thousands of years. Traditional societies and traditional costumes are identifiable as such not because of their actual antiquity, but because those who belong to them and wear them possess a traditionalist ideology which is based in steady-state time, defensive of the status quo and belligerently opposed to change.

Western style groups (even the mods, despite their name) all possess just such a traditionalist world view. Teddy Boys boast that 30 years on they haven't 'hung up their drapes' (the long 'Edwardian' style jackets which are the badge of their identity). Rockers, Bikers, Punks and Skinheads use tattoos of group allegiance as a buttress against change. And original and second generation hippies, mods, preppies, psychedelics, gothics and so forth have each stuck with their original styles of dress and decoration despite constantly changing fashions in society at large. Like those who belong to tribal and peasant societies, the members of Western style groups, by means of the time capsule which is costume, seek to preserve their socio-cultural status quo 'forever'. (Whether they will succeed in this project is, of course, another matter.)

Although fashion has periodically copied and recontextualized the costumes of these Western style groups (e.g., Zandra Rhodes' ripped and safety-pinned designs of 1977/8), those who are actually members of these groups deplore such fashionalization and trivialization of their costumes. Within the boundaries of these style groups themselves there is no such thing as 'this year's punk look' or the latest thing in biker gear. Mods might wear suits which were seen to have a 'modern' style but they also originally made of them a traditional, 'timeless' costume.

Another characteristic which today's 'tribes' share with all other traditional communities is an emphasis on stylistic, behavioural and ideological conformity. While we who are not Gothics, Skinheads, Hippies, Mods and so forth may tend to see their appearance as 'different' and 'rebellious', this is only from the perspective of 'normal Western society'. *Within* such groups there are always strict rules which govern how any would-be member must dress, behave and even think. Thus Hippies can't wear suits, Gothics can't wear flower prints, Mods can't wear scruffy clothes and Skinheads mustn't grow their hair long. Of course this uniformity is not absolute, but then neither is it in peasant or tribal communities. What is important and fascinating is the fact that such a high degree of conformity should be accepted – even sought out – in the West where, as we have seen, individuality usually reigns supreme.

Finally, as in the case of traditional tribal and peasant communities, style groups' costumes are symbolic and their meaning is the culture, values and beliefs of those who wear them. For example:

1. This does not, of course, apply to those who, like Princess Diana, have 'moved up' into the Royal family. We should not be surprised that *anyone* who has benefited from upward social mobility should exhibit pro-fashion tendencies.

Hippy couple with Teddy Boy (and fashionable friend) at Wembley Rock and Roll Festival, London, 1972.

(A) BEATS

(Originally Washington Square/Left Bank style with lots of black existentialist jumpers and 'On the Road' casualness. Influences: modern jazz, folk, Kerouac and Ginsberg. This style group has had a new lease of life in the '80s with the revival of jazz and 'cool'.)

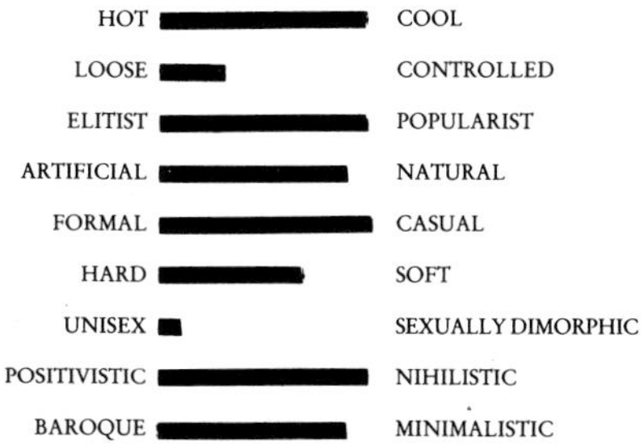

(D) MODS

(Definitive 'sharp' style with trim, Italian suits for men worn with thin ties and pointed shoes. For women: pencil skirts/mini-skirts, tights, minimal jewelry and sharp, shortish haircuts. Music: '60s soul and Motown.)

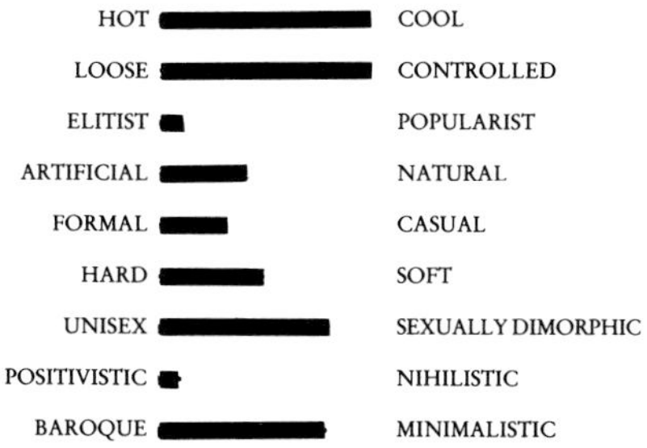

Classic rockabilly style as shown in Gerald Manliegh ad in *New Musical Express*, 1952.

(B) TEDDY BOYS

(Predominantly working class, British style which symbolically repudiates 'common' origins. Men wear expensive 'Edwardian'-style drape jackets and huge quiffs. Women wear full circle skirts with lots of petticoats and enormous beehives. Music: Elvis Presley and Carl Perkins.)

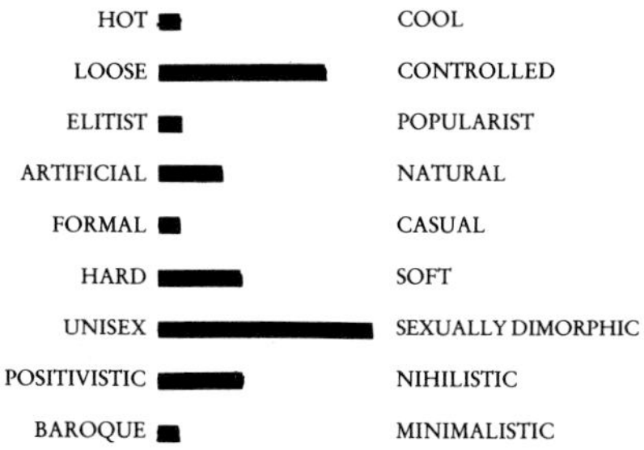

(F) PUNKS

('No Future' anarchy, anti-hippies.* Both sexes wear studded, ripped leathers and gravity-defying hairstyles in da-glo colours. Music: Sex Pistols to PiL.)

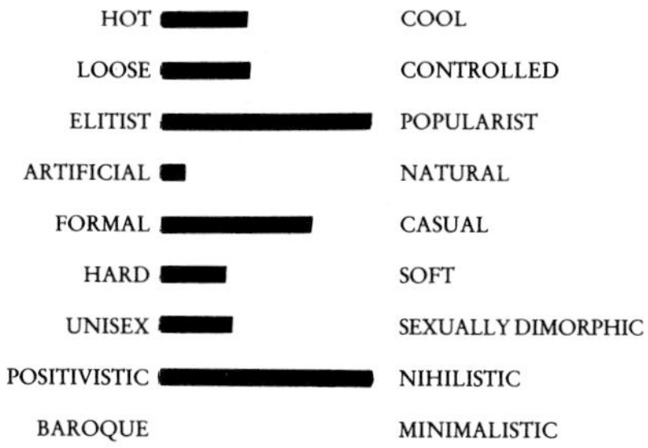

* Although originally devoutly anti-hippy, there is today a new sub-group which might be called Hip-punks which combine both styles and ideologies.

(C) ROCKERS

('Live Fast Die Young', 'Born to Lose' style with butch leather jackets with lots of studs worn by both sexes. Optional extra: motorcycle. Influences: Billy Fury, Gene Vincent, James Dean in *The Wild Ones*.)

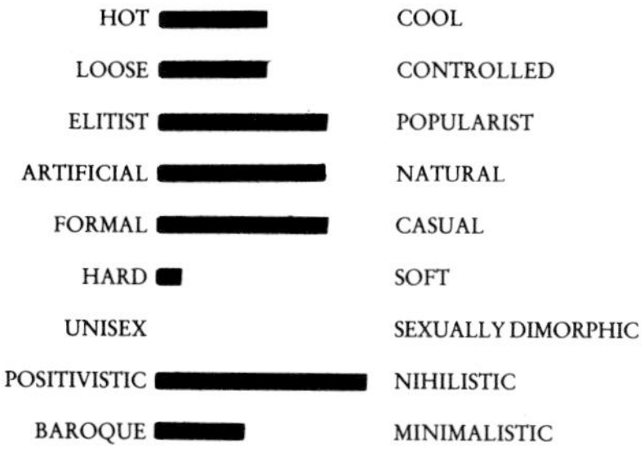

Punk costume, Kings Road, 1983.

(E) HIPPIES

('Love and peace', long hair, ethnic influences and anything natural. Essentially up-beat beats gone to seed. Music: Grateful Dead and Pink Floyd.)

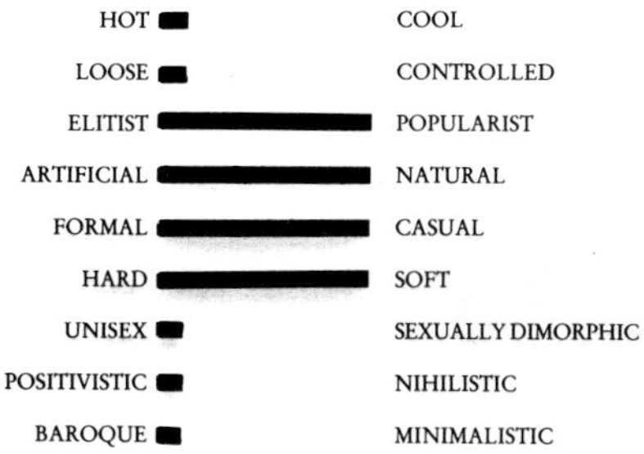

(G) GOTHICS

(The Undead. Both sexes wear vampire black clothes with skull-like make-up. Music: The Mission and the Cramps. Essential reading: Mary Shelley. Morticia Adams lives.)

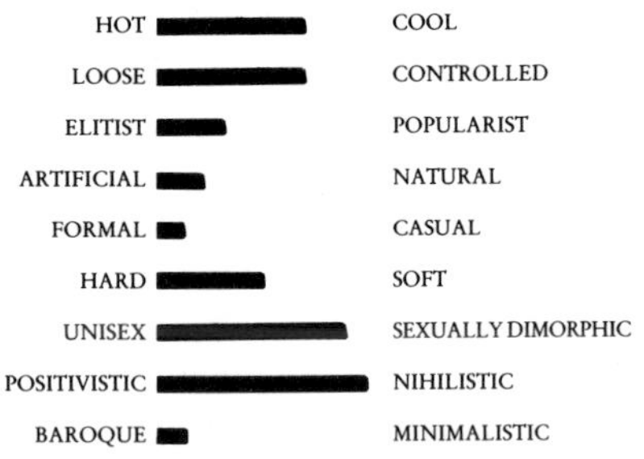

(H) SKINHEADS

(Originally British, working class and proud of it. Now international but still proud of national and lower-class origins. Cropped hair, braces, Fred Perry shirts and Dr Martin 'bother boots' for both sexes. Definitive hard but controlled style. Music: Reggae and ska.)

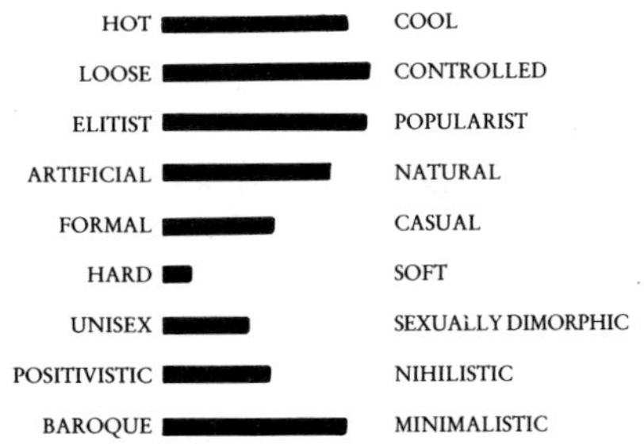

(J) PREPPIES

('Ivy league college chic and cashmere blazers, with a credit account with Ralph Lauren. It's clean-cut conservatism with a compact disc – casual display of wealth.')*

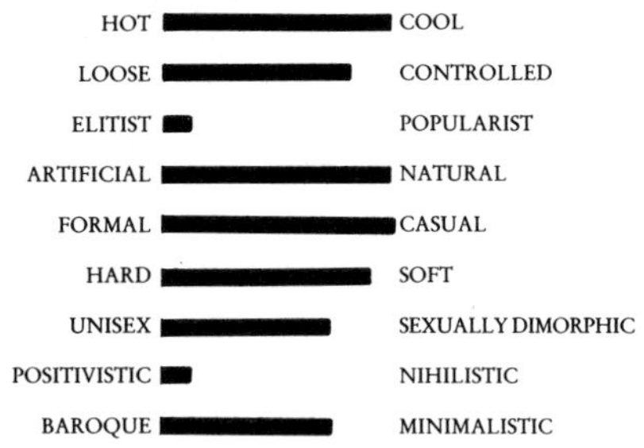

* Quote from *The I-D Bible*. Recommended reading.

By means of such a semiotics of attire and adornment the members of style groups can advertise the most fundamental beliefs and values of their culture to each other and to the rest of us. While (as I suggested in Chapter 21) the clothing and decorations of the would-be fashionable are arbitrary signs which generate meaning (ahead of the times/now/ behind the times) only in relationship to fashion history, the costumes of Western style groups (like those of most tribal and peasant peoples) are meaningful in and of themselves and they signify symbolically and 'naturally'. Because they are not arbitrary signs, these costume symbols are not interchangeable – thus it would be semiologically and ideologically inappropriate for hippies to dress like punks

(I) PSYCHEDELICS

(Pro-plastic hippies. Both sexes wear da-glo and/or Op Art clothes and make-up. Music: Jefferson Airplane to Zodiac Mindwarp.)

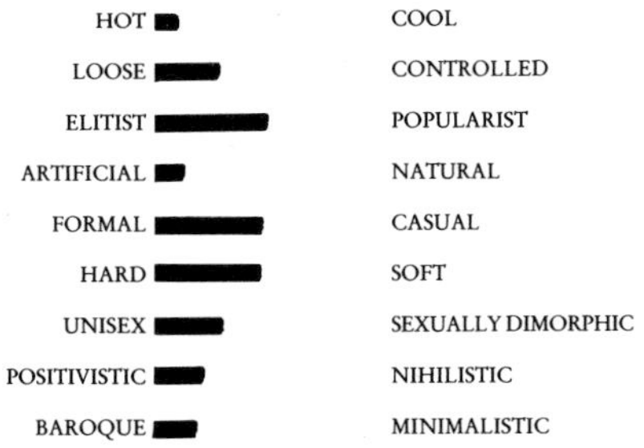

(K) B-BOYS AND GIRLS

(Flashy street style. Casual but ostentatious. Ghetto blasters blaring hip hop sounds. 'Steals the good life and takes it to the street.'*)

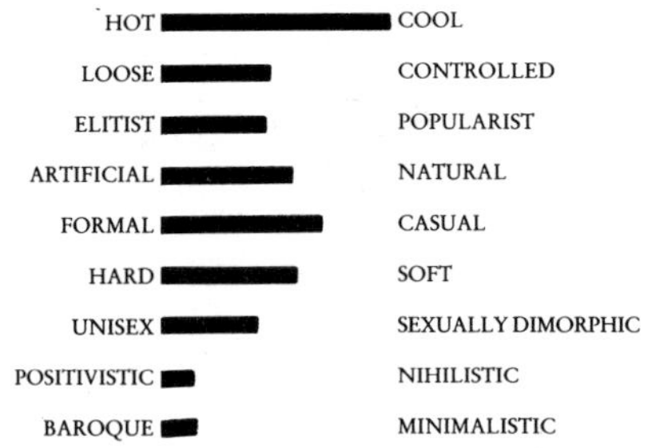

* *The I-D Bible*, p.46.

or vice versa. And because such costumes are 'natural' symbols, they constitute a direct, visible expression of the cultural system of those who wear them. In a sense, therefore, punk costume *is* punk culture and hippy costume *is* hippy culture, etc.

While this is also true of the garments and decorations of peasant and tribal societies, it is particularly relevant with regard to Western style groups. Since such 'tribes' lack the social, economic and kinship networks which are the foundations of any Third World tribe or peasant community, their costume/adornment style (and the world view which is symbolically conveyed through it) is all that they have to link themselves together and to share as a culture. Thus, while a tribe in the Amazon or a peasant community in Moravia Slovakia expresses its social system through its adornments and costume (thereby affording it a greater inter-subjective reality), Western 'tribes' attempt to *create* an entire social system out of only their costume.

The amazing thing is that it seems to work. From London to Tokyo, New York to Sydney, hundreds of thousands – if not millions – of young people are enjoying a sense of belonging to 'tribes' which, in the sense that anthropologists would normally use this word, do not really exist at all. And what is perhaps even more ironic is the fact that this system would not work at all were it not for the global communications system (the dreaded media) which did so much to destroy the traditional communities of the West and thereby created the need for such 'tribal' groupings in the first place.

The reader will have noticed that our modern day 'tribes' seem to be populated almost exclusively by teenagers and young adults. There is a good reason for this. It is precisely during this period of our lives that we are most likely to be estranged from a sense of social belonging. From birth to adolescence we are socially and culturally supported by our parents and the family relationships which network out from them.

From mid-life, on the other hand, we have usually succeeded in creating a family of our own which, together with career and neighbourhood-based relationships, ideally creates around us a social and cultural cocoon. During our teenage and young adult period of life, however, we have usually moved away from (if not literally, at least figuratively) our first family but have not yet created our second. It is for this reason that the West is producing hundreds of youth-oriented 'tribes' within the embrace of which teenagers and young adults can achieve a much needed sense of incorporation and belonging.

We would, however, be mistaken if we were to assume that this phenomenon is as unique to the young as is generally presumed to be the case. While the costume styles (and therefore the cultures) of the young are highly distinctive, provocative and generate a great deal of media attention, and while the young (for the reasons cited above) have a particularly strong motivation for organizing themselves into 'tribes', the fact of the matter is that in recent years people of *all* ages within the West have been doing precisely the same thing for precisely the same reason – the need for a sense of socio-cultural belonging and involvement.

Our adult 'tribes' are stylistically and semiologically more subtle and (according to the aesthetic and ideological principles of 'normal' society) less disturbing and less visible, but they exist just the same. The advertising industry – which cannot afford to make too many mistakes – has in recent years noted a drastic increase in 'market segmentation', the bottom line of which is that products today have to be aimed at particular factions within the overall population. Thus particular groups will buy products only in particular styles – styles which clearly reflect differences of world view. It would appear, therefore, that Western 'society', like some enormous protozoa, is in the process of subdividing into hundreds of different social groups, each with its own ideology, its own aesthetics and its own costume.

Examples of these contemporary, adult style groups are:

(A) MINIMALISTS

(Designer basics. Soho meets SoHo. No frills fundamentalism. Any colour as long as it's matt black.)

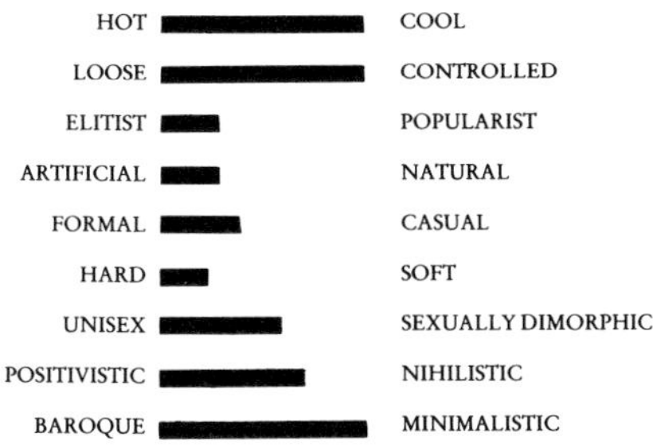
HOT
COOL
LOOSE
CONTROLLED
ELITIST
POPULARIST
ARTIFICIAL
NATURAL
FORMAL
CASUAL
HARD
SOFT
UNISEX
SEXUALLY DIMORPHIC
POSITIVISTIC
NIHILISTIC
BAROQUE
MINIMALISTIC

(C) COSY COUNTRY

(A soft rural style/ideology found primarily in cities and suburbs. Laura Ashley, stripped pine, Agas, green wellies and Land Rovers. Optional accessory: black labrador or golden retriever.)

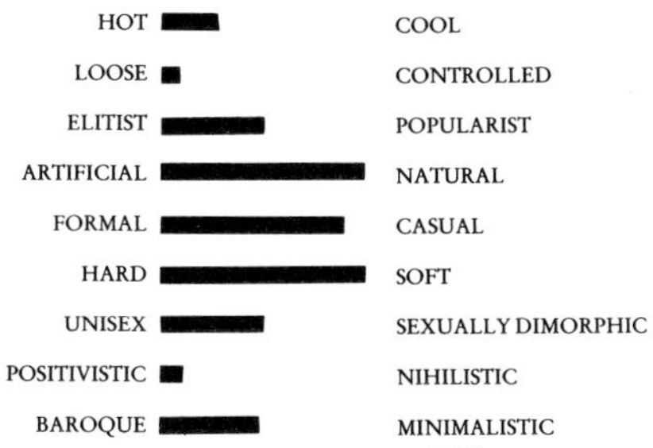
HOT
COOL
LOOSE
CONTROLLED
ELITIST
POPULARIST
ARTIFICIAL
NATURAL
FORMAL
CASUAL
HARD
SOFT
UNISEX
SEXUALLY DIMORPHIC
POSITIVISTIC
NIHILISTIC
BAROQUE
MINIMALISTIC

2. The only exception to this is the music which, like costume, embodies and expresses the distinctive culture of each of these groups.

(E) DISCO GLITZ

(Fringes, tassels, beads and bangles on everything to go go. Nouveau money style and pretensions. If you've got it flaunt it.)

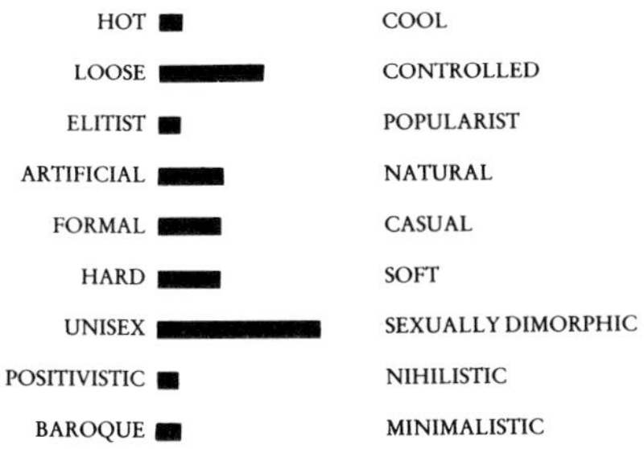
HOT
COOL
LOOSE
CONTROLLED
ELITIST
POPULARIST
ARTIFICIAL
NATURAL
FORMAL
CASUAL
HARD
SOFT
UNISEX
SEXUALLY DIMORPHIC
POSITIVISTIC
NIHILISTIC
BAROQUE
MINIMALISTIC

(F) EXECUTIVES

(Dressing for success. Expensive looking suits for both sexes. For men: Next, Brook Brothers. For women: Options at Austin Reed, Donna Karen. Drives: Escort XRi with car phone.)

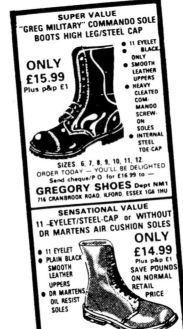

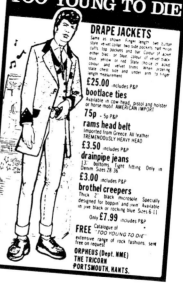

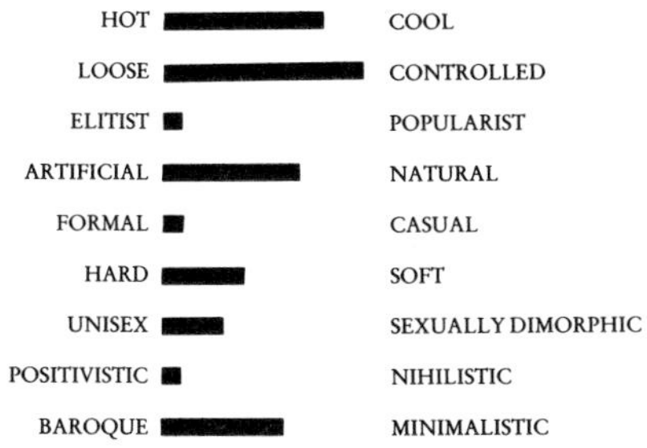
HOT
COOL
LOOSE
CONTROLLED
ELITIST
POPULARIST
ARTIFICIAL
NATURAL
FORMAL
CASUAL
HARD
SOFT
UNISEX
SEXUALLY DIMORPHIC
POSITIVISTIC
NIHILISTIC
BAROQUE
MINIMALISTIC

(G) BABYTIMERS

(Adults who refuse to grow up. Infantile style primarily in primary colours. Soft shoes, bow ties, badges, ephemera, kid's lunch box, chunky plastic glasses in jelly baby colours.)*

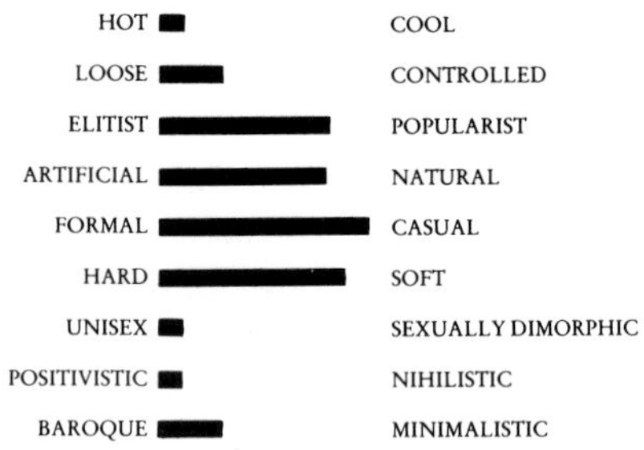

* The name of this group was invented by Peter York whose book *Modern Times* deals with many of the style groups listed here and is recommended reading.

(D) RUGGED COUNTRY

(Marlboro Man or Woman. Both sexes wear well-worn/stone washed denim jackets and jeans. Ironically, a society of would-be individualists. Optional extra: Renault Alpine with roof rack for skis or wind-surfing board.)

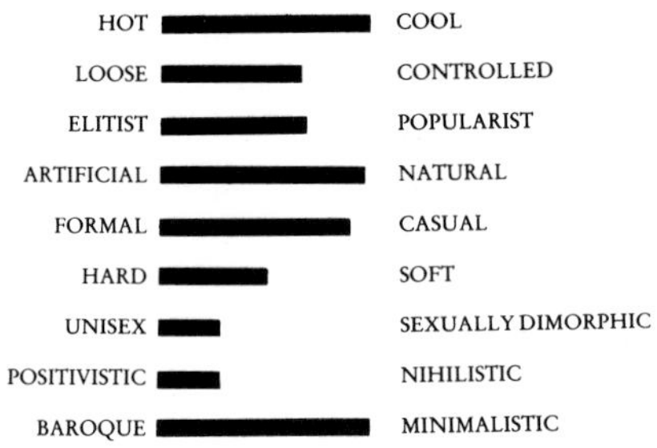

(H) WOOLIES

(Deliberately tired tweeds, baggy cords, elbow patches, knitted waistcoats and ties, pipes, earth shoes and bushy moustaches or beards for men. For women: voluminous woollen skirts, flat shoes, thick tights, ill-fitting homemade jumpers, shawls. An anti-style style. Muesli maniacs and lentil lovers. Drive: 2CV, VW Beetle or ride push bike.)

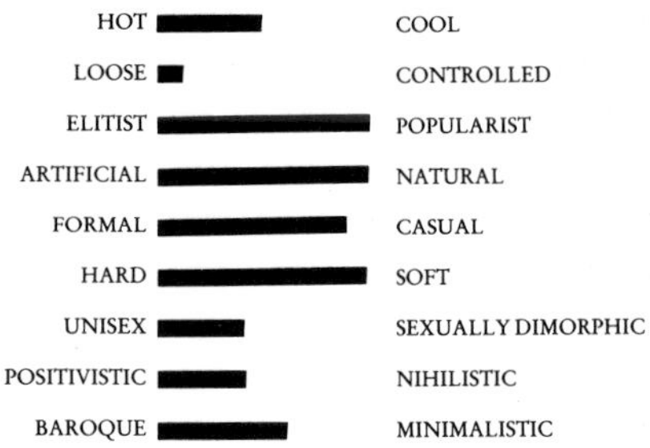

(B) FOGIES

(Traditional conservatism with old money flavour.)

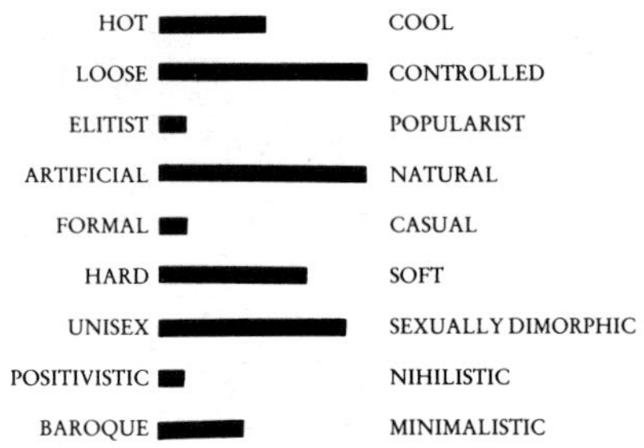

(I) SPORTY CASUALS

(Track suits and more track suits – Le Coq Sportif, Lacoste, Adidas, Nike, etc. 'Natural look' make-up for women. A must for men: Aramis grooming kit. Optional extra: exercise.)

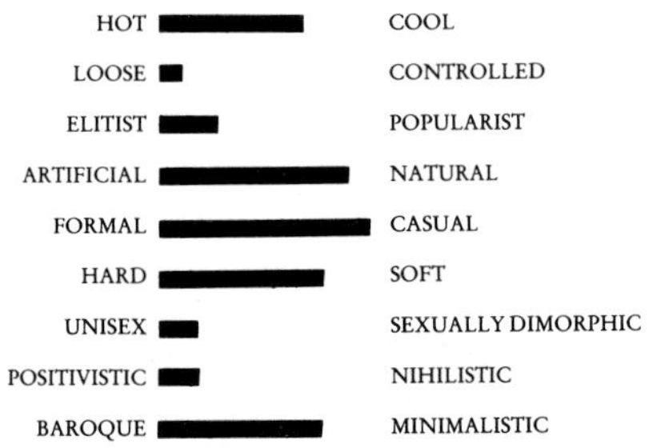

There are actually dozens of these groups – most of which are themselves divided into distinctive subgroups. Although it is usually assumed that style groups such as these are 'fashions', this is clearly not the case because (even though the media tends to spotlight them in a lineal sequence) they co-exist *next to* one another in social space. In any major Western city or suburb one can find, for example, a Minimalist couple living literally next door to a bunch of Fogies who, themselves, live above a pair of Disco Glitzers. And while fashions may come and go, many of these people remain true to the aesthetics and ideology of their particular group – theoretically, 'forever'.

The roots of this phenomenon are located within the same disintegration of traditional community life which prompted the rise of the teenage 'tribes'. Clearly, a great many people are finding that their nuclear family and career-based social networks are not (and here we clearly are talking about millions) providing a sufficient sense of social and cultural belonging and participation. Our response to this unsatisfactory situation is to try to create a 'community' of like-minded people 'out there', beyond the limits of our tiny and socio-culturally insignificant nuclear units.

The entailments of this phenomenon are of enormous importance. Western 'society', despite itself, is once again becoming a narrow-cast world divided into innumerable communities – not, as once was the case, according to region, religion, class or ethnicity, but according to ideological differences as expressed in the semiotics of aesthetic principles. The fact that each of these groups possesses its own 'timeless' costume may, at first glance, seem like an insignificant part of this all-pervasive revolution, but it is, in fact, the trigger and focus of the entire phenomenon. And this return to costume, in and of itself, has far-reaching ramifications. Most importantly, as we will see in the next chapter, the decline (if not death) of fashion.

5
Clothing

24 Fashion Today

From the Renaissance to the present day, fashion – against the odds – has managed to come up with a new look each 'season'. The rate of this change (and hence the length of each 'season') and the enthusiasm with which new styles have been leapt on by the public have, however, fluctuated from one era to the next. While the production of new styles has been (largely? completely?) determined by the internal structure or programme of the fashion system itself, the extent to which each era could be said to be 'fashion crazy' has been dependent upon changes in the social, economic and cultural environment.

As we saw in Chapter 21, the circumstances which first gave birth to fashion were as follows: the social mobility of the rising bourgeoisie, economic optimism and a belief that the future would be better than the present (which itself, for the first time, was seen as an improvement on the past) all conspired to break the mould of steady-state traditionalism and to replace it with a progressive and modern social construction of reality.

This world view did not die with the Renaissance; whenever and wherever the socio-economic conditions which first triggered the shift from traditionalism to modernism have predominated – but only during such times – fashion has been an obsession of most of the people most of the time. Aside from the Renaissance, the second half of the 18th century, the second Empire, the 1920s, and the 1960s were all futuristic eras in which *everyone* (not literally, but it must have seemed like it) danced to the frantic rhythms of fashion change.

Let's look at the period of the 1960s in some detail. There can, I'm sure, be no doubt that this was a thoroughly 'modern' age. In the '60s, to label a building, an outfit, a way of life or even a person as 'modern' or 'progressive' was the highest compliment. There was relative prosperity throughout large segments of Western society and there was considerable social mobility. Not, of course, for everyone, but the important thing is that an overwhelming majority *believed* that their chance at the jackpot was just around the corner. Had not The Beatles, David Bailey, Twiggy and countless others gone from rags to riches? Such people seemed to be living proof of a pattern of social mobility which – even if, for many, it remained but a myth – became a centrepiece of the '60s perception of reality.

In the '60s the future certainly looked bright. So bright in fact that no one could wait to get there. Science fiction sold like hot cakes – and not the gloom and doom stuff we see today, where mutants from the final holocaust fight in the streets over something to eat. The science fiction of the '60s (especially the early to mid-'60s which are, of course, the real historic boundaries of this era) looked towards a wonderful future where there was prosperity for all and robots saw to the hoovering. The dream of a futuristic Eden

Where once there was fashion uniformity there is now stylistic diversity. Contemporary alternative styles for different style groups from (left) Kahniverous and (right) Boy. Both sold in London's Hyper Hyper market. (Kahniverous dress by Jane Kahn, photo by Robert Chouraqui; Boy photo by Jack English).

– an Arcadia located in time rather than remote geographic space – had been brewing for a long time (I suppose since the Renaissance) but in the '60s you could almost reach out and touch it.

In such a linear-progressive climate the traditional, the backward, the classic and the timeless had few takers. If something was new it was automatically improved and, not surprisingly therefore, fashion reigned supreme. Even in the American suburban backwater in which I grew up, *Life* magazine's reports from Paris (and later London), although initially greeted with derision, were always in the end obeyed as my mother and her friends (all of whom claimed to be 'not the fashion type') would get out a needle and thread and raise the hem lengths of last year's dresses and skirts. As Peter York comments in *Modern Times*:

'In a time gone by what people now call style [and which I would call costume] was then called fashion and fashion had to be followed. It had its own establishment, a kind of Vatican, in the fifties and sixties and in this set-up they had dictators who set the lines for everybody to follow. The lines were set like edicts in the way of the old world . . . they were set by magazine editors for magazine readers. *Vogue* used to announce the colour of the season and up and down the land shops presented clothes in banana beige or coral red or whatever . . . And the point was that everyone wore it, your sister, your auntie, the gym mistress, everyone. For truly THERE WAS NO ALTERNATIVE. You were either with them or against them'. (p.10)

To summarize: the '60s were a period when virtually everyone perceived themselves to be members of some enormous, ever-expanding and ever-rising bourgeoisie. Everyone, in other words, had great expectations. The vast majority believed that they had *prospects* and they welcomed change as the doorway which led to a sunny, SF future. Standing still, looking back, putting up with the status quo and unchanging traditionalism was frowned upon. Ever more rapid fashion changes symbolically celebrated the desirability of social change and progress. A particular style of garment was, therefore, either old-fashioned, in fashion or avant-garde and there was no room in this system for alternatives. Because style was completely defined by its temporal dimension, it was uniform and easily recognizable (by the public as well as fashion journalists) as *the* fashion.

1987 (left) and 1988 (right) evening dresses by British designers. From top: Zandra Rhodes, Benny Ong, Gina Fratini, and Roland Klein. (Sketches by the designers).

In the 1980s things appear to be very different. Instead of embracing the futuristic we embrace the *post*-modern – a style which looks back with affection rather than anger or superiority and which unashamedly salutes that which used to be seen as *passé*. This may not (in so far as dated styles are deliberately re-contextualized) be a straightforward traditionalism but it certainly is a world away from the approach of the '60s which labelled as suspect anything whatsoever which was tainted by time and therefore not 'modern'. Clearly the 1980s are a whole new ball game.

(Even men's underwear is indicative of this change of attitude: whereas in the '60s we wore futuristic, space-age 'briefs', today's styles tend towards post-modern boxer shorts which are reminiscent of what your father and his father before him might have worn.)

Perhaps our problem is that we have seen the future and it doesn't work. Or perhaps, social mobility isn't as fluid as it once was (or as we once thought it to be). Certainly the kind of great leap forward which the majority experienced in the post-war period up to, perhaps, the mid '70s is no longer as statistically likely as it once was. Whereas parents in the '50s or '60s could hope and expect that their children would 'have it better than we did', parents in the '80s can typically only hope that their children will do *as well* as they did. (And this was true long before the stock market crash of '87 further reduced expectations.) Clearly it is not only the punks who suspect that we have '*no future*'.

I cannot claim to know the true cause – or even the extent – of the post-modern world view, but it is easy to see that it has had a profound effect upon fashion's previous dictatorship of style. Today, just as in the '60s (twice yearly in Paris, New York, London, Milan and Tokyo), fashion designers launch their new collections and each season the fashion journalists dutifully report that this year's colours are such and such, this year's hem length is such and such, and so forth. On the surface it all seems like business as usual, but closer inspection suggests that something very different is going on.

Figure 24.1 shows 1987 and 1988 designs by several influential British designers. As we can see, the stylistic differences from one designer to the next are more pronounced than are the generic differences from one year to the next. Indeed, it is very difficult to find *any* common denominator which effectively summarizes this yearly fluctuation. One could make the same point using Italian designers such as Armani, Missoni or Valentino, French designers such as Saint Lauren, Lagerfeld or Givenchy, or American designers such as Lauren, Calvin Klein or Karen. And if we were to try to compare and contrast *all* of these designers' collections for the years '87 and '88 (etc.) we would find even more difficulty in pinpointing a common factor of fashion change.

My point is simply that in the '80s, yearly fluctuations are not as distinctive as are the 'timeless' signatures of particular designers. And although fashion journalists may each year make valiant (if misguided) attempts to neatly summarize the themes, colours, hem lengths, etc., of that season, this has clearly become a rather meaningless exercise. Whereas in the '60s, 'this year's colours' might have been limited to two or three per season, we are now given a list as long as your arm which takes in practically every conceivable shade and hue (and then, as we read on, we discover that 'of course' X, Y and Z are continuing to buck the trends by using some other colour which somehow managed to slip through the long list which the journalist provided at the start).

In the 1980s it is the differences *from one designer to the next* which are important, while yearly fluctuations are no longer as marked or as significant as they were in, for example, the '60s when one really could pinpoint the common denominator of a given season's direction. In glossing over the differences between different designers, journalists are obscuring the fact that large segments of the so-called 'fashion industry' are no longer engaged in the business of producing fashion in a strict sense of the word.

There is, of course, nothing wrong with a designer stepping outside of fashion. Britain's Jean Muir many years ago rejected the label of 'fashion designer' and loudly and clearly announced that her objective was to produce 'timeless classics' – clothes which could be worn 20 or 30 years after they first appeared on her catwalk. In other words, Muir was declaring a career shift from fashion to costume. The fact that she could do so and remain highly successful is a clear indication that what the public wants – in terms of the relationship of clothing and time – has changed drastically since the 1960s.

It would be a mistake, however, to give the impression that no one these days is interested in fashion and that no designer in the '80s can rightly be described as a fashion designer. Vivienne Westwood is a case in point. Each year since she first became a designer, Westwood has been turning out something new and fresh and then almost immediately moving on.

In 1971, together with Malcolm McClaren, Westwood opened a shop on the King's Road called 'Let It Rock', for which she designed 'Teddy Boy' styles with a difference. In '72, the shop became 'Too Fast To Live Too Young To Die' and Westwood turned to fashionalizing 'The Biker Look'. Then in '74 the same shop was transformed into 'SEX' and Westwood became the first to explore the fashion potential of rubber fetishism – the earth-shaking result was the look which the punks latched onto as their badge of visual identity. But unlike the punks who took her to be their patron saint, Westwood kept restlessly and innovatively moving on. The shop became 'Seditionaries' in 1977 and a rapid-fire series of stylistic changes resulted in 'World's End' in 1980 and the 'pirate' and 'dandy' looks which Adam Ant and Bow Wow Wow brought to international attention. While the little shop was allowed to keep the same prophetic name, Westwood introduced the 'Savage Collection' in '81, 'Buffalo Girls' in '82, the 'Hobo Look' in '83, 'Witches' in '84 and 'The Clint Eastwood Collection' in '85. Money problems closed the shop from June '85 until June '86, but Westwood came out of her corner with the (now internationally acclaimed) 'mini-crini', the 'Aristocratic Collection' in '87 and the 'Goddess Look' (and a lot else besides) in 1988.

The only thing which is constant and unchanging about Westwood's designs is their capacity to outrage. Each 'year' (some of her years are admittedly longer than others) she moves one step further in linear-progressive fashion time and each year everyone applauds like crazy but privately wonders if the stuff will sell. In a good year they sell just about well enough for Westwood to get by until the next year. In part this limited commercial success (sometimes even failure) is a product of this designer's unwillingness to compromise stylistically and erotically, but it is also a product of her choice to continue as a progressive, futuristic *fashion* designer in a post-modern age which hankers after steady-state traditionalism and which finds costume more ideologically comfortable than the new and the different.

It is not my intention to suggest that Vivienne Westwood is a 'better' designer than, for example, Jean Muir. My point is simply that their respective creations are expressions of different kinds of time. Muir's designs are costumes which (like costume everywhere) embody and project a steady-state conceptualization of time: classics which hold onto the status quo. On the other hand, Westwood's designs (again, taken in historic relationship one to the other) are fashions which embody and project a linear-progressive conceptualization of time – each announces that the times they are a changing.

Whether we find the work of Westwood or Muir to be more attractive/desirable is a product of our own personal social situations, histories, values and beliefs – everything which leads us to celebrate either change or, alternatively, the status quo. Westwood designs clothes for the *rising* bourgeoisie (those on the way up) while Muir designs clothes for the *established* bourgeoisie (those who already have it made).

Ironically – given the consistent shock value of Vivian Westwood's designs – it is actually Jean Muir's approach and intentions which, historically, are the more unusual. While Westwood carries on the process of perpetual revolution which was born in the Renaissance and which has been the cornerstone of Western society ever since, Muir's work is unusually *anti*-fashion. Unusual, that is for the West which has traditionally been anti-traditional. But in the 1980s, even within the 'fashion industry' she is far from unique. Zandra Rhodes, Ralph Lauren, Saint Laurent, Armani, etc. have all developed a 'timeless' style which cuts across and ignores fashion fluctuations.

This is a far cry from the 1960s when, although different designers may have experimented in different directions, constant change was the constant preoccupation of the clothing industry and to be out of step with the accepted 'New Look' was a one-way ticket to obscurity. In the 1980s, on the other hand, designers like Jean Muir can go on year in and year out ignoring 'the fashion', while doing very nicely thank you and without fear of being stigmatized as 'old fashioned'.

The continuing success of these designers of costume classics suggests that the public is no longer enamoured of the thrill of the perpetual motion machine that is fashion. In 1987 the fashion press announced with great fanfare and conviction that 'THE MINI IS BACK' and true enough in '87 and '88 one began to see many more mini-skirts on the streets and in the shops. But one also saw a great many women (perhaps even the majority) who were prepared to thumb their

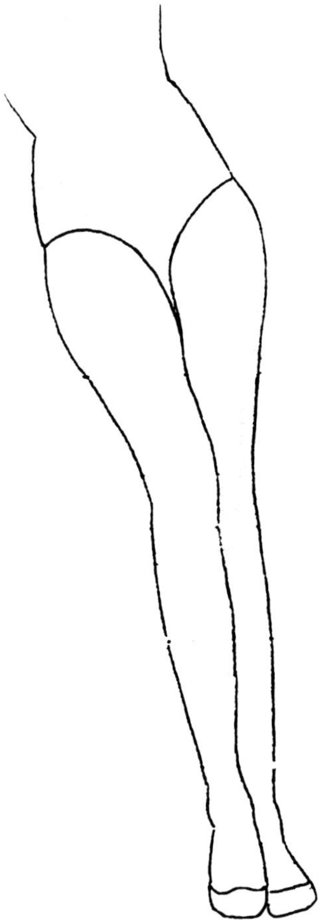

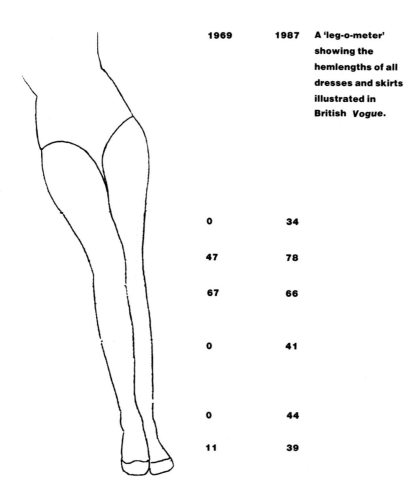

1969	1987
0	34
47	78
67	66
0	41
0	44
11	39

A 'leg-o-meter' showing the hemlengths of all dresses and skirts illustrated in British *Vogue*.

noses at the fashion pundits and fashion designers and carry on wearing that which 'suited' them (aesthetically and ideologically).

As we have seen, back in the '60s, the opprobrium of being labelled 'old fashioned' caused everyone ('your sister, your auntie, the gym mistress, everyone' as Peter York puts it so well) to get out a needle and thread and (even if reluctantly) attempt to 'keep up with the times'. Today, on the other hand, it is only a minority who appear to feel compelled to follow the latest looks.

We can see this change even in the pages of a magazine like *Vogue* which, as it name implies, is built upon the shifting sands of fashion change. A leg-o-meter, if you will, is a record of the hem lengths shown in all the photographs and illustrations (including editorial, advertising, etc.) in the January, February and March 1969 issues of British *Vogue*. As we can see, there is not a single violation of the 1969 fashion law which decreed that hem lengths should fall either above or below the ankle. For the January, February and March 1987 issues of *Vogue*, although it is true that the most frequently found hem length in these three 1987 issues of *Vogue* is that which falls above the knee (this is, of course, especially true in the fashion features) there are also plenty of examples of hems of *every* conceivable length. Clearly, even amongst the readers of *Vogue* there are plenty of women prepared to ignore fashion trends. And on the streets, at the supermarket, etc. this phenomenon is even more pronounced.

What seems to be going on in the 1980s is that fashion – and, by impliction, the linear-progressive model of time – is the obsession of only some of the people some of the time. For a significant segment of the population (the majority?) it is the 'timeless classics' (i.e., costume) which have the most appeal. As Kathryn Samuel says in her book *Lifestyles/Fashionstyles*:

'Today, dressing well is all about developing a personal style, rather than religiously following fashion. Indeed, the obsessive follower has been labelled a 'fashion victim' by the style-conscious eighties – a far greater insult in current terms than being regarded as anti-fashion or just having given up on the battle of looking good. For style, not fashion, has become the watchword of the decade.

The fashion victim swallows seasonal directives whole, wearing each new look without individuality, regardless of whether it suits her or not – mindlessly seduced by all and everything trendy. Victims don't plan their wardrobes, they just veer wildly from one new fad to the next in an expensive hit-and-miss manner.' (p.6)

While I would use the term costume instead of style and while I would wish to suggest that at least some of the apparent 'individuality' to be found today is actually an expression of style group affiliation (as Samuel herself shows in her compartmentalization of '80s styles into groups such as 'Dynasty', 'Country', 'Action Girl', 'Sloane', etc.), I am in complete agreement with this author's (and Peter York's) point that fashion change seems to be going out of fashion.

What interests me is to try to pinpoint the sociological and cultural roots of this phenomenon. The clear implication is that the Renaissance-like conditions and world view of the '60s are no longer as predominant as they once were. The shift away from the progressive and the modern in clothing, architecture, interior design, music, etc., which is going on in the '80s and which has been labelled post-modernism, suggests that the golden age of endless opportunity, bright prospects and blind faith in the future is in decline. Our society – or at least our perception of it – is not, apparently, what it once was.

This may be a temporary phase but then again it may not. Meanwhile, however, the preconditions and mentality of the Renaissance – social mobility, an expanding rising bourgeoisie and a thoroughly modern futurism – are beginning to appear in places in the West like Spain (which, under Franco, was a 'yesterday' culture and which is only now experiencing something akin to our '60s) and in the Third World.

Although this is hardly true of the majority of people in places like Rio, Dar es Salaam, Singapore, Port Moresby, Buenos Aires or Bombay (and although, in comparison with their counterparts in the West, such people might still be economically disadvantaged), it is nevertheless the case that some sort of Renaissance *is* in progress beyond the boundaries of 'the West'. For a minority of people in the urban Third World (and let us remember that even in our own Renaissance it was, at least at first, only a tiny minority who benefited from social mobility and who embraced modernism) the future looks brighter than the past and change looks more promising than the traditional steady state.

For these people, changing fashions are inevitably more attractive than traditional costumes – which are symbolically laden with connotations of a past which is now seen as *passé*. Perhaps in ten, twenty or thirty years time the West will be completely fragmented into countless 'tribes', each with its own timeless costume, and tomorrow's 'New Looks' will each season be unveiled on the streets or even the catwalks of the Third World where, not that long ago, the only clothing and adornment to be seen was that designed for killing time.

Photographic Acknowledgements

Front cover: Make-up artist and singer Rimba Wildman (photo: Ted Polhemus)
Back cover: A reconstruction of the tattoo designs of a 5th century-Scythian chief (photo: Henry Ferguson)
Endpapers: Some tracings of anthropomorphic figures found in prehistoric caves in Spain. (After Abbe[/] Breuil. From M.C. Burkitt, *Prehistory*, 1925, Cambridge University Press. Reproduced with kind permission of the publishers.)

Picture Credits

(NOTE: b = bottom; t = top; l = left; r = right; c = centre)
1) By kind permission of the Papua New Guinea High Commission [p4 t, p66 t l];) 2) Photographs and illustrations by Marcus Podilchuk [p4, p5, p9 b l, p16 t, p43, p51, pp66-7 b, p119, p120]; 3) By kind permission of Cambridge University Press (illustrations from *Prehistory* by M.C. Burkitt, 1925) [p9 t l, p9 l, p19]; 4) By kind permission of Dover Publications, Ltd. N.Y. (illustrations from *African Designs from Traditional Sources* by Geoffrey Williams, 1971) [p9, p16 b, p17, p18 l, p18]; 5) Illustrations from Robert Brown, *The Races of Mankind* (4 vols. Cassell Petter & Galpin, London, 1873) [p14, p28 t r, p53 b l, p75]; 6) Photographs by Robyn Beeche [p15 (model: Scarlot, body painting; Richard Sharples), p29 (make-up: Phylis Cohen, collar by: Richard Sharples. Courtesy of Vidal Sassoon), p59 [make-up; Phylis Cohen, hair by Robert Lobetta. Courtesy of *The Observer*]; 7) Photographs by kind permission of Adel Rootstein Display Mannequins (Shawfield House, Shawfield St, London SW3 4BB) [p20L (photo: David Bailey), p20 t r, p20 b r]; 8) Photographs by Ted Polhemus [p20 b c, p44, p49 t, p53 b r, pp54-5, p67 b c, p67 t, p94 b, p101, p113t r, p113 b l, p131 b c, p34 l, p34 r, p35, p36 b r, p37 t, p37 b, p39, p40, p58, p60 t, p62 b, p63 t, p82, p86 t, p86 b, p87 b l, p87 b r, p108 b, p110 t, p110 b l, p110 b r, p111 t, p111 b l, p111 b r, p112]; 9) Photographs from the BBC Hulton Picture Library [pp22-3, p24 c, p28 t c, pp124-5 c, p125 b l, pp130-131]; 10) Illustration from Samuel Soemmerring, *Ueberdie Wirkungen*, Berlin, 1793 [p24 b]; 11) Illustrations from Adolfo Dembo and J. Imbelloni *Deformaciones Intencionales del Cuerpo Humano de Caracter Etnico*, Humanior, Biblioteca del Americanista Moderno, Buenos Aires, 1938) [p25 t l, p26, p49 b r, p74]; 12) Photographs by Grace Lau [p25 c l, p25 b r]; 13) Illustration used by kind permission of Dover Publications Inc., N.Y. (from *Vecellio's Renaissance Costume Book* by Cesare Vecellio, reprinted by Dover, 1977) [p28 l]; 14) Illustrations used by kind permission of Dover Publications, Inc. N.Y. (From *Men: A Pictorial Archive from Nineteenth-Century Sources* selected by Jim Harter, 1980) [p28 b r, p53 t c]; 15) Photographs by Henry Ferguson [p45, p61 l, p61 r]; 16) Illustrations from Sydney Parkinson, *Journal of a Voyage to the South Seas in His Majesty's Ship the Endeavour*, 1773; printed for Stanfeild Parkinson (the editor), London [p52, p73]; 17) Illustration from Robert Brown, *Countries of the World* (5 vols., 1876, Cassell Petter & Galpin, London) [p53 t r]; 18) Illustrations used with kind permission of Dover Publications Ltd, N.Y. (from *Historic Costume in Pictures* by Braun & Schneider, reprinted by Dover, 1975) [p66 b l, p67 b r]; 19) Illustration used with kind permission of the Bibliotheque Nationale, Paris [p71]; 20) Photographs from the Murray Wren Picture Library [p77 l, p77 r, p90, p95]; 21) Photograph by Lynn Procter [p78]; 22) Photographs by Trevor Watson [p94 t l, p113 t l]; 23) Cartoons by Tony Husband (with thanks to *Fiesta* magazine) [p80]; 24) Cover reproduced with kind permission of *Skin Two* Magazine (BCM Box 2071, London WC1 N3XX) (photo: Garrard Martin) [p104 t l]; 25) Illustration by Melinda Gebbie [p104 b l]; 26) Photographs reproduced by kind permission of She-an-me (P.O. Box 171 Gerrards Cross, Buckinghamshire, SL9 8YZ) [p104 t r]; 27) Photographs reproduced with kind permission of Atomage [p104 b c, p104 b r]; 28) Photographs by Kevin Davies [p113 b c, p88]; 29) Illustrations used with kind permission of Dover Publications Inc., N.Y, (from *Victorian Fashions and Costumes from Harper's Bazaar* 1867-1898, Stella Blum (editor), 1974) [p113 b r, p115]; 30) Illustration reproduced with kind permission of the Ashmolean Museum, Oxford [p128]; 31) Photographs reproduced with kind permission of Hyper Hyper (London) [p135 b l (photo: Robert Chauraqui), p135 b r (photo: Jack English)]; 32) Illustrations reproduced with kind permission of Zandra Rhodes [p136 c t]; 33) Illustrations reproduced with kind permission of Gina Fratini [p136 c l]; 34) Illustrations reproduced with kind permission of Benny Ong [p136 c r]; 35) Illustrations reproduced with kind permission of Roland Klein [p136 b]; 36) Photograph by Chris Moore; 37) Photographs from The Hutchinson Library [p33, p38, p83, p87 t by Michael MacIntyre, p81, p63 b by Jesco von Puttkamer, p57 by Charlie Nairn, p62 t, p106, p107 by Sarah Errington, p105 b by Brian Moser]; 38) Photograph from the Susan Griggs Agency Ltd. (photo: Victor Englebert) [p36 l]; 39) Photograph used with kind permission of Tanta Fash (21 Wayside Ave. Harrogate, North Yorkshire, HG2 8NL) [p60 b]; 40) Photograph by Mal Stone [p85]; 41) Photograph used with kind permission of the Japan National Tourist Organization [p105 t]; 42) Photograph by David Hughes. Used with kind permission of Arbor Films [p108 t]; 43) Photograph used with kind permission of Liberty's (photo: James Cotier, art director: Billy Mawhinney) [p109].
All possible attempts have been made to obtain permission for use of all illustrations and photographs. In a few cases, however, this has not been possible and if copyright has unwittingly been infringed please contact the author via the publishers.

Bibliography

ABLEMAN, PAUL
Anatomy of Nakedness [Orbis, 1982, London]

ARGYLE, MICHAEL
Bodily Communication [Methuen & Co, 1988, London]

BARTHES, ROLAND
Camera Lucida [Fontana, 1984, London]

BARTHES, ROLAND
Elements of Semiology [Jonathan Cape, 1967, London]

BARTHES, ROLAND
The Fashion System [Jonathan Cape, 1985, London]

BARTHES, ROLAND
Mythologies [Paladin, 1973, London]

BATESON, GREGORY AND MARGARET MEAD
Balinese Character [Special Publications of the New York Academy of Sciences, Vol. II, N.N., 1942]

BATTERBERRY, MICHAEL AND ARIANE
Fashion: The Mirror of History [Greenwich House, 1982, N.Y.]

BENTHALL, JONATHAN AND TED POLHEMUS (eds)
The Body as a Medium of Expression [Allen Lane, 1975, London]

BERGER, PETER L. AND THOMAS LUCKMAN
The Social Construction of Reality [Penguin Books, 1971, London]

BERNARD, BARBARA
Fashion in the '60's [Academy Editions, 1978, London]

BILLY BOY
Barbie: Her Life and Times [Columbus Books, 1987, London]

BINDER, PEARL
The Peacock's Tail [George G. Harrap & Co, 1958, London]

BLACK, J. ANDERSON AND MADGE GARLAND
A History of Fashion [Orbis, 1985, London]

BLUM, STELLA (ed)
Victorian Fashions and Costume from Harper's Bazar: 1867-1898 [Dover Publications, 1974, N.Y.]

BODY ART MAGAZINE
[Publications Ltd, Blake House Studios, Blake End, Rayne, Braintree, Essex, CM7 8SH, UK]

BOGATYTEV, PETR
The Functions of Folk Costume in Moravian Slovakia [Mouton, 1971, The Hague]

BOUCHER, FRANCOIS
A History of Costume in The West [Thames & Hudson, 1987, London]

BRAIN, ROBERT
The Decorated Body [Hutchinson, 1979, London]

BRAND, CLAREL
Fetish [Luxor Press, 1970, London]

BRAUN AND SCHNEIDER
Historic Costume in Pictures [Dover Publications, 1975, N.Y.]

BROWN, ROBERT
The Countries of the World Vol. I - V [Cassell, Petter, Galpin Co. 1876, London]

BROWN, ROBERT
Races of Mankind Vo. I - V [Cassell, Petter & Galpin, 1890, London]

CARTER, ERNESTINE
The Changing World of Fashion [Weidenfeld and Nicolson, 1977, London]

CARTER, ERNESTINE
20th Century Fashion [Eyre Methuen, 1975, London]

CLAPHAM, ADAM AND ROBIN CONSTABLE
As Nature Intended [Heinemann/ Quixote, 1982, London]

CLARK, KENNETH
The Nude [Penguin, 1970, London]

CLARKE, ARTHUR C
Childhood's End [Pan, 1977, London]

COHEN, SIDNEY
Drugs of Hallucination [Paladin, 1970, London]

COX, HARVEY
The Secular City [SCM Press, 1967, London]

DOUGLAS, MARY
Natural Symbols: Explorations in Cosmology [Barrie and Rockcliff, The Cresset Press, 1970, London]

DOUGLAS, MARY
Rules and Meanings; The Anthropology of Everyday Knowledge [Penguin Education, 1973, London]

EBIN, VICTORIA
The Body Decorated [Thames & Hudson, 1979, London]

EVANS-PRITCHARD, E.E.
Kinship and Marriage Among the Nuer [Clarendon Press, 1951, Oxford]

EVANS-PRITCHARD, E.E.
The Nuer [Clarendon Press, 1940, Oxford]

FARIS, JAMES C.
Noba Personal Art [Duckworth, 1972, London]

FELDMAN, PHILIP AND MALCOLM MacCOLLOCH
Human Sexual Behaviour [John Wiley & Sons, 1980, Chichester]

FISHER, ANGELA
Africa Adorned [Collins Harrill, 1987, London]

FISCHER, H.
The Clothes of Naked Nuer in Ted Polhemus (ed) Social Aspects of the Human Body [Penguin, 1978, London] (Org in: International Archives of Ethnography, 50 (1964), pp 60-71)

FISHER, SEYMOUR
Body Consciousness [Calder & Boyars, 1973, London]

FISHER, SEYMOUR AND SIDNEY E. CLEVELAND
Body Image and Personality [Dover Publications, 1968, N.Y.]

FLUGEL, J.C.
The Psychology of Clothes [The Hogarth Press, 1971, London]

FORD, CLELLAN AND FRANK BEACH
Patterns of Sexual Behaviour [Eyre and Spottiswoode, 1952, London]

FREUD, SIGMUND
The Standard Edition of the Complete Works (James Strachey, gen.ed.) [The Hogarth Press, 1974, London]

FRIDAY, NANCY
My Secret Garden: Women's Sexual Fantasies [Quartet, 1980, London]

GLYNN, PRUDENCE
Skin to Skin: Eroticism in Dress [George Allen & Unwin, 1982, London]

GOFFMAN, ERVING
Behaviour in Public Places [The Free Press, 1966, N.Y.]

GOFFMAN, ERVING
Interaction Ritual: Essays on Face-to-Face Behaviour [Penguin Books, 1972, London]

GOFFMAN, ERVING
The Presentation of Self in Everyday Life [Penguin, 1971, London]

GOFFMAN, ERVING
Relations in Public [Penguin Books, 1972, London]

GOUDE, JEAN-PAUL
Jungle Fever [Xavier Moreau, Inc., 1981, Vitry, France]

HALL, JOHN
'A World Elsewhere' in Denys Hay (ed) The Age of the Renaissance [Thames & Hudson, 1967, London)

HEBDIGE, DICK
Subculture: The Meaning of Style [Methuen & Co, 1979, London]

HERALD, JACQUELINE
Renaissance Dress in Italy 1400-1500 [Bell — Hyman, 1981, London]

HOEBEL, E. ADAMSON
Anthropology: The Study of Man [MacGraw-Hill, 1966, N.Y.]

HOLLANDER, ANNE
Seeing Through Clothes [Avon, 1978, N.Y.]

HOLMBERG, A.R.
The Siriono [Unpublished Ph.D. dissertation, Yale University, 1946]

HOWELL, GEORGINA
In Vogue: Six Decades of Fashion [Allen Lane, 1975, London]
The I-D Bible [Levelprint Ltd, 1987, London]

KONIG, RENE
The Restless Image: A Sociology of Fashion [George Allen & Unwin, 1973, London]

KUNZLE, DAVID
Fashion and Fetishism [Rowman and Littlefield, 1982, Totowa, New Jersey]

LAVER, JAMES
A Concise History of Costume [Thames & Hudson, 1969, London]

LEVI-STRAUSS
The Savage Mind [Weidenfeld & Nicolson, 1968, London]

LEVI-STRAUSS, CLAUDE
Structural Anthropology [Allen Lane, 1969, London]

LEVI-STRAUSS, CLAUDE
Tristes Tropiques [Penguin Books, 1984, London]

LEWIN, ROGER
'When Obesity is Unreal' in World Medicine, Oct 18, 1972, pp 17-19

LEY, DAVID
Portuguese Voyages: 1493-1663 [J.M. Dent & Sons, 1947, London]

LINDEN, EUGENE
Apes, Men and Language [Penguin Books, 1976, London]
LIVINGSTONE, DAVID
Missionary Travels [John Murray, 1857, London]
LOWEN, ALEXANDER
The Betrayal of the Body [Collier, MacMillan, 1975, London]
LURIE, ALISON
The Language of Clothes [Hamlyn, 1983, London]
MARLY, DIANA DE
Working Dress: A History of Occupational Clothing [B.T. Batsford, 1986, London]
MAZRUI, ALI
'The Robes of Rebellion: Sex, Dress and Politics in Africa' in Ted Polhemus (ed) Social Aspects of the Human Body [Penguin, 1978, London] (Org in: Encounter, XXXIV, 2 (Feb. 1970), pp 19-30)
McDOWELL, COLIN
McDowell's Directory of Twentieth Century Fashion [Frederick Muller, 1984, London]
MEAD, MARGARET AND FRANCES COOKE MacGREGOR
Growth and Culture: A Photographic Study of Balinese Childhood [G.P. Putnam's Sons, 1951, N.Y.]
MERKER, M.
Die Masai [D. Reimer, 1904, Berlin]
MERLEAU-PONTY, M.
The Phenomenology of Perception [Routledge & Kegan Paul, 1970, London]
MORRIS, DESMOND
Body Watching: A Field Guide to the Human Species [Grafton Books, 1987, London]
MORRIS, DESMOND
Man Watching: A Field Guide to Human Behaviour [Jonathan Cape, 1977, London]
NATIONAL GEOGRAPHIC SOCIETY
Vanishing Peoples of the Earth [National Geographic Society, 1968, Washington, D.C.]
NEWTON, STELLA MARY
Health, Art and Reason: Dress Reformers of the 19th Century [John Murray, 1974, London]
PARROT, NICOLE
Mannequins [Academy Editions, 1982, London]
PERUTZ, KATHRIN
Beyond the Looking Glass: Life in the Beauty Culture [Penguin, 1972, London]
POLHEMUS, TED (ed)
Social Aspects of the Human Body [Penguin Books, 1978, London]
POLHEMUS, TED AND LYNN PROCTER
Fashion and Anti-Fashion: An Anthropology of Clothing and Adornment [Thames & Hudson, 1978, London]
POLHEMUS, TED AND LYNN PROCTER
'Fetish Fashion' in The Fashion Year, Vol.II (Emily White, ed.) [Zomba Books, 1984, pp 115-126]
POLHEMUS, TED AND LYNN PROCTER
Pop Styles [Vermilion, 1984, London]
RACHMAN, STANLEY
'Sexual Fetishism: an experimental analogue' [Psychological Record Vol.16, pp 294-XXX, 1966]
RACHMAN, STANLEY AND RAY HODGSON
'Experimentally induced Sexual Fetishism: replications and development' [Psychological Record Vol.18, pp 25-XX, 1968]
RIBIERO, AILEEN
Dress and Morality [B.T. Batsford, 1986, London]
RICHARDSON, JANE AND A.L. KROEBER
'Three Centuries of Women's Dress Fashions: a quantitative analysis' in Anthropological Record, Vol.5, Number 2, (1940)
RICHIE, DONALD AND IAN BURUMA
The Japanese Tattoo [Weatherhill, 1982, N.Y.]
ROACH, MARY ELLEN AND JOANNE BOBLZ EICHER (eds)
Dress, Adornment and The Social Order [John Wiley & Sons, 1965, N.Y.]
RUDOFSKY, BERNARD
The Onfashionable Human Body [Ruper Hart-Davis, 1972, London]
RUITENBEEK, HENDRIK M.
The New Sexuality [New Viewpoints, 1974, N.Y.]
SAINT-LAURENT, CECIL
The Great Book of Lingerie [Academy Editions, 1986, London]
SAMUEL, KATHRYN
Life Styles/ Fashion Styles [Orbis, 1986, London]
SARTRE, JEAN-PAUL
Being and Nothingness: An Essay on Phenomeno-logical Ontology [Methuen & Co, 1976, London]
SAUSSORE, FERDINAND DE
Course in General Linguistics [Fontana/Collins, 1974, London]
SAYER, CHLOE
Mexican Costume [Colonnade Books (British Museum), 1985, London]
SCOTT, RONALD AND CHRISTOPHER GOTCH
Skin Deep: The Mystery of Tattooing [Peter Davies, 1974, London]
SONTAG, SUSAN
On Photography [Farrar, Straus and Giroux, 1978, N.Y.]
STRATHEVIS, ANDREW & MARILYN
Self-Decoration In Mount Hagen [Duckworth, 1971, London]
SUREN, HANS
Man and Sunlight [The Sollux Publishing Co., 1927, Slough]
THEROZ, MICHEL
The Painted Body [Skira/Rizzoli, 1984, N.Y.]
TURNER, VICTOR
'Colour Classification in Ndembu Ritual' [in Michael Banton (ed), Anthropological Approaches to The Study of Religion, Tavistock, 1966, London]
UCKO, PETER J
'Penis Sheaths: A Comparative Study' in Proceedings of The Royal Anthropological Institute of Great Britain and Ireland for 1969 pp 27-67
VEBLEN, THORSTEIN
The Theory of the Leisure Class [Unwin, 1970, London]
VECELLIO, CESARE
Habiti Antichi, et Moderni di Tutto il Mondo [Giovanni, Bernardo Sessa, 1598, Venice] (Reprinted by Dover Publications, 1977, N.Y.)
VITEL, ANDRE
Decorated Man: The Human Body as Art [Harry N Abrams, 1980, N.Y.]
WHITMAN, WALT
'Specimen Days' in The Complete Poetry and Prose, Vol.II [Pellegrini and Cudayh, 1948, N.Y.]
WILLIAMS, GEOFFREY
African Designs From Traditional Sources [Dover Publications, 1971, N.Y.]
WILSON, ELIZABETH
Adorned in Dreams: Fashion and Modernity [Virago, 1985, London]
WOODFORDE, JOHN
The Strange Story of False Hair [Routledge & Kegan Paul, 1971, London]
YORK, PETER
Modern Times [Futura, 1984, London]
YORK, PETER
Style Wars [Sidgwick & Jackson, 1980, London]
ZANER, RICHARD, M.
The Problem of Embodiment: Some Contributions to a Phenomenology of The Body [Martinus Nijhoff, 1971, The Hague]
ZICREE, MARC SCOTT
The Twilight Zone Companion [Bantam Books, 1982, N.Y.]

Index

A
Aborigine 41, 54, 123
Adam & Eve 71, 72, 74, 76, 79, 91
Adamites 90
Adornment 6, 7, 29-71
Africa, Peoples of 73
Age of Discovery 73, 92, 128
AIDS 119
Amazon, Peoples of 68
Andes 10
Anorexia 7
Anthropologists 12
Arab peoples 92, 93
Artificial Bodies 13-20, 26
Ashanti 18
Asoro 46
Augustine, St. 4, 6

B
Baboon 8, 98
Baby timers 134
Bafo 18
Bailey, David 135
Bali, People of 9, 11, 12, 16, 24, 29
Barthes, Roland 11, 89, 122
Bateston, Gregory 11
Bath houses 90
Beach, Frank (and Ford, Clellan) *Patterns of Sexual Behaviour* 10
Beatles, The 135
Beats 131
Beauty 4-27
Beauty Contest 22
Berber 46
Bikers 49, 130
Biological Reality 19
Biologists 22
Binet, Alfred 102
Black is Beautiful Movement 23
Blind Date (TV Programme) 70
Blondes 96
Body Building 25, 50
Body Decoration 6, 15, 29, 30, 41, 43, 45, 54, 92
Body Hair 10
Body Image 7, 8
Body Modification 26
Bogatrev, Peter *Folk Costume in Moravia Slovakia* 123
Bolina, People of 10
Botocudo 74, 76
Bourgeoisie, Rise of 126-128
Boy George 67
Boys and Girls 132
Brain 6
Brazil, People of 74
Breasts 10, 16, 73, 76, 80, 115, 116
Brown, Robert *The Races of Mankind* 15, 75
Burma, People of 24, 46
Bushman 9, 16, 17
Bustle 114, 115
Butterberry, Michael & Arianne *Fashion: The Mirror of History* 127
Buttocks 10, 92, 93, 98, 99, 114, 115, 116

C
Caduveo 29, 30, 32, 46, 74
Cameroon, People of 18
Caminha, Pedro Vaz de 75, 76
Cap d'Agde 78, 79
Caricature 16
Carnivals 90, 91
Caroline Islands, People of 153
Cave Paintings, Prehistoric 9, 18
Charms 42
Childhood 8, 100
Chimpanzees 30
Chinook 24, 25
Circumcision 31
Clark, Kenneth *The Nude* 89
Clarke, Arthur C *Childhood's End* 4
Clones 6
Clothing 120-139
Cohen, Sydney *Drugs of Hallucination* 121
Coiffure 65, 68
Colburn, Theresa 67
Corsets 24
Cosy Country 133
Courtesans 117, 118, 119
Cranial Deformation 24, 26, 48
Crinoline 114
Crucifix 46, 47
Crusaders 48, 126

D
Delgado, Dr. Jose M.R. 6
Dembo, Adolfo 49
Descartes 4, 6
Diet 24
Dinka 31
Dior, Christian 115, 120, 122
Disco Glitz 133, 134
DNA 45, 70
Dolls 13, 19, 21-23, 26
Dogon 46
Douglas, Mary *Natural Symbols* 12
Duchamp, Marcel 18
Durville, Gaston & Andre 78
Dyer, Catherine 20

E
Ears 74
Easter Island, People of 49
Ebin, Victoria *The Body Decorated* 29
Eden, concept of 75, 77, 79, 97, 135
Elizabeth II, Queen 120
Embarrassment 79
Eroticism 17, 44, 95-119
European Culture 72
Evans Pritchard, E.E. 121
Evolution 22, 23
Executives 133
Exploration, Age of 72
Eyes 21

F
Face-lift 25, 27
Faces 10, 41, 90
Facial Decoration 43
Facial Expressions 4
Fall, The 75
Fanon, Franz *Algeria Unveiled* 92, 93
Farthingales 98, 115, 116
Fashion 30, 48, 65, 135-139
Fattening House 8, 17, 25, 27
Features 41, 54
Feet 24
Feminists 56
Fete Bresilienne, Rouen 70
Fetish Clubs 100-101
Fetishism 99-113
Flugel, J.C. *The Psychology of Clothes* 55
Fogies 134
Folk Tales 14
Foot Binding 48, 99
Ford, Clellan (and Beach, Ford) *Patterns of Sexual Behaviour*
Foucault, Michael 98
France 66
Frankenstein 14
Fratini, Gina 136
French Revolution, The 55, 56, 100
Freud, Sigmund 100, 101
Friday, Nancy *My Secret Garden* 102
Fulani 21, 22, 23, 54

G
Garter 99
Genital Organs 73, 75, 79, 93, 97, 99, 100
Gerewol, the 21, 23, 55
Ghana, People of 18
Ghandi 93
Gloves 91
God 73, 91
Godiva, Lady 93
Goffman, Irving *The Presentation of Self in Everyday life* 68
Golem, the 14
Gothic 65, 113, 130, 132
Goude, Jean Paul 16, 17-18, 19
Jungle Fever 13, 16
Greeks 78, 89
Greer, Germaine *The Obstacle Race* 65

H
Hair 70, 71
Hands 90
Hawaii, People of 95
Heads 24, 25, 90
Heliopolis 78
Hells Angels 6, 27
Hippies 27, 65, 68, 76, 96, 130, 131, 132
Hips 6, 16, 115
Hitler 78
Hodgson, Ray 102
Hollander, Anne *Seeing through Clothes* 89
Hollywood 79, 102
Homosexuals 96, 100
Husband, Tony 80

I
Ideal Beauty 21
Ideal Body 8, 10, 11, 18, 89
Imbelloni, J. 49
Impotence 102
Industrial Revolution, The 56, 100
Islam 92, 93

J
Japan 46, 47, 50, 53, 65, 129
Jewellery 30, 32, 41, 46, 67, 70, 71, 74, 113

K
Kayapo 54
Kilt
Kings Road 55, 103
Kinshasa 9
Klein, Roland 136
Kuhn, T.S. 75
Kunzle, David 103

L
Labrets 74
Labrodor, Sanchez 29
Language 30, 41, 45
Laver, James 115
Leather 101, 102, 103, 104
Levi-Strauss, Claude 29, 46
Life Class 80
Lingerie 101, 102
Lips 21, 24, 25, 29, 47, 52, 74, 75
Lonely Hearts 70
Los Angeles 32
Lowen, Alexander *The Betrayal of the Body* 4

M
Make-up 29, 43-47, 65, 70, 71, 95, 97
Mannequins 20
Maori 29, 42, 48, 52, 93, 123
Masai 10, 91, 92
Masks 18, 90
Mazrui, Ali 91, 92, 93
Mead, Margaret 11
Medici, Catherine de 118
Middle Ages 48, 75, 89, 115, 116, 126
Minanacho 90
Minimalists 133, 134
Mini-skirts 92, 95, 97, 138
Mirrors 1-8, 73
Miss World 21, 28, 123, 124, 125
Model 10, 14
Modesty 72-93, 95, 116
Mods 65, 130, 131
Moqui 46
Moravia Slovakia 124
Muir, Jean 137, 138
Mura 53
Mythology 14

N
Nakedness 89, 92
Naked Savages 72-74
Narcissism 4
NASA 43
Naturists 43, 77, 78, 79, 89
Neck 24, 25
New Guinea, People of 6, 10, 29, 41, 42, 46, 66, 68
New psychedeleics 65
Nigeria, People of 9, 92
Nipples 13
Nordenskiold, Baron Von 74
Noses 22, 75
Nuba 31, 54, 74
Nuer 79, 93, 121

O
Ong, Benny 136

P
Padung 24, 25, 26
Parkinson, Sydney *Journal of a voyage to the South Seas in His Majesty's Ship Endeavour* 52, 73
Penis 10, 100, 101, 117
Perutz, Katherine *Beyond the Looking Glass* 25
Phallo-plethysmograph 102
Piercing 31, 44, 49, 53, 74
Pigments 30
Plastic Surgery 24, 26
Polynesia 73
Pornography 89
Prehistoric Man 9, 19
Preppy 97, 129, 132
Primates 30
Prostitutes 96, 118
Psychedelics 130, 132
Punks 6, 27, 32, 42, 47, 49, 65, 95, 96, 97, 130, 131, 132, 137
PVC 102, 103, 119
Pygmalion 19

Q
Quant, Mary 103

R
Rachman, Stanley 102
Reflection 7, 8
Relationships 4, 49, 69
Religions 14, 90
Renaissance 48, 115, 129
Rhodes, Zandra 130, 136, 138
Ritual 7, 68
Rockabillies 130
Rockers 130, 131
Rome 21
Rootstein, Adel 20
Roro 29
Rubber 101, 102, 103, 104, 113
Rugged Country 134
Ruitenbeek, Hendrik *The New Sexuality* 101

S
Sahara 10
Saint-Laurent, Cecil *History of Women's Underwear* 117
Samuel, Kathryn *Lifestyles/Fashion Styles* 139
Saturnalia 90
Sayer, Chloe *Mexican Costume* 124
Scarification 29, 41, 49
Scythian 48
Semiotics 11, 45, 96, 99, 118
Sex 8, 10, 41, 42, 95, 99, 117-119
Shaving 29, 31
'Sick with Desire' 54
Signifier 11
Signs 11
Siriono 10
Skinheads 46, 49, 130, 132
Sloane Ranger 97, 98, 129
Slut, Johnny 67
Social Body, The 12
Soemmerring, Dr Samuel 24
Sontag, Susan 89
South Africa, People of 9, 16, 18
Sport Casuals 134
Star of David 46
Star Trek 32
Status 48, 68
Steady State 121
Street Gangs 32
Stiletto heels 95
Stockings 95, 99
Stonier, Tom 6
Strip-tease 76, 93, 102

Suren, Major Hans 78
Der Mensch und die Sonne 77
Suspenders 114
Switzerland 67

T
Talisman 42
Tanzania 91
Tattoo 29, 30, 31, 41, 44, 46, 47, 48-53, 69
Tchikrin 25, 26, 27
Teddy Boys 49, 130, 131
Teeth 21, 29, 46, 48
Tits 13
Toukie 13, 16, 17, 18, 19
Tribal Peoples 49, 50, 55, 72, 92
Tribal Societies 6, 7
Tupi 76, 77
Twiggy 20, 135
Twilight Zone, The 27

U
Ucko, Peter *Penis Sheaths: A Comparative Study* 117
Ungewitter, Richard 77
Underwear 91, 114-116

V
Vanity 4
Vecellio, Cesare 28
Venice 90, 128
Venus de Milo, The 19
Venus of Willendorf, The 13, 16, 17, 18, 19
Vince, Leonarda da 127
Virginity 47
Voyager I 43, 71
Vogue 136, 138
Vulva 10

W
Warhol, Andy 121
Wells, H.G. *The Invisible Man* 56, 65
West Africa 8
Westernization 23, 26, 50, 54, 129
Western Society 10, 25, 26, 41, 42, 47, 48, 65, 69, 76, 89, 92, 95, 99, 100, 138, 139
Westwood, Vivienne 115, 137, 138
Whitman, Walt 76
Wigs 54, 95
Wooden Sculpture 18
Woolies 134

X-Z
Yorke, Peter 138
Modern Times 136
Yoruba 9
YMCA 79
Zimmermann, Werner 77
Zulu 18